Hoteko's Laws

Other Books by Sarge Hoteko

On The Fringe Of History:
A riveting behind-the-scenes look at the war on drugs and terrorism from a
"fed" who fought the fight

Hoteko's Laws

✦

A Manager's Guide to Success, Survival and Sanity in the Federal Government

Sarge Hoteko
Chief Inspector (Retired)
United States Customs Service

iUniverse, Inc.
New York Lincoln Shanghai

Hoteko's Laws
A Manager's Guide to Success, Survival and Sanity in the Federal Government

Copyright © 2005 by Sergei A. Hoteko

iUniverse books may be ordered through booksellers or by contacting:

iUniverse
2021 Pine Lake Road, Suite 100
Lincoln, NE 68512
www.iuniverse.com
1-800-Authors (1-800-288-4677)

ISBN-13: 978-0-595-37674-2 (pbk)
ISBN-13: 978-0-595-82058-0 (ebk)
ISBN-10: 0-595-37674-6 (pbk)
ISBN-10: 0-595-82058-1 (ebk)

Printed in the United States of America

Dedicated to the ten percenters; you know who you are

Contents

Authors Note

Hoteko's Laws evolved over the course of my career with the U.S. Customs Service, which no longer exists within the Department of the Treasury. On March 3, 2003, it was merged with the parts of the Immigration and Naturalization Service and sections of the Department of Agriculture to form US Customs and Border Protection within the newly created Department of Homeland Security.

Any references or characterizations in this book should not be construed by anyone to be intentionally harmful or embarrassing since this was not my purpose. I have changed some names, some locations and some characteristics of people in this book to protect their privacy. The events that I have referenced are recreated to the best of my memory. The views reflected in this book are mine, and they do not reflect the official views of any government agency.

Acknowledgements

I owe an enormous debt of gratitude to all the *ten percenters* who showed me the way. These noble beings kept the government running in spite of the obstacles in their way. You will learn some of their names in the following pages. They could have easily climbed the private corporate ladder and been rewarded with benefits far beyond what Uncle Sam gave to them. Instead, they chose the path of public service because they believed in the United States of America.

I firmly believe that if government *ten percenters* like a Sam Banks or Richard (Corky) McMullen were in charge of Tyco, Enron, WorldCom or Arthur Andersen; these corporate giants would have been spared from the needless catastrophes that befell them. If Chicago Mayor Richard M. Daley had a Banks or McMullen as his chief of staff, he would not have suffered from embarrassing scandal-after-scandal-after-scandal in his various city services departments over the last number of years.

Contrary to that famous line in the Oliver Stones' 1987 Hollywood blockbuster *Wall Street*, Banks and McMullen believed that *greed isn't good*. They believed that honest management is good management, whether it is in government or private industry. I salute these *ten percenters* for their dedication to the mission, their ethics and their integrity which they freely shared with me.

I will forever be indebted to my loving and understanding wife, Donna, for all the support she has given to me throughout the years. I also want to extend a huge thank you to my talented editor, Jean Sneed, Ph. D., for her efforts in making this book a reality as she so ably did with my first book. Lastly, I want to thank all those in government who have sincerely helped and supported me throughout my career. You always did what I asked of you. I couldn't have gotten the job done without you. You made it a memorable ride. A *Doff-O-The-Hat* to one and all!

Prologue

I spent 27 years in the United States Customs Service. It was a unique agency chartered in 1789, tasked with revenue collection and the examination of people, merchandise and conveyances entering and leaving the United States to ensure compliance with the law. The Customs motto was *to collect and protect the revenue*. It sounds very simple, but in fact Customs was a very difficult agency to manage, given the diversity of our mission in a geographical and a legal sense. We faced a tremendous workload, and unlike most federal agencies, we were open for business 24 hours a day, 7 days a week and 365 days a year.

In 2002, we collected $24 billion in duties and fees for the US Treasury Department, our parent agency. We were responsible for the 5,000-mile border with Canada, the nearly 2,000-mile border with Mexico, 95,000 miles of coastline, 300 seaports and 429 international airports. This nationwide operation was directed from 312 port offices scattered across the country in such diverse locations as New York City; Eagle Pass, Texas; Los Angeles; and Sweet Grass, Montana.

Nearly 330 million people crossed our land borders in 118 million vehicles or on foot. Over 70 million people arrived at our international airports aboard 760,000 commercial aircraft or in 130,000 private airplanes. Ocean vessels numbering 7,500 made 51,000 ports of call, delivering over 20 million 40-foot shipping containers crammed with imported goods. Crossing our borders were 11.2 million trucks and 2.4 million railcars from Mexico and Canada that year. All were subject to a Customs examination. In addition US Customs was also responsible for the enforcement of over 400 laws for 40 different federal agencies at the border.

It's obvious that Customs couldn't look at everybody and everything crossing our borders. International commerce would have had to come to a screeching halt, our land borders would have had backups of a hundred miles or more, vessels would have been anchored for weeks waiting for a berth at the pier and passengers have been camped out in our international airports waiting to get into the United States. Our mission was complex, diverse and challenging.

In 2002, there were approximately 5,000 uniformed inspectors deployed across our land borders and at our sea ports as well as stationed at our international airports, all were tasked with enforcing the Customs mission. During that year this *thin blue line* seized nearly 1.4 million pounds of marijuana, 170,000 pounds of cocaine and 5,600 pounds of heroin. In addition, they confiscated nearly $45 million belonging to drug, terrorist and criminal organizations in outbound enforcement operations. These inspectors had to make the final decision on which person, which cargo shipment, which airplane, which vessel, which vehicle or truck, which container or railcar to search physically for contraband or on whether to let them go without inspection.

You can have all the best technology available, but, if you do not have dedicated people and good managers to direct their efforts, it's all for naught. Being a manager in Customs was not only challenging, but could be downright daunting at times because you had to make decisions in real-time minutes at the border, airport or seaport, and you had to live with consequences of those actions. You didn't have the luxury of studying the ramifications of a decision as a manager in the Social Security Administration or the Railroad Retirement Board could do while leisurely mulling it over when drinking his morning coffee. This was the Customs Service I knew and for whom I worked.

Introduction

I think it was on the 150-yard, par 3, 14th hole at Sportsman's Country Club that I mentioned to my good friend, the late Noel Kaplan, that I was writing this book. Noel was a retired vice president of the fast food giant McDonald's and always sported a sharp wit and keen sense of humor. I can still recall his response on that sunny day as he said, "Sarge, managing the federal government is an oxymoron."

He's not the first person to say or think that. The federal government has become a wily and nearly uncontrollable beast with an insatiable appetite for growth, power and money—meaning congressionally appropriated tax dollars. Nearly two million civilians labor, or perform a reasonable facsimile of work, for the federal government. They are employed in hundreds of large or small and obscure agencies whose budgets run into the trillions of dollars. Many of these agencies have well-defined purposes and missions; however, some provide little if any useful service, while others have nebulous charters at the best.

◆ ◆ ◆

I retired as a Chief Inspector with the U.S. Customs Service in 2002, after a 27-year career, serving in various mid-management positions throughout Chicago. I was a recipient of the prestigious Albert Gallatin Award presented by the Secretary of the Treasury, Paul H. O'Neill. I also received prominent recognition from the US Commissioner of Customs, Robert C. Bonner, from the Director of the FBI, Richard S. Mueller III; and from Chicago Mayor Richard M. Daley. My public service career was honored by the 93rd General Assembly of the State of Illinois in House Resolution 25. I had the distinct privilege of being selected as only the third recipient of the coveted US Customs Supervisor of the Year Award in 1991, presented by Assistant Commissioner Charles W. Winwood. In 1996, I was the second honoree of the O'Hare Airport Wings of Vision Award, the first being Mayor Richard M. Daley.

I enjoyed a very successful career because I was blessed to have worked with many dedicated people who relished the challenge of achieving the overwhelming

Customs mission. Yet, during my 27 years on the job I've witnessed numerous managers, both within Customs and other agencies, struggle to accomplish the simplest job. On many occasions these managers had some of the very same people under their supervision that had made my operations shine. I began to wonder what the difference was; just what factor was missing or was present that caused them to flounder or fail where I had succeeded?

After much reflecting on my career and after talking with numerous people with whom I've worked, I came to certain conclusions which I call Hoteko's Laws. Just what are Hoteko's Laws? Well, they are a series of practical axioms that have guided me throughout my career. Many have helped me to succeed, and many have assisted in keeping me out of harm's way. Some of Hoteko's Laws were developed solely by me through trial-and-error, and others were born through the first-hand privilege of observing and learning from good managers at work such as Sam Banks and Richard (Corky) McMullen.

My laws aren't based on what you would learn at the John F. Kennedy School of Government at Harvard University or any other such prestigious institute of higher education. I wasn't lucky enough to go to Harvard. In fact, I was an average blue-collar kind of guy who learned how to manage the old-fashioned way—from the bottom up. Hoteko's Laws are a down-to-earth, simple nuts-and-bolts guide to management, born of my experiences, successes, frustrations and failures as a federal manager.

◆   ◆   ◆

An Ivy League school once invited the late alderman Vito Marzullo to speak at a seminar in 1971. Why did they invite a crusty, old-school Chicago machine politico to lecture about politics? I believe simply because Marzullo was very successful. He always got out the vote and got it out in the way the late *Boss,* Mayor Richard J. Daley, liked it—a 100 percent turnout and a 100 percent straight-line Democratic vote in the old west side 25th Ward. A phenomenal feat year after year!

How did he do it? This self-professed nonintellectual ward boss knew people; he cared about them and knew what made them tick. Vito didn't need an Ivy League university study or a sophisticated scientific polling organization to tell him how to get out the vote; he only needed his experience with people and his gut sense. He listened to his constituents and he delivered on his promises. I grew up in his ward and admired him as a man who kept his word. I learned an early lesson from Vito—that your word is your reputation and your golden bond with the people. Once your word is gone, it's gone forever.

◆   ◆   ◆

Managing in the government is vastly different from private enterprise. I know that many people will disagree with me. They will emphatically state that *management is management*—period. To a small extent they are correct. Whether you are the Ford Motor Company (FMC) or the Federal Emergency Management Agency (FEMA), a budget is a budget, time and attendance is just that, health benefits, sick leave and vacation time are expected by employees, and a boss is a boss. In my opinion, however, there is a big difference.

Private industry has a bottom line—it's called *profit*. Profit is obtained when the consumers purchase the product being offered in large enough numbers that will pump enormous volumes of dollars into the company's coffers. This cash infusion allows the company to grow, to modernize, to expand its markets and to stay competitive. A company can only last so long without turning a profit before the board of directors fire the CEO. If, after a number of fired CEOs, and the company is still losing money, the factory will probably close and all the workers will be out on the street.

A good friend of mine, Chief Inspector Zoran D. Knezev, had a folksy way of getting this point across. He said, "If there is a shoe factory and the employees aren't producing shoes what happens to the manager? Gone!" He also went on to state, "If there are no shoes to sell in stores, what happens to the factory and the employees? Gone!" He accentuated the word *gone* with a dramatic sweep of his right hand as if clearing all the pieces off a chessboard in one fell swoop.

In the federal government it's vastly different. There really isn't a bottom line, meaning *profit*. The American people do not expect a profit from government; they expect a *service*. Nobody in their right mind would expect the US Army to turn a profit. The American people expect the army to defend our country against any and all evils. Albeit you can say that profit and service are both end-run products, and you would be technically right. They are. Yet, in private industry the shoe factory would close if it wasn't profitable, but the government agency would remain open without giving good or any service at all. Why? One big reason is the *congress factor*.

In those agencies that do not provide a good nor needed service, the Congress may feign shock, indignation and make windy speeches about frugality with appropriated tax dollars. With a wink-and-a-nod, however, they continue gleefully to shovel over your tax dollars to keep these federal *shoe factories* open in their respective districts or states. Government employees are constituents, and, most importantly, voters too, and that fact isn't lost on the congressmen and senators. Hence, the employees know that their agency (i.e., shoe factory) will stay open whether they give service or not, because their representative or senator will vote to keep it open.

◆   ◆   ◆

One of Hoteko's Laws is the 10 percent rule. Ten percent of those in management actually run their government agency; the other 90 percent are along for the ride. As a good manager you have to know that, accept that and work around that. It was my policy to let the *90 percenters* enjoy the ride, simply because I couldn't do anything about it. It was also my policy, however, to keep them out of the way to let the *ten percenters* run the show.

As a *ten percenter* it is of utmost importance that you are able to identify the cast of characters that populate the ranks of federal government management. It is critical that you place them with care depending on what category they fall into. You will either succeed or fail by your selection process. Many of the *90 percenters* can be further broken down into these categories—the *yes men*, the *wackos*, the *stargazers*, the *sandbaggers* and the *clowns*.

Yes men are indigenous to both private industry and government. If you apply common sense and lack delusions of grandeur, you can easily identify these self-serving syncopates. They cheerfully chime in on your every word as if you are revealing the Gospel according to St. Mark to them for the first time.

The *wackos* are much more difficult to identify. They usually only come to light after they have caused some damage. It is critical to your survival to closet these nuts in such a way as to protect yourself and your agency. Most of the *wackos* are just that—*wacko*; they're just simply nuts and cannot help themselves.

The *stargazers* pose a true problem. They are usually very intelligent; they occupy positions of higher authority and issue idiotic orders that affect you and your ability to get the job done. It seems as if one day they wake up, divinely look to the heavens and miraculously see what normal mortals can't see. They're convinced that they're the only ones who can read the stars and unlock their cosmic mysteries.

Beware of the *sandbaggers*. This is a unique species that defy logic. It would seem that their sole purpose in life is to do you in. They are smart and they have malice in their hearts. They are dangerous because they know what they are doing to you and they do it deliberately. Once they are uncovered, you need to bury them in some useless job where they can do no more harm.

The *clowns* are everywhere, whether private industry or government. They are generally good-natured people who truly want to do a good job for you. It's just that they are missing some simple elements like a logical thought process and/or common sense.

◆　　　◆　　　◆

So, here are my musings, my perspective, my inside look at a career in management. This is the way I saw it. Whether I'm judged right or wrong, this is what I learned in 27 years in government.

- I learned to manage.
- I learned to accept challenge.
- I learned to take risks.
- I learned to take responsibility.
- I learned integrity doesn't take a back seat to anyone or anything.
- I learned to turn corners.
- I learned to adapt.
- I learned to bring projects in under budget and ahead of schedule.
- I learned when to speak up.
- I learned when to keep quiet.
- I learned when to fight.
- I learned when to let go.
- I learned when to ignore.
- I learned be wary.
- I learned to trust.
- I learned to keep my word.
- I learned that leaders lead by example.
- I learned that one person can make a difference.
- I learned to be that person.

- I learned to pass it on to others.

These are the basic principles that formulated Hoteko's Laws.

Sarge Hoteko
Chicago, Illinois
August 2005

PART I
The Cast of Characters

The government, like any company large or small, is populated with some unique characters. I use this term affectionately since most of these characters are good-natured and good-intentioned people. We all have our limitations. Some people are born to lead, some are born to follow, some are born to deal with problems and issues, some are born to duck them, some are born to trouble shoot, some are born to cause trouble and some are born simply to make you laugh.

If you seek to become one of the *ten percenters* who really run the government, you have to be able to identify the cast of characters who make up the other 90 percent of people in the government. You need to do this so you can deal with them effectively. Your success or failure will depend upon your selection process.

1

The Sandbaggers

We had two very good midlevel managers within our Customs region; each in his own right was a *ten percenter*, someone who could get the job done. Let's call them Don and Jim (not their real names) from Buffalo and Minneapolis respectively. There were two promotional openings, much sought-after, at a major west Texas land border crossing that were vacant, the district director and assistant district director jobs. It is quite unusual for the two top positions to be vacant in a major district at the same time. Some *stargazer* in HQ had made a cardinal mistake of allowing that to happen.

It would be akin to the Chicago Bears being minus their head coach and offensive coordinator in week eight of the NFL season. The general manager could bring in two new people, but I guarantee you that the team would be lucky to win one or two games in the next eight weeks. If they had only been minus the head coach, however and brought in a new guy and still you had your offensive and defensive coaches in place, you're probably going to win four or five out of the last eight because you have some continuity in your game plan. In our case the HQ *stargazer* willfully did what private industry, i.e., the Chicago Bears, would never do—leave their organization vulnerable by having the two top jobs open at the same time.

Each applicant was judged to be best qualified for the jobs they had applied for and both were selected. Neither Don nor Jim were native to Texas, or had southern land border experience, but this was not necessary. Nobody, however, in that west Texas town really welcomed there selections. I suppose that's only natural considering that Customs had nearly 500 employees in that large district, many of whom thought they were also best qualified for the vacancies and should have been selected. Don and Jim were going into hostile territory and should have proceeded with due caution.

At this major Customs district as many as 20,000 vehicles a day crossed the border over the three bridges which span the shallow Rio Grande River that divides the United States from Mexico. It is also a major thoroughfare for commercial truck traffic that can bottleneck the highways with ten-mile backups. It is also one of the primary commercial rail crossings between the two countries. It's a very busy place.

Needless to say, both Mexico and the United States realize the huge financial gain that the Mexican migrant workers and Mexican manufactured goods impact upon both economies. Backups at the border usually mean lost dollars for US industries that rely on these workers and the Mexican imported goods. It behooves the United States to expeditiously move vehicle and pedestrian traffic across the border.

This facilitation has to be delicately balanced to comply with the Customs enforcement mission of various laws and regulations. They run the bizarre gamut of dealing with illegal immigration, the Mediterranean fruit fly and narcotics. Over 90 percent of the cocaine flowing into the United States does so through the southern land border. The President, Congress, the governor of Texas, the Texas ranch owners and retail industries and department stores across the United States are certainly aware of and care about the drug problem in America.

When it gets down to the nitty-gritty, however what really matters in private industry is making a profit. No workers and no goods equal no profit. So, in essence what our Texas business friends most cared about was getting their migrant workers and Mexican products quickly across the border and through U.S. Customs so they can make money. It's simple economics.

When money speaks, Congress listens. Congress had appropriated many millions of dollars to build a special container examination facility at that district border crossing. This facility was to be solely used to conduct enforcement examinations on Mexican trucks that were considered high-risk for smuggling contraband—items like marijuana and cocaine. By using this facility for that single purpose, it would free-up the other container examination sites so they could expedite the legitimate cargo trucks going north to their commercial destinations. Congress and their special interest groups like to see that their appropriated tax dollars go to the intended purpose; in this case moving the imported cargo and the workers across the border as fast as possible so money can be made.

◆   ◆   ◆

As a good government manager, a *ten percenter*, you have to be sensitive to the needs and wishes of Congress. Why? They vote on your budget each year and what congress giveth one year, Congress can taketh away the next. In plain

English, never alienate a member of Congress or embarrass a commissioner of Customs, especially one who happens to be traveling to your location to view the golden egg the member has benevolently bestowed to Customs. Hell hath no fury like a member scorned.

That's the mistake our newly appointed northern brethren made one day in that major district. The commissioner of Customs and a member of Congress were visiting the border crossing. The member had been very instrumental in obtaining funds to build the enforcement examination site that would alleviate congestion in the commercial truck lots. He had listened to the Texas titans of industries, or rather their well-paid Beltway lobbyists, and had gotten the big bucks to build the building. Imagine his chagrin, the commissioner's embarrassment and the burning hole-in-the-stomach feeling our boys from the north felt when they visited the new state-of-the-art examination facility, and it looked more like a ghost town than a busy interstate truck stop.

There wasn't a single truck or a single container in sight. All they saw were some inspectors waiting around on the empty dock for the visiting brass to show up. Not good. What should have been a bustle of enforcement examination activity turned out to be a bust, not a big bust of narcotics, but the bust of two careers. Don and Jim had been *sandbagged*. They relied on a couple of their key supervisors to insure that all would go well on the site visit. They didn't establish accountability and they didn't do their homework.

Their homework should have started the day they arrived in Texas. They should have realized they were going into hostile territory and that they would be viewed as northern carpet baggers who stole jobs that should have belonged to a couple of Texans. Not a pretty scenario, but unfortunately that's not only the southern border mentality, but seems to also extend to the northern border as well. These areas do not take kindly to those that they view as an outsider. Both Don and Jim should have been aware of that issue, but, for whatever reason, they either ignored it or they suffered delusions of grandeur that they would be welcomed the same as the American army liberating Paris in 1944.

◆   ◆   ◆

When Ray Kelly, named twice as NYPD's top cop, was commissioner of Customs, he tried to institute a program where newly hired inspectors would have to spend their first five years on the job in a place different from their home town before they could apply for any transfers. There was a prevailing view that both the southern and northern border ports only hired local people. In fact, in many of these locations there were numerous generations of the same family working for Customs throughout the years. It was as if they could inherit the job. This practice fostered a culture that excluded the acceptance of outsiders.

Under Kelly's plan if a Chicago person was hired, they may go to El Paso; the Brownsville, Texas person would start perhaps in New York and the guy from Pembina, North Dakota, might go to Miami. I think he hoped that this program would not only break up the border mentality issue, but also insure more integrity. Apparently he felt the less familiarity, the less opportunity for corruption among the troops. It was a good idea, but it didn't last long and was quickly discarded once Kelly left Customs.

In the aftermath of that fiasco Don retired and Jim was shifted to a glorified analyst's position of no real authority or responsibility. Two fine careers went down the tubes, but it didn't have to be that way. There were two factors that led to their downfall: one they had no control over and the other they certainly did.

The factor that they didn't have control over was their own selection for the jobs. Both were eminently qualified, and each would have been a good selection if only one position was being filled. This scenario would have ensured the stability and continuity of operations within the district. The current district director could have easily broken in the new assistant or the current assistant could have shown the new boss all the ropes.

This would have made it much more difficult for the *sandbaggers* to do their thing. If one of the two top people in the district were still in office, that person would have a vested interest in not wanting to see his operation sabotaged. It would be his professional reputation at stake. The new comer, if he were a *ten percenter*, would ask the salient question, just what am I responsible for and what are you responsible for? Feet would be held to the fire and accountability established, both of which would impede the *sandbagger*. With both positions being vacant however it was an invitation for disaster. It created a situation eagerly pounced upon by the *sandbaggers* to do the two new outsiders in.

◆   ◆   ◆

The HQ *stargazer* was never criticized for his blunder of allowing both jobs to be open at the same time. Remember, *stargazers* never accept responsibility for their idiotic decisions, but they will take full credit for all your successes in the field. Don and Jim could have succeeded if they followed Hoteko's Laws. Remember, they had no control over their selection for the job. They could have controlled how they approached their new jobs, however by exercising due caution by ensuring each had a clear understanding of their areas of responsibility. If they had done that, all the bases would have been covered.

One of Hoteko's Laws states that there can only be one BIG PICTURE person. Usually that person is the boss because he's ultimately responsible for the success or failure of the mission. His job is to keep the ship on course. He needs freedom to chart the waters without the distractions of the day-to-day responsibilities of running the ship. The boss can't be bogged down with trimming the sails, pumping out the bilge or seeing that crew is fed. He has to rely on his number two man to do that. In this case it would be the assistant district director who would be his DETAIL MAN.

Disaster strikes when both the boss and second-in-command are BIG PICTURE guys. This is what happened to our northern boys. Both were BIG PICTURE guys and nobody attended to the details—nobody except the *sandbaggers*. For whatever reason Don and Jim didn't sit down and cover their bases on who was going to do what. Instead of being cautiously wary in their new jobs, they blindly trusted people in their new district, ignoring the fact that some of them may be *sandbaggers* waiting in the weeds, people who had wanted those jobs in the first place and had been denied. It was a classic *sandbaggers'* sting opportunity!

◆   ◆   ◆

They should have known better since both were *ten percenters* who individually ran good shops back in their original districts. Don should have saddled Jim with being the DETAIL GUY in no uncertain terms. If that had happened, the new enforcement examination facility would have been a beehive of activity during the member's and the commissioner's visit. Being new to the district, Jim should have been out at the facility at the crack of dawn to ensure that manifests were being reviewed and high-risk trucks and their cargo were being sent for examinations. Instead he was with the district director, the member and the commissioner, enjoying breakfast and basking in the momentary glory of being in the presence of these temporary deities.

Usually when you are *sandbagged* you let it happen to yourself, although there are times when you'll never see it coming until it's too late. Remember, they had no control over their selection for the jobs but had all the control in the world over their actions once on the job. Also, remember, the *sandbagger* is smart and vicious and can usually only succeed if you give him an opportunity. Don and Jim gave him that opportunity.

◆   ◆   ◆

Hoteko's law:—*Only one BIG PICTURE guy is allowed in a division or branch—PERIOD. The DETAIL MAN is just that—he crosses all the T's and dots all the I's. The combination of a good BIG PICTURE guy with a good DETAIL MAN spells success.*

2

The Clowns

Every organization has their *clowns*, their funnymen. Some are intentionally humorous by their good nature, some are entertainingly comedic due to their lack of competence and some will never get their act together no matter how hard they may try. The government isn't any different from private industry in this respect with one exception: we may actually employee more *clowns*. As a matter of fact; we may have more *yes-men, sandbaggers, wackos and stargazers* aboard per capita than private industry. Why? Simply because it's much more difficult to fire them. They know that and hence they seek the safety of the wide protective umbrella of government shelter. They also know they will be continuously fed at the generous public trough.

◆   ◆   ◆

The Civil Service Commission was created in the late 19th century to stabilize and professionalize the federal government. Prior to its adoption, hiring and firing was a political willy-nilly beast that stalked Washington with terror. Whoever was in office brought all his cronies along for the ride whether or not they were qualified to do the job. To the victor go the spoils. Once he was out of office, all his buddies went with him. Government services essentially came to a halt until the new group learned what it was they were supposed to do. This was no way to run a railroad or to perform the greater good of serving the people.

The old political spoils system was also deeply rooted in graft and bribery. One had a de-facto purchase of a job. Political contributions were not only expected but demanded by politicians of both current and potential federal employees. It created an unhealthy and unprofessional atmosphere in which to do the people's work. Hence, the Civil Service Act was born to professionalize the federal government, to stabilize it and to protect employees from wanton shake-downs and firings by the corrupt fat-cat politicos. Along with that reform protection came a plethora of rules and regulations. All personnel actions had to stand up to a third-party review. Over the years more and more *stargazers* piled on more and more protections that have resulted in the near impossibility of firing a federal employee. It was a good idea gone very wrong.

◆   ◆   ◆

Firing is another major difference between managing in government and private industry. In the shoe factory if an employee repeatedly produces inferior quality shoes, he's gone—*out the door!* This is not so in government. The employee is usually retrained, or reassigned to another job, or perhaps even promoted or just ignored, because no one wants to take on the near impossible task of trying to fire him. The inability to terminate an employee is one of the most frustrating facts facing a government manager, especially a *ten percenter*, one who really cares about getting the job done.

What is worse, however than not being able to fire him is seeing him get promoted into a management job to get him out of the way. This is a favorite action of the *90 percenters* who usually pass the buck. As a midlevel manager you inherit these people. You have to able to accept that fact, and unless they commit capital murder, with witnesses who will testify against them, with a smoking gun in hand and without a high profile criminal attorney defending them, you can't fire them. So what do you do with them?

You don't promote them but place them where they will do as little damage as possible. Most of them are quite harmless, unlike the *sandbaggers* who are actively out to do you in. Many of these *clowns* actually have the best of intentions, but God didn't bless them with common sense; the wire isn't connected to all parts of their brain. Many of these *clowns* are capable of doing a good job if nurtured, directed and stroked. They just can't be the BIG PICTURE person. They can under certain circumstances be the DETAIL MAN. Usually, however they can only be assigned minor tasks that allow you, as the BIG PICTURE person, to run the show.

◆   ◆   ◆

There was one fellow, with good intentions and absolutely no malice in his heart, who was assigned to take pictures at a major convention that would be attended by the commissioner of Customs. He was our version of the world famous photographer, Ansel Adams. So, he was given a camera and four roles of film. Off he went to the event with the sole propose of snapping pictures. This was not a difficult job at all. He didn't have to research and write a paper, give a presentation in front of a large audience, or be subjected to a tough questions-and-answer period. No, all he had to do was just point and shoot.

During the course of the event he happily snapped away the four rolls of 36 exposures; a total of 144 clicks of the camera shutter. When he came back, he gave the film to an underling to take to the camera shop to have them developed and printed. A couple of days later the associate gave him four rather thin envelopes.

The underling said with a happy smile on his face, "Wow! The shop didn't charge us anything. It must be because we give them so much business."

Our Ansel Adams smiled back in agreement. It was only after he opened the envelopes that he realized why Customs had not been charged a dime. All 144 negatives were black, and the film had never been exposed. No pictures were there to develop, hence no charge by the camera shop. What happened? Had the camera shop made an error in the development process? No, the raw unexposed film had never made it out of its cartridge.

Our Ansel Adams never loaded the film correctly into the camera. It was a point-and-shoot camera, the type that an idiot can use. It was a camera that always takes great photographs, provided you load the film correctly. He placed the film in the camera but didn't pull the leading edge out to the red line that is marked by the take-up reel. So when he closed the camera and pressed the button to wind the film, it didn't wind into the take-up reel. However, he heard the whir of the winding motor and thought all was *A OK.*

He happily snapped away, frame after frame, and when he saw the film counter was at 36 exposures, he manually pressed the rewind button. He did that with all four rolls, apparently oblivious of the fact that these cameras have an automatic rewind that is triggered at the end of the roll of film since it's not unusual to get more than 36 exposures. The automatic rewind did not engage which should have been his first clue that he hadn't loaded the first roll properly. But no, he repeated the same mistake with the next three rolls.

Now mind you, our Ansel Adams is a midlevel government manager. He was within the GS-13 to GS-15 pay level, the grouping just below the senior executive service (SES) which is the top pay grade in government. He was genuinely embarrassed and heartbroken that he had failed to get the photographs. This was an assignment that couldn't be replicated. It wasn't as if he made a mistake collating copies of a research paper and could go back and do it right. The opportunity was lost for all time.

For his explanation said, "Well, my camera at home is different. I have to rewind it manually."

No disciplinary action was taken nor should there have been. It was obvious he wasn't a *sandbagger*. He was just a good-natured person who tried his best at a simple task and failed. One silly mistake shouldn't ruin a career. Our fine friend was given another simple responsibility. He was to pick up a group of HQ managers and drive them to a conference being held in close-by neighboring state. He bundled them into his car at the airport and off they went.

Our Ansel Adams was a longtime resident of a major Customs port city and had worked out at the airport as well. The group left the airport on a sunny day. After driving about 20 minutes, one of the HQ people noticed a highway sign that indicated they were headed south to an east-west toll road, so he asked Ansel, "Say, is this a short cut? We seem to be headed south. Shouldn't we be going north?"

Well, a light bulb must have gone off in Ansel's brain. He sheepishly smiled and replied, "Oh, yes, I think we're going the wrong way. We need to turn around and go north, isn't it? I guess I forgot that. Geography confuses me."

He obviously couldn't be out on his own. He needed to be deskbound where he could be carefully directed which the BIG PICTURE guy then realized. So, Ansel was given a job compiling statistics, creating pie charts and graphs which are a necessary evil that the bureaucracy thrives on. He had found his niche as a DETAIL MAN, or rather the BIG PICTURE guy found the right niche for him and for Customs.

◆   ◆   ◆

There was one person who was in charge of a narcotic enforcement team in a major city. Matt (not his real name) was one of those people who were never successful in their own right, even though they had many of the same people under their supervision who had made others successful. Instead of concentrating on the job at hand, he concentrated on keeping the office clean. Apparently Matt thought that cleanliness is next to godliness.

When first assigned to that critical narcotics enforcement job, Matt didn't have a team meeting to outline goals, objectives and the mission. No, Matt called everyone in on their day off to clean the offices. The floors were stripped of wax and mopped, the windows washed and the light fixtures were cleaned. The desks were washed, including the drawers which were taken out and the insides washed with a scented soap. Some people are clean freaks and Matt was one of them.

Needless to say, Matt's enforcement team was one of the least productive in the history of that Customs district. When the boss is a *clown* who concentrates on cleaning the offices, the Customs mission is lost and the team members lose their focus. If the boss isn't keeping the ship on course, the sailors will simply go through the motions of sailing the ship when in actuality the ship is floundering at sea.

One example of that was when Matt's team did an enforcement examination on a cargo shipment destined for another city. This type of inspection entails taking the entire shipment apart at its first port of arrival to search for narcotics, leaving no stone unturned. The problem was when the shipment got to the next Customs port the inspectors there found heroin inside that Matt's team missed. Apparently they were only going through the motions of doing their job. The only dope that the team could find was the dope leading the team at the end of the day in Matt's spotless office.

After that debacle, to improve morale and make his team more productive, Matt came up with a real harebrained idea. Matt had the entire team meet at a local park for a day of relaxation and motivation. He then photographed them in various positions frolicking around the colorful spring flowers. It was ridiculous, but Matt thought after the team tiptoed through the lilacs they would start finding drugs! Needless to say, the BIG PICTURE guy finally had enough and buried Matt in an innocuous job that had little if any contact with the human race.

◆   ◆   ◆

We had a senior midlevel manager who made an interesting decision one winter day. The old adage is that if you don't like the weather in Chicago, wait five minutes and it will change. Being close to the Lake Michigan we have lake effect snow, so the physically closer you are to the water the more snow you can get. Our district office is very close to the lake.

One bright, sunny winter day it started to snow downtown. The flakes were thick and coming down like someone was shaking goose down feathers from a ripped open pillow. Sheridan (not his real name) looked out his office window and saw nature's keen display of a winter wonder land rapidly coating the streets of the Loop. It was 10 a.m. He was in charge that day since the district director was out of town as was the regional commissioner. He was the man for Customs in Chicago and the 18-state region.

He called me at the airport and said, "Sarge, it looks like another horrible winter storm. I'm sending everybody home early with the exception of essential people."

My office at O'Hare didn't have a window, so I couldn't see just how bad the storm was. I replied, "O.K., most of my inspectors are essential and have to stay to process incoming flights or handle diversions. I'll call over to cargo and have them shut down their operation and send the people home."

The 300 or so employees who got to leave early that day were happy; happy to be able to beat the snow home and happy to get the rest of the day off. Snow storms in Chicago have a fierce reputation of being able to paralyze the city. Everybody who wasn't essential immediately evacuated their work site. The problem was 20 minutes after he called with the go-home-early order, the snow stopped.

When he looked out of his downtown office window he could see the blue sky, the brilliant sun and he actually heard the birds singing. Prior to issuing his go-home-early order he hadn't called the weather service, turned on a radio for a forecast or called other agencies to see if they were closing operations. He saw the initial snow, panicked, shot from the hip and sent everybody home.

When he called the district director, who was in Washington with the news about the snow storm and its sudden demise, the district director replied, "You did what? Well, call everybody and tell them to get back to work." Click went the telephone.

The damage was done. There was no way he could have called anybody to come back because they wouldn't answer their telephones anyway. The employees knew a good thing when they saw it! The entire workday was lost. Needless to say he was never in a position to make that call again; rain, snow or shine! He wasn't a *sandbagger*. His intentions were good and he didn't want to see employees stranded overnight at work. He didn't do his homework, however to find out more about the weather before making a decision that would greatly impact the district.

◆   ◆   ◆

These are just a few examples of the multitude of people I've classified as *clowns* in government. Please realize that there isn't any malice in their hearts for they are good-natured people. It's just that they shouldn't be the BIG PICTURE guy. Some, however like Matt, our enforcement team chief who actually was a borderline *wacko*, unfortunately need to be buried. Many of these people actually think that they should be running the show. They have no idea that the wires in their brain are not connected or will ever be connected to make a good circuit for decision making. It's critical that you as the BIG PICTURE person (i.e., a *ten percenter*) correctly evaluate people and get them where they can do you some good and do the least amount of harm. If you are able to accomplish that, it will help you to keep your sanity too.

◆   ◆   ◆

Hoteko's law: *Judge each person according to their ability or lack thereof and each according to your needs, and not necessarily theirs.*

3

The Wackos

If you study people long enough just by looking at their nonverbal communications such as facial expressions, hand gestures, eye contact, etc., you can at times identify a *wacko* before he can do harm to you. Usually though, a *wacko* only comes to light when he's done some damage. A *wacko* differs from a *sandbagger* in one major way: once the *wacko* raises his head and does his damage you know who he is, and you can effectively deal with him. A *sandbagger* can remain submerged for years on end doing some serious damage before you really know who he is, and that can be disastrous. A *sandbagger* is very smart and knows exactly what he is doing. A *wacko* is, well, a *wacko* is just plain nuts and apparently cannot help himself.

So, how can you tell a *wacko* by looking at him? Behavioral scientists will scoff at my explanation, but my theory is that it's mostly in his eyes. When you are asking him a question or when he is replying to you, watch his eyes. The eyes get a sort of glazed-over look, and their gaze goes out about three feet and then crosses over in an X-like pattern. The best example would be to visualize a straight line that narrows from each eye going out about three feet until they intersect and then the left eye line crosses over the path of the right eye line and vice versa. Now both lines continue in opposite, nonparallel paths that vector right out into space, never to meet again.

It's only in those first three feet he has eye-to-eye contact with you as a normal person would. Once the X-crossing is made, his eyes have the same dead quality that the eyes of a Great White shark have: absolutely no life to them, just a dull, unfixed stare. Like the Great White shark, beware of the person with that stare. I don't know what causes this at all, but I do know I've observed it in people who did indeed turn out to be *wackos*!

◆   ◆   ◆

We had a fellow named Rodney (not his real name) in Washington D.C. who was in charge of our national firearms program. All Customs inspectors are armed and must qualify quarterly to maintain their proficiency to carry their weapon. I was assigned to our region office at the time and administered the program in 18 states. We also had a commissioner at the time who was very conservative; some believed that his politics were slightly to the right of John Birch.

I met Rodney at a conference. Our commissioner had tasked him with finding a new firearm for our inspectors, so he was soliciting opinions. He asked me, "Sarge, what do you think about our current revolver, the Smith and Wesson model 36?"

"It's a fine weapon, easy to shoot and to maintain," I replied.

Obviously it wasn't the answer he was looking for. He said, "The commissioner thinks Customs should have their own model, developed just for us and I agree with him. What do you think about the ammunition we shoot?"

Again I gave the wrong answer when I said, "The .38 P-plus-P is a good, solid round. It will stop a violator from doing damage if necessary. It's all we really need."

That's when I saw the glaze in the eyes begin to develop and the X-pattern crossover when he stated, "Well, we're going to ask Smith and Wesson to develop a new .357 magnum revolver and we're going to call it the CS 1. The commissioner thinks that's a hot name; the CS 1 and only Customs will have it. He wants us to adopt a stronger load, like a .357 hollow-point cartridge as standard issue and I agree with him that we need more stopping power. What do you think?"

By now the glaze was so intense that his right eye was focused on Venus and the left somewhere on Mars, he was standing in front of me, but he wasn't seeing me. I told him, "I think that's just stupid. Why spend the money to develop another weapon when the production model 36 is good enough? Why shoot .357 magnums when a .38 P-plus-P will do the same job at a lesser cost? A P-plus-P will stop a person. What more do you want?"

I could see he wasn't even listening to me, but he seemed locked into some form of cosmic energy that was beaming down from the heavens. So I interjected, "But let's go a step further; let's equip each inspector with a small, personal nuclear device in the event of an emergency. That way we can really stop a person and protect the borders."

Obviously I was being sarcastic but you would have never known that by his reply, "No, I don't think there is such a thing as that available, but I'll look into it."

I don't know what it is with people and guns. Most people who are into guns do not just have one. Most have ten and a crate of ammunition. It becomes an obsession. If person is a true collector of historical firearms that's one thing, and I don't have an issue with that. However, never have a *wacko*/part *stargazer* gun collector in charge of a firearms program, because he will go to the extreme. For whatever reason Rodney had gained the commissioner's ear by apparently appealing to his dark side, and that access gave him carte blanche in the firearms program.

At a substantial cost to the government Rodney, with the commissioner's joyous blessing, did have Smith and Wesson develop the CS 1 revolver which we were shooting with the new hot loads too. We had nothing but maintenance problems because the tolerance levels were too close between the cylinder and the frame. This caused a carbon built-up when firing the new weapon with the hot loads which caused cylinder rotation jamming. A few years later we junked the CS 1 and reequipped our 5,000 inspectors with another new weapon.

◆   ◆   ◆

We had a computer guru in a major Customs region that did an outstanding job computerizing the office. He was a self-taught whiz kid of the motherboard, and he became a GS-14 midlevel manager in charge of Automatic Data Processing. The only problem was the more he learned the more he became convinced that only he should have the knowledge contained in the data bases. Knowledge is power, and one or both become dangerous in the hands of a *wacko*, especially one who is a borderline *stargazer*.

In the mid1980s our HQ decided to upgrade TECS, the Treasury Enforcement Communications System. TECS was a multifunctional electronic data base that stored records, reports, border and intelligence alerts. It interfaced with the FBI National Crime Information Center (NCIC), INTERPOL, the U.S. State Department, DEA, ATF, Secret Service and a host of other agencies' data bases. It was one of the most valuable enforcement tools that a Customs inspector utilized.

Over 495 million people cross our borders each year, and 70 million do so at an international airport. Their names are queried through TECS to ensure that there isn't an active NCIC arrest warrant, prior drug arrest record or suspect criminal activity report contained within that huge data base. If the name queried *hits* against any one of the data bases, the passenger is subjected to a more in-depth examination. TECS gives the inspector a quick way to process passengers effectively, while still keeping the borders safe and secure.

Our Sam (not his real name) wanted to restrict access to TECS II, as the powerful upgrade was called. He told me, "Sarge, the new TECS allows inspectors to be able to have too much access. It's too powerful for them to use. We need to restrict it. I'm going to see the commissioner about this. I think that I should be the only one to have complete control and then I'll make the decision on who gets what access."

All the while he was talking to me his eyes glazed and did the familiar three-foot X crossover. I replied, "Sam, just think a while about this. Why was TECS developed in the first place? It was developed as a tool to help the inspectors. Why would we restrict it? It has to be available to the inspectors in the field. If you restrict it, that action defeats the purpose of having the system and upgrading it."

So, off he went not having heard a word I said. Well, thankfully a *ten percenter* BIG PICTURE guy agreed with me and not with Sam. TECS II and all the valuable data bases were made accessible to all the inspectors. The BIG PICTURE guy realized that Sam had limitations. Although nobody ran the IBM 36 computer system better than he did, Sam was not a decision maker nor should he be. The BIG PICTURE guy used him where his talents lay best; programming data and maintaining the system, and most importantly in not making any decisions.

◆   ◆   ◆

We actually had a few people that I think would have committed murder if asked. I'm serious. We had one character in Chicago, Gordon (not his real name), who would do anything to get ahead in the organization. He was a first-level supervisor who dealt very well with the troops, getting them to produce superior enforcement results. Every once in a while I'd figuratively have to rearrange the nose on his face to keep him in line. Without that verbal reminder he could go *wacko*. I had learned early on that he needed to be watched.

If I had asked him, "Gordon, I need you to kill so-and-so."

He wouldn't be shocked or reply that I asking him to commit murder. No, he would most probably answer, "Sarge, do you want it to be quick or do you want him to suffer?"

This is why you have to be very careful of what you ask someone to do, especially if you suspect they are a *wacko*. In Gordon's case if I had said, "You know, so-and-so is really getting on my nerves. My job would be easier if he retired or was dead."

I think we've all thought that from time-to-time when releasing pent-up frustration with an incompetent boss. I never said that in front of Gordon because I never wanted to find out if he would do the deed. In my mind I knew he was capable of doing anything, especially in his overzealousness to please the boss and to be promoted. That was his mindset, and coupled with his lack of scruples, he was capable of anything.

I could just hear the police asking him why he killed so-and-so. He would reply in a matter-of-fact voice, thinking he had done something good for the boss and the police would understand, "Well, Sarge asked me to."

Gordon was one of the *wackos* who didn't have the telltale glazed eyes or X crossover syndrome. I only discovered his nuttiness after he committed several stupid deeds. Once I knew that he had the perchance of going *wacko*, I watched him closely. He was one of my best subordinate supervisors when kept in check. He would have jobs done that nobody else could or would do. He had value to the organization if carefully watched over but could never be a BIG PICTURE guy out on his own.

◆   ◆   ◆

We also had a fellow, George (not his real name), who had a master's degree as did Gordon and Rodney. The problem was one of his shingles would occasionally slide open on top of his head and the bats would fly out of his belfry. If I wasn't around to slam the shingle shut, he could manage to do damage. It was not serious damage, but embarrassing things like talking to arriving international passengers while eating a large wedge of lettuce topped with creamy Roquefort cheese dressing.

I actually saw this one day. I then called him over and asked him, "George, what on earth are you doing eating lettuce while talking to passengers?"

His reply was classic George. He started off with his trademark laugh of five or six Porky Pig yuckity-yucks, all the while some pieces of partially chewed lettuce shot out of his mouth. His eyes glazed over and he said, "Well, I was eating lunch at my desk and an inspector came in to get me. He stated a passenger wanted to talk to a supervisor."

George just didn't think and that was his problem. He consistently put in for promotions and was consistently denied promotions for just that reason. He was a good first-line supervisor who needed constant watching and because of that he could never be a good BIG PICTURE guy.

Years later he was forced into retirement when he did a stupid thing. I'm sure he didn't think it was stupid; most *wackos* don't think their actions are stupid. He tried to obtain sensitive, non-government personal records of a manager he was suing for denying him a BIG PICTURE guy promotion. Nobody was there to watch George, as I used to, and it cost him dearly.

◆　　　◆　　　◆

One of the most amazing cases of a *wacko* was a fellow with the Immigration and Naturalization Service. He was a member of BORTAC, the INS Border Patrol Tactical Team. This elite unit is mobile, highly disciplined and expertly trained to respond to emergency situations. They are often dispatched to provide security at border crossings, including airports.

I can't recall the exact situation when I first was in contact with BORTAC. I think, however it was some type of terrorist alert and we were located at O'Hare Airport Terminal 4 at the time. The INS chief, Orrie DiChristofaro, came into my office and said, "Sarge, our commissioner has mobilized BORTAC and put them on alert at major airports. We'll have a unit here and I'll introduce you to the team leader when he arrives."

A day or two later, Orrie returned with a fine fellow all decked out in a sharply pressed green uniform that would have made the toughest Marine proud. This BORTAC team leader explained their function, where they would be stationed and what they would do in certain situations so as not to conflict with my Customs security procedures. All the while he was speaking his eyes glazed and I saw the very familiar X crossover of a *wacko*.

He stated, almost standing at attention as if the *Star Spangled Banner* was playing in the background, "Sir, I'm here, and my men are here to take a bullet for you and your inspectors. Yes sir. You have nothing to worry about. They won't get you. I want you to know that I'm personally here to take a bullet for you."

◆　　　◆　　　◆

As you can see some of the *wackos* will even take a bullet for you. Withstanding that, the *wackos* can be productive if put in the right place and carefully watched. As a *ten percenter* BIG PICTURE guy this does make your job more difficult, but what you can gain is worth the effort. In essence you have to protect them from themselves. By doing so, you help keep yourself out of trouble and still reap the value that they can give to the organization.

◆   ◆   ◆

Hoteko's Law: *Know the difference between a wacko and a sandbagger. A wacko can be of use to you and the agency but only if carefully watched. If not watched, they will become a disaster waiting to happen. A sandbagger is an incurable cancer who should be removed and buried.*

4

The Yes Men

Where would the world be without *yes men*? We'll never know because there isn't likely to be a shortage any time soon. They prosper everywhere. They are like weeds and cockroaches. You can see them, try to kill them and they come right back, usually bigger and stronger than ever. Why will we always have *yes men*? One simple word will do—ego.

We all have an ego, some have a larger version, but we all succumb to the age-old proverb of wanting to be loved and praised. I have fallen victim to my ego many times. I have learned, however, from my mistakes and have always tried to keep it in check. As long as the boss has an ego, there will be scores of *yes men* to stroke, stoke and nurture that ego.

Yes men are generally very intelligent and thus can be very useful to your agency. Their biggest flaw, however, is their inability to tell the truth. Many have a fear that if they are the bearer of bad tidings, they will lose their head. Hence, they will paint a bright and shiny picture to each and every boss with which they come into contact. Many of these *yes men* even believe the fluff they are spinning off to the brass themselves. I refer to this as a cocoon of self-denial that protects them from the reality and evils of the world.

◆　　◆　　◆

A case in point is the retail giant Sears. After nearly cornering the department store market by the 1950's, Sears began to suffer from self-induced delusions of superiority from their success. Their corporate mentality through the 1960's and 1970's was simply that the public had to buy from Sears; where else could they or would they want to go for tools, clothing or appliances? After all, Sears had every-thing.

When Sears corporate HQ moved into the world's tallest building in 1974, they did indeed feel on top of the retail world. There was, however, a growing group of dissident stockholders who were looking at the bottom line. They were increasing their scrutiny of the top brass, the board of directors and how they were doing business. By 1990, a shareholders' revolt was beginning to pick up steam. Two individuals were key to that movement, Robert A.G. Monk and Nell Minow.

One was denied a seat on the board although eminently qualified. Eventually CEO Ed Brennan had to face the fire to quell the revolt. In the end run Sears divested itself of their real estate company and stock brokerage firm as well as one-fifth of their insurance company to concentrate on their core business, retail merchandising.

What caused the success of this revolt? The answer is *yes men*, plain and simple. The Sears Tower was filled with hundreds of *yes men* who were afraid to tell the truth to the brass. They had been weaned on a diet of propagating the Sears doctrine of superiority in the retail market. Nobody wanted to hear the news that Sears was losing that market because it was concentrating on the divergent entities of buy and selling your home, investing in Wall Street and car and life insurance policies.

These *yes men* didn't have malice in their hearts. They wanted to see Sears keep succeeding. They were proud of Sears, yet none stepped up to the plate to tell the truth. They all wanted to be known as a team player and not a malcontent. By doing so, however, they nearly ruined the retailing giant.

In the end members of that revolt were granted a meeting with CEO Ed Brennan. As they rode the elevator up to his lofty office, one of the *yes men* said, "This is the first time that bad news has gone this far up the tower."

◆   ◆   ◆

When I was able to identify a *yes man*, I would work with him to overcome this fear. I would say to him, "Don't tell me what you think I want to hear; tell me what you know."

This approach generally worked. It wasn't, however, a quick or easy fix. You have to be patient and work with the *yes men*. Reinforce the fact that you need to hear bad news. You can't jump down their throat in a moment of anger if the news is really bad. If you do that, they will quickly revert to telling you what they think you want to hear.

Some *yes men* will always be *yes men* no matter what you do or how hard you try to work with them. They just cannot overcome their fear of telling the boss bad news. These *yes men* are not saboteurs nor are they saviors as evidenced at

Sears. They are like children who cover their eyes when faced by fear of the unknown. Unless you can get them to open up, they'll really never provide a service to the organization.

Some *yes men*, however, are very devious and will try to manipulate you to their advantage. It's in their blood. They can cause trouble if you blindly heed their advice. It's these *yes men* who have an agenda, and they bear careful watching, for it's these *yes men* who can do you in.

◆   ◆   ◆

In my estimation the consummate *yes man* was Henry Kissinger. He told Richard Nixon anything and everything that he wanted to hear, and he did it in a very subtle and manipulative way. He did it to get his own agenda across to the president and that wasn't a bad thing since he was a brilliant man. Many times Kissinger's agenda was the right agenda for our country. In all fairness we would not have had the Paris Peace Accord that ended the Vietnam War in 1973 or the opening to Red China without him. Like most *yes men*, however, he had a flaw. In his case it was his ego too.

He worked Nixon's ego like a lady of the night works a glitzy bar in Las Vegas rubbing up against some overweight, sweating truck driver who has been playing the slots for six hours straight and telling him, "Hey big hunk, I just love your cologne and your muscles turn me on."

Kissinger could apparently goad Nixon into action by playing to his ego and saying things like, "Mr. President, if you don't do this, the world will think you are weak."

If Nixon succumbed, however, to what was suggested by Kissinger and it backfired, old Henry would step away from the policy as quickly as if a leper were trying to reach over and shake his hand. That's the norm in the Beltway to survive and stay in power: distance yourself from embarrassment and ruin and do it quickly. Kissinger apparently took it a step further in those instances; he would surreptitiously contact someone in the press and subtly question the president's judgment as if he didn't have anything to do with the flawed decision.

Being a good *yes man*, Henry burned his candle at both ends and played each side against the other in his quest for historical immortality. Nixon, being a brilliant *ten percenter* himself, finally realized what Kissinger was doing behind his back. So why did he keep him? He realized Kissinger's talents and made an objective decision to take the good with the bad in Henry, because the good outweighed the bad.

Kissinger was always protective of his image and would stoop to any length to protect and project it. He apparently told a member of the press after Nixon had left office something like this, "Nixon was a funny-looking man with a complex character." I wonder if Machiavellian Kissinger ever looked in a mirror.

◆   ◆   ◆

One of the most persistent and prevalent *yes men* was Simon (not his real name). He nearly put old Henry Kissinger to shame with his acute cunning guile. I think that Simon had been born a *yes man*, either that or he was the fastest study I've ever seen of someone who adapted well to willingly placing his lips on the boss's derriere.

Simon was a first-line supervisor in a major Customs district. He was very well educated and a top enforcement supervisor. People enjoyed working for him. At one point in his career he had been unceremoniously dumped into a boring paperwork desk job, and he desperately sought to get back into action. There was a vacant position for a deputy operations chief. John (not his real name) was a BIG PICTURE guy who could have chosen anyone for that job, but he picked Simon. He had recalled Simon's kindness to him when he had first come on board Customs and wanted to repay that gesture.

Many managers criticized his selection of Simon to be the deputy, one of them told him, "John, are you crazy? He's a *yes man*. He'll tell you anything to your face, but he's a back-stabbing SOB!"

John couldn't disagree with that assessment, but he desperately needed some-one who could be out in the field and motivate the troops. Simon was his man. John had given him new life, and in gratitude Simon was producing enforcement results. As with most *yes men*, he was loyal to a fault. You had to be weary, how-ever, of just what he might be doing behind your back. He had his own agenda.

As hard as Simon tried, he couldn't help but lapse back into his old habits of back-stabbing, plotting and conniving. All of this was in a vain attempt to try to get to his next unobtainable promotion. You see, Simon was not only a *yes man*, but was a bit of a *clown* who could never be a BIG PICTURE guy. Simon would tell John anything he wanted to hear in order to curry his favor, and yet when John turned his back out came the knife ala Kissinger with Nixon.

◆　　　◆　　　◆

Simon would sink to any level to show his supposed loyalty, thinking John was buying it hook, line-and-sinker. John hosted a party one year at a local tavern to reward the troops for a job well done. The place was a dive, but the beer was cold and the pizza was spectacular. He had his entire branch there, about 30 people, and they were having a merry old time.

Some of the employees had gotten Simon to drink whiskey, shot for shot with them. They knew that those libations would ultimately lead to some fun with this *yes man*. Like everyone whoever prided himself in his own bravado, Simon kept throwing glass after glass of whiskey down his throat while the two other people were downing shots of vodka. They were, however, really only drinking water. They had duped the wily Simon into a drinking contest that was a sure loser for him from the start.

All the while this was going on, they were peppering him with questions seeking his opinion about this boss and that boss. His tongue being freed by copious amounts of whiskey he rattled off his darkest innermost thoughts that damned any and all names put forward. The deep fury of his wrath was evident and provided a comical overtone to the evening. He would spout off that every manager was an idiot except himself and that he should be running the entire district. John sat back and enjoyed the scene.

One of the people then asked him, "Simon, what about John? What do you think about him?"

Now he had been doing shots for over an hour and was certainly near the point of complete inebriation or very close to it. John was sitting in an area just to his left and Simon couldn't readily see him, if he could focus his eyes at all at this point. Everyone waited with bated breath for his answer to see if he'd give John up like he did every other manager whose name came forward.

He leaned back in his chair, and being the *yes man* he was, stated, "John is a great man! He is a great manager!"

With that being said everyone burst out laughing. Simon had very subtly glanced sideways and in his peripheral vision caught sight of John still sitting there. The caging old fox was wily enough not to step in the trap and damn John while he was still in the room.

◆   ◆   ◆

Like Kissinger, Simon thought he had everybody duped. John knew what he was doing behind his back. When his boss asked him why he still kept him, John replied like Nixon had regarding Kissinger, "He gets the job done. In fact he does things I can't do because I have a conscience. He has no morals or shame. He's worth his weight in gold. I'll take the good and the bad with Simon."

John knew that Simon was a *yes man* from day one. John kept careful watch over him and would confront him if his behavior turned vicious. Simon would then change. It would only last a short time, however, until he would lapse back into his old habits. Simon had great ability and potential, but his need for conspiracy and Machiavellian politics always did him in, just as his reputation of being a *yes man* followed him throughout his career.

◆   ◆   ◆

When John was reassigned to another branch, Simon was hooked up to a chief inspector who was not a *ten percenter*, not a good BIG PICTURE guy. This person couldn't, and apparently, didn't try to handle him. As a consequence Simon really ran amok causing problems across the board. They had to reassign John back to that branch primarily to rein him in. When Simon got wind that John was going to be his boss again, he tried his best to block the move.

He called Jim (not his real name), a HQ assistant commissioner and slyly told him, "Jim, if John comes back to our branch, there will be big problems. John is nothing but bad news and he's not a real leader. He's a liability and that liability just might extend to Washington, and to you, Jim. I'm only calling to protect you, since you're my friend. Jim, you are a great leader and I don't want to see anything bad to happen to you."

The wily old fox thought that he had done John in. What was his motive? He knew if John came back he'd be held accountable. Simon enjoyed working under the other chief because this *90 percenter*, although a very nice fellow, let Simon do anything he wanted without oversight. Simon enjoyed the free rein and didn't want John back at any cost.

What Simon didn't know was that John received a call from HQ, "John, this is Jim. I understand that you're coming back to run the branch again. I think it's a good move; the other chief wasn't providing the leadership I wanted. Oh, by the way, Simon called me and tried to get me to kill your reassignment. Just thought you should know that. Do you think we should get rid of him?"

John replied, "Jim, that's our boy. What did you expect? No, I'll keep him. If I ride herd over him, he'll produce the results we need. He just needs to be watched. I'll keep him."

When John became his boss again, Simon told him, "John. I'm so glad you're back! You have the leadership skills we need. I can't wait to work with you again. My friend, we'll accomplish great things!"

Simon never understood that John and Jim knew the silly duplicitous game he was playing. He thought he had pulled the wool over their eyes. John didn't care because Simon did a great job for him, as Kissinger had done for Nixon. He had value to the agency but could never be a BIG PICTURE guy because of his being a consummate, but devious, *yes man* and a bit of a *clown*.

◆　　◆　　◆

Once a *yes man,* always *a yes man. Yes men* are the easiest to identify if you don't let your ego get into the way. They can be some of the best people you can surround yourself with. You have to work with them, however, to get them to tell you the real truth and not what they think it is you want to hear. Remember nobody likes bad news, but better the bad news upfront so that you can deal with it before it becomes an unmitigated catastrophe for you and the agency.

◆　　◆　　◆

Hoteko's law: *Park your ego at the door and be wary of those who are always cheerfully singing your praise. If you always question why they are saying what they are saying, you'll keep everything in perspective.*

5

The Stargazers

The *stargazers* are among the most difficult category of employees for you to deal with as a manager. They are mostly very bright, creative and usually very polished. Most are totally married to their ego with no earthly boundaries. Some *stargazers* just play the game. They are part of the *90 percenters* who are along for the ride. These *90 percenters* put very little effort into the job. This is what makes them all-the-more reprehensible since they actually know better and can do better. However, they consciously choose to be along for the ride.

There are also *stargazers* who are *ten percenters,* BIG PICTURE guys who really believe in what they are doing, but only within their vision of things. They are so smart that common sense doesn't come into play. They see things in the cavernous abstract of outer space where normal people dare not travel with their thoughts. As opposed to the *90 percenter stargazers*, these guys can't help themselves, for they border on being nuts. Unfortunately, both types will plague you throughout your career.

One of the problems with the *stargazers* is that they are usually upstream of you in the pecking order. Hence, you have to do what they say and that makes it all the more unpalatable. I do not believe that people are born as *stargazers*. They have a propensity to dream the undreamable dream and to think the unthinkable thought, while they apparently fall victim to their own super-sized ego. This combined with the skillful stroking they receive from *yes men* makes them firmly believe that they know what is best for one and all. In essence, you can't talk common sense to them; it's their way or no way.

◆   ◆   ◆

Very rarely will you find a *stargazer* downstream of you. If you do, you can cure him. If a subordinate supervisor dreams up a nutzo idea or foolish program, charge him with accomplishing the task. One of two things will happen. First off, most will relish the fact that the boss, the BIG PICTURE guy, thinks enough of their idea to try it. This is fine.

So, task him with a writing a detailed SOP, preparing a budget and organizing a manpower work schedule to accomplish the program that will not affect other essential operations. You must hold him to a measurable standard, and, most importantly put him on a timetable to have this on your desk. You must also give him the time and the support to complete his project.

A majority of the time the happy camper will come up with a program that is nothing more than a mishmash of unworkable parts. So, sit down with him and explain the reality of the world. Go point by point and break all the tasks down that you have given him. Then, detail why it isn't worth the effort. Usually this educative process, which I admit is cumbersome, works. It leaves a lasting impression upon the young supervisor of how not to waste time and effort on a furtive dream, but to concentrate on reality. If you explain why it will not work, that will have a lasting value on the new manager.

On the other hand, if you can't make a good case against his project, it just might be worth pursuing. Remember, you are not the end-all of ideas. Be open-minded. Your objective as a BIG PICTURE guy is to encourage and nurture good people to accept a challenge, take responsibility, make decisions and get the job done. This is the only way your employees and the agency can grow.

In critiquing the project you should spend your time with the person in a positive way, rather than just stating, "That's the most stupid idea I've ever heard."

There is nothing more devastating to a new supervisor than to hear a slam like that from their boss. Their creative juices will dry up and they will retreat into becoming a *90 percenter*, someone just along for the ride. It's your obligation to make the effort to ensure your downstream people grow in the right way so that they can become a *ten percenter*, someone who might actually run the government one day.

Remember, many are slow learners and need to learn by their own mistakes. Just don't let them make those mistakes without your oversight and critique. At the opposite end are the fast learners who are a true joy. A fast learner may also suggest an idiotic project. If so, task him with the same criteria listed above. If he's really a fast learner, he'll be back at your desk in a short day or two.

He'll say, "I've really thought my project over again given the criteria you tasked me with completing. I don't think it's that workable."

If he's sincere and really a fast learner, he'll explain exactly why he has found his project to be classified as nutzo, point by point. If he can't articulate why he no longer wants to do the project, you have to begin to suspect either he's lazy and didn't want to put in the effort or he had hoped that you would have tasked someone else with his idea. This can be the beginning of someone becoming a *stargazer* or a *90 percenter* along for the ride. They love to pontificate an idea and have everyone else do the work.

If you feel the project is doable and will reap good benefits for the agency, hold his feet to the fire and make him do it. You must be available to assist him. If, however, you're not going to support him, he'll probably still get the job done, but you'll never see another positive effort from him. Sometimes it's a very thin line between a person becoming a *90 percenter* or a *ten percenter*, a thin line from becoming a *stargazer* or a BIG PICTURE guy. The supervisor is usually the deciding factor in these situations.

◆   ◆   ◆

Can you combat an established *stargazer*? When I was assigned to our region office, I was tasked with putting together a conference. Corky McMullen visualized the need for uniform Customs processing along the northern border. McMullen's North Central Region was responsible for the major portion of the border with Canada, and regional commissioners in Los Angeles and Boston had sections of the border too. Each region supported a different way of doing business and that wasn't good.

Corky called me into his office and said, "Sarge, I want you to develop an agenda for an all-northern border conference. What I envision are all our northern border district directors from Maine to Blaine, the two other regional commissioners, HQ program officers, the Northern Border Brokers Association, all the Canadian regional collectors of Customs and our staff in attendance. We all need to be on the same piece of paper regarding the processing of commercial cargo crossing the border. It needs to be uniform across the board."

Mr. McMullen was a BIG PICTURE guy, and I was the detail man in this venture. This was a historic first. The magnitude of this gathering had never before been attempted. He had laid out what he wanted and left it up to me to compile the agenda and the logistics. Pretty heady stuff for a newly promoted mid-manager. The only problem was he threw in a road block.

He told me, "Coordinate this through Rob."

Unfortunately, Rob (not his real name) was a *stargazer*. What made that worse was that he was a *stargazer* who knew better, a *90 percenter* along for the ride. He was ambitious and was determined to put his stamp upon this historic first.

There was no getting around Rob, I had to funnel the agenda through him, for he'd be the one briefing Corky along the way.

Corky wasn't interested in the minor nuts-and-bolts of the agenda or who was going to speak when and on what. He was only interested in the crux, the end-run product of Customs uniformity along the northern border. This would result in better service to the importing community. He left details to his staff, a staff he trusted and respected.

It took weeks and weeks just to coordinate the schedules of the 11 district directors, the 10 Canadian regional collectors, the three U.S. Customs regional commissioners, our HQ deputy and assistant commissioners and the Northern Border Brokers' Association. I had to identify appropriate subject matter experts, block out times for their presentations in a manner that logically accentuate the uniformity theme of the conference. I had to budget money for travel, contract hotel rooms and a conference facility suitable for the large group. I also had to organize after-hour activities that would keep the people together so they could network on the issue at hand.

Each time I had the agenda finalized, I'd go into see Rob. He'd look it over, think for a while, make some notes and tell me, "Sarge, I think we need to eliminate this, change that and include this."

After four or five times that became really old. Some of his suggestions were off-the-wall. He thought that we were negotiating the North American Free Trade Agreement, except we weren't. He visualized himself in some historic role dramatically signing the treaty while the media cameras rolled while he was holding a press conference. His mind was in outer space. He lost the entire focus of the conference as he dreamed his lofty dreams. The more he dreamed, the more he fed his growing ego. It was an endless cycle.

At one session I told him, "Rob, this is all about uniformity. In the end-run what Mr. McMullen hopes to accomplish is this; when a Customs broker submits entry documentation to clear a shipment of automobile parts in Buffalo, it will be handled in the exact same way in Blaine, Pembina or Detroit. Same classification, same duty rates, same examination procedure. The same service regardless of where they file."

Rob leaned back in his large leather chair, lit a cigarette and spoke his words as if communicating with an astral deity. "Well, it's bigger than all that. I guess you can't see what will come out of this. What I see is a consolidation of the border with Mr. McMullen being in charge from Maine to Blaine. I don't see a Los Angles or Boston or headquarters role at all. We will do it all. Chicago will run the entire Canadian border. Maybe one day you'll be able to see the big picture the way I do."

Time was running down and I had to finalize the agenda and send it out along with the schedule. It was time to stop changing speakers and agenda items. It was time to stop dreaming. So I went in with my final agenda and handed it to Rob for his approval. He looked it over and over again.

He then said, "Well, it looks good. Did you make all my last changes?"

"Sure," I replied.

He looked at the agenda and then at me and said, "Sarge, how do I know you did that. Where is the last agenda with all my notes and suggestions?"

I looked him straight in the eyes and stated, "I threw it away after I made the corrections."

Rob kind of smiled and said with a nervous laugh, "How do I know you changed it if I can't compare it with my notations?"

"You don't," I answered. "I would have expected that you would have remembered your changes. Besides, you simply have to trust me."

This is how I finally got the agenda out and away from this *stargazer* and his increasingly delusional characterization of his own importance. I never changed anything on the agenda that final time. I had to take a gamble that he didn't have a copy of his notes, which he didn't. If his changes were that crucial, he would have kept his notes or he would immediately found the omissions as glaring errors. He didn't, so he approved the agenda rather than admit he couldn't remember his changes and suggestions. His ego was at work.

Rob as a *stargazer* had the luxury of sitting in his office and dreaming. He'd have thoughts and ideas and pencil them in on the agenda. He did it because he could and because it gave him a sense of power and control. Each day, however, he'd make different changes that countermanded his previous changes. Whatever cosmic thought invaded his brain, he'd write it down. You can't run a railroad like that. You have to have an action plan and follow it; otherwise, nothing gets done.

I played a risky game and won. I had to get the agenda out or the conference would fail. Curtain time was upon us. I needed this *stargazer* out of the way for the good of the agency. Neither Rob nor Corky ever knew the real story behind the final agenda. Corky's idea became a reality because we had a solid agenda and that produced a successful conference. His vision became an annual conference that brought great continued uniformity to the northern border and better service to the importing community.

◆   ◆   ◆

This was an example of a *stargazer* who knew better. He really didn't have malice in his heart, but his dreams were gumming up the works. We also have *stargazers* that do indeed have malice within their hearts and they are trouble. Again, they are usually very brilliant and are easily and rapidly promoted into positions of authority before anyone realizes the mistake.

Rob did take full credit for the success of that venture, as is the tendency with most *90 percenters* and *stargazers*. It didn't bother me at all. It was my job to get the job done. I have always remembered what President Harry Truman once said, "In Washington it's amazing what you can get done if you let the other guy take all the credit."

◆   ◆   ◆

Hoteko's Law: *If you're under the direction of a stargazer, know what's legitimate and what's not. Don't spend any more time than necessary on his daydreams; concentrate on what's important and not on who gets the credit.*

PART II
External Factors

Like anything in life, there are situations we can control and situations we can only respond to after the fact. Outside influences will make an impact upon you and your agency whether you like it or not. It's better to be aware of what's out there. If you're aware, you can be prepared. If you're prepared, you can succeed in situations where the unprepared will falter, stumble and fail.

Fat cat politicos, hack reporters and shysters all share something in common. They hide among the decent politicians, respected journalists and ethical lawyers in an attempt to gain legitimacy. They are, however, also very different in one respect. While the rest of us have to tell the truth, they don't, and they are rarely held accountable for their actions. When dealing with these dregs of society, smile and be wary of each and every word you say to them. If you do that, you just might survive your encounter with these ravaging locusts.

6

The Politicians

As a midlevel government manager I was always acutely aware of the happenings on Capitol Hill. All federal budgets are funded with appropriated tax dollars that are doled out in varying degrees by members of the House and Senate. Congressmen and senators, even those not from your district or state, have an enormous amount of power and influence. They are not ordinary people. They expect you to know that and to act accordingly. They fully expect you to bow and kiss the ring when you meet them.

In my career I had many more dealings with congressmen and senators than most government managers since many would pass through Customs from their usually unnecessary junkets around the globe. Assisting an elected official is a no-win situation. Glad-handing a senator upon his arrival from London really doesn't do your career any good because he expects to be glad-handed. If you fail to so, however, I can assure you that Mr. Senator will make sure that the commissioner of Customs becomes aware of your shortcomings. At best, it is a break-even situation when dealing with them.

So, don't sweat it. Just do it. Many managers question why we would give preferential treatment to these already pampered beasts. They would say, "Let them wait in line like anyone else. They don't have diplomatic immunity, so let them wait."

I've never agreed with that assessment. I've always swallowed my pride and kissed their derriere after shaking their hand and feigning what an awesome privilege it was just to be in their presence. So, park your ego at the door, feed their ego and get them out the door as soon as possible.

◆　　　◆　　　◆

Some politicians are more pleasant to deal with than others and you can truly enjoy their company. I recall one encounter I had just after former Senator John

Tower had been killed in an airplane accident in Brunswick, Georgia, in 1991. Senators Phil Gramm and John McCain had been out of the country and were rushing home for the funeral.

I met their aircraft upon arrival from Japan. Their staff had called me and asked for the *courtesy of the port* and for my assistance in getting them to their next flight. These were both powerful Republican senators. We had a Republican-appointed commissioner of Customs, and we had a Republican in the White House at that time. With that having been said, I wasn't about to let one of my *90 percenters* handle this and chance a screw-up. Some things cannot be delegated.

Texan Phil Gramm shook my hand and thanked me, but Senator John McCain put his hand on my shoulder as we walked down the long concourse to their next flight. This former P.O.W. had a genuine smile on his face. His kind words of appreciation made the effort all the more memorable. He made a positive impression on me with his personal touch.

He said to me, "Sarge, thanks for the special treatment. I know we've taken you away from your job. But we really wanted to get back to Texas for the funeral, and I don't think we'd have made it without you. And thank you for the good job Customs is doing in taking drugs off the street. Keep it up!"

◆   ◆   ◆

Knowing who is who can work to your advantage. I recall one situation where I was waiting for the arrival of a VIP on a flight from Hong Kong. I was with my boss, Larry Shirk, when aircraft door opened. Out stepped a familiar face and this person headed straight toward me. It wasn't our VIP, but I recognized the person as the governor of Georgia, Zell Miller.

I had never met Zell Miller before in my life, but I recognized his face from some magazine articles and news programs. I didn't hesitate one bit as I held out my hand and said, "Mr. Governor, welcome to Chicago. Let me escort you through Immigration."

He had a wide smile on his face as he replied, "Why, thank you. It's always good to be back home and to get such good service."

Obviously, he had expected to be greeted upon arrival. Miller never suspected there wasn't anyone to meet him, since his staff failed to call ahead; however, he left a happy camper. Afterward Shirk said, "How did you know him?"

I explained how I recognized him. What did we gain from escorting the governor of Georgia through? Perhaps nothing other than he might remember the courtesy he received in Chicago. Could the governor of Georgia do anything for me or for Customs? Probably not, but a few years later he was elected to the US Senate, and perhaps he just might have recalled our goodwill when voting on our appropriation bill. Remember, you venerate the office and not the person.

◆   ◆   ◆

Unfortunately, many politicians are demanding, arrogant and condescending. There isn't anything you can do about it, except to do your job. One such person was the former Illinois governor, George Ryan. Ryan was an old-time hack politician who wouldn't give you the time of day unless you were a campaign contributor. My experiences with him went all the way back to the days when he was the lieutenant governor and the Illinois secretary of state.

In one of my first encounters with him he was returning from some unnecessary foreign trip. His assigned state troopers came into my office to inform me of his arrival later that day. I didn't know that the lieutenant governor of any state would rate "secret service" type protection. I thought it was not only ridiculous, but a waste of taxpayers' money to have two plainclothes troopers fawning over Ryan like he was the president. So, I decided to have a little fun with them.

When they told me they were his protection detail and asked for my assistance and I replied, "Who did you say was arriving today?"

"George Ryan," one trooper replied.

I shook my head and said, "Who's he?"

The other trooper interjected, "He's the lieutenant governor."

"Of what state?" I asked.

By now both were squirming, thinking I wasn't going to help them. One trooper gulped as he replied, "Illinois."

I figured I had worried them enough, they were only doing their job and I had my moment of amusement. I assisted them in clearing Ryan through Immigration and Customs because that was my job. What I found appalling was that Ryan had the dutiful troopers carry his bags out to his waiting car. He used them more as valets rather than bodyguards. Apparently, throughout the rest of his political career Ryan used his security detail in the very same way.

He wasn't the only one to do so. In 2004, the current Illinois governor, Rod Blagojevich was caught having his security detail carrying suitcases and baby strollers for his wife as if they were personal servants. Blagojevich was also exposed on a trip to Washington, D.C., when the media uncovered that he had a nine-man, multi-vehicle security detail that zipped him around running red lights as if he was the president. He must have learned from old George how to travel in style at taxpayers' expense.

On December 17, 2003, George Ryan was indicted by a federal grand jury on charges of racketeering, fraud and conspiracy. He was caught with his hand in the cookie jar. An indictment does not mean Ryan is guilty, only a trial jury can issue that verdict. If that happens, I wonder if old George will have his state troopers carry his knapsack into his jail cell or will he finally carry his own baggage?

◆   ◆   ◆

Former Illinois Governor Jim Thompson and Mayor Richard M. Daley were among two of the most courteous and friendly politicians it's ever been my pleasure to deal with and know. Both were outgoing and unpretentious with a genuine happy nature. Each would stop and talk with passengers waiting for their suitcases, and each insisted on leaving from the main public lobby exit rather than a covert side door for "security purposes" as some politicians insisted upon.

Fortunately most public officials are not like Ryan, but are like McCain, Thompson and Daley. Regardless, you must be professional and not personal when dealing with them. As with your ego, park your personal politics and personal opinions at the door. I recall one instance when a rookie inspector (still on probation) was asking a few questions of a federal district court judge who was returning from a trip to England. He was traveling with an assistant who happened to be an attractive young woman.

The inspector asked with arched eyebrows, "I suppose you always travel with your secretary?"

The clear implication being that the lady wasn't his assistant but perhaps a lady of the night companion. It was an unnecessary comment that was personal and judgmental in nature, and the federal judge didn't appreciate it one bit. He told me he was going to inform the commissioner of Customs of the lack of respect he received in Chicago. Later that week we received a call from our personnel office that the inspector was terminated. The reason given was that he had failed his background investigation. Was that a coincidence or did the judge pass sentence upon the cocky rookie?

◆   ◆   ◆

There are times when you have to take a stand with public officials whether they are elected or appointed. If the city of Chicago isn't still the most politically controlled municipal government in the United States, then I don't know which city is. It is nearly impossible to obtain a management job with the city unless you're connected to an elected official or a Democratic ward committeeman.

There are, however, many good people in city government who are professional, who do not abuse their authority and who provide good service to the public. On the flipside there are those "ward heelers" who find themselves in jobs way above their potential and ability. They are stubborn, opinionated and arrogant. They do more harm than good for the public. They are difficult to deal with since they know that their clout will protect them against any and all who seek to challenge their authority. It's their way or no way.

When international terminal five was being built to stem the serious overcrowding of terminal four, I was selected as the federal inspection service spokesperson representing all agencies in negotiation with the city regarding employee parking. As a *ten percenter* you have to be aware of what's important to those you supervise. Employees can care less about the aesthetics of a new terminal, but they are very concerned about where they will be able to park their car.

All the top federal managers made parking a primary issue when dealing with the city because of our employees' concerns. For whatever reason the city refused to consider the issue even reasonably. They flatly told us that our employees would park where their employees parked, which was in a remote parking area where they had to be bussed to the terminal. On face value, you would think that is reasonable, federal employees shouldn't be any more privileged than city employees.

Unfortunately, there was a hitch. International arrivals were nearly operating 24 hours a day, seven days a week at O'Hare Airport. Unlike city employees who worked a straight eight-hour shift and went home, federal employees were required to work on the average of a 10-hour day and were subject to callback assignments in the middle of the night to process incoming flights. They would then have to go back home, try to sleep and still report back to duty at the beginning of their normal shift the next morning. The extra 15 to 20 minutes, both at the start and end of their workday that the bussing to-and-from the remote area added, caused an undue burden to the federal employees. Due to that factor the federal government had a requirement that any airport constructing a new international terminal was required to provide the federal employees parking in close proximity to the new building.

It was the wording in that regulation that caused the problem—close proximity. The assistant aviation commissioner I was dealing with defined close proximity as a remote parking area about four miles away. I defined it as within walking distance of the new terminal. Since the federal government wasn't paying to build the new terminal, the city thought that they had the upper hand, but I wouldn't budge.

It wouldn't be fair to the federal employees to add those unnecessary hours onto an already long workweek. I made my case to the city. If the inspectors had to spend an extra hour each day commuting from a remote area, eventually they would call in sick for their regular shift. This would impact our ability to process arriving international passengers. We would be experiencing logjams in the new terminal which was built for the sole purpose of alleviating overcrowding as it existed in terminal four. This argument and the requirement for close proximity parking fell on deaf ears.

In the best Chicago tradition, they tried to buy me off, but not with greenbacks then I was told, "Sarge, we'll give you and your top managers parking right at the terminal. You wouldn't have to ride the bus from the remote lot, only your employees will."

It didn't work. I wasn't going to sell out our employees. I assure you that there would have been many of the *90 percenter* federal managers who would have jumped at that opportunity. These people are just along for the ride and once they see difficulty ahead, they try to run and hide from it. If that fails, they cave in using the *shrugged shoulder syndrome* but only after accepting their preferential parking spot.

They shrug their shoulders, toss their hands in the air and justify their actions by saying, "Well, there wasn't anything I could do about employee parking. The city wouldn't give it to us. Fifteen or 20 minutes extra each way from the parking lot isn't too bad for the employees. After all, it's free parking. I just couldn't do anything about it."

In one testy encounter I was lectured by the commissioner of aviation's chief of staff, "Sarge, you're not getting the parking you want. Who are you to question us? We own and run the airport. I'm not dealing with you anymore. Who's your boss?"

I could hear and feel the high testosterone level in his voice that was emanating from his ego. I gave him my boss's name and telephone number. The only thing I did was to dial faster than he did. I told my *90 percenter* boss not to cave in, but to tell the city I was the point man on parking. I kept one telephone call ahead of him and got all the federal agency district directors to do the same thing. The city was stuck dealing with me.

A month went by and nothing happened. They then asked for a meeting and I was told in threatening terms, "Sarge, you've become an obstructionist on the parking issue. We're considering calling Washington and telling them that. Do you know what that might do to your career?"

I guess they thought that veiled threat would cause me to cave in. Two, however, can play the threat game. I simply replied, "Tom, I started out at this airport under Mayor Richard J. Daley, then there was Michael Bilandic, Jane Byrne, Harold Washington, Gene Sawyer and now Richard M. Daley. Do you know how many people I've seen sit in your seat? A lot, but they're all gone and I'm still here. Go make your call. And by the way, I have a letter on my desk with all the federal agency directors' signatures. It informs the mayor that the department of aviation is the one holding up the new terminal project by refusing to honor federal employee parking as required in the regulations. The letter also mentions you by name."

He shot back, "You can't send that letter. You have to go through the chain of command and start with the commissioner of aviation."

I smiled and told him, "Tom, that's your chain of command, not mine. I am sending the letter."

Of course, I never had to mail the letter. As soon as I returned to my office, I was called and informed the city would acquiesce to our parking requirements. They asked me if we could wait a few months while they enlarged the public lot in front of the new terminal and have our employees park in the remote area. I told them no, we park in the adjacent lot on day number one. I wasn't risking the possibility of their not expanding the lot to accommodate us. I didn't trust them.

We went through this long and bitter experience because someone in the city didn't want to honor the parking requirement. Some ward heeler with an arrogant attitude wasn't going to let the "feds" tell him what to do. The threat of my letter to the mayor must have made that ward heeler a little bit nervous because they caved in.

If you're going to fight city hall, do your home work before you strike a blow. Have all your ducks in a row. Know what's worth fighting for and know the consequences of your actions, so pick your battles wisely. Compromise when you can, for it gives the other fellow a way out. When it comes to what's right, however, do the right thing and stand your ground.

◆   ◆   ◆

As a government manager you will get letters and inquires from elected officials. Some are routine and some are complaints, not necessarily complaints from that official, but complaints from their constituents, meaning a VOTER. I don't care who the elected official is—a congressman, senator, alderman or dog catcher—believe me, they listen to their constituents. Their tenure in office depends on their being responsive to the people who will either keep them in or vote them out of office.

The one thing that irked most managers in Customs was being tasked with answering complaint correspondence from a congressman or senator. I have to admit it was one of my least favorite tasks because nearly all the complaints were bogus in some form or fashion. Yet, it was my job to insure that each one was investigated point by point and if corroborated to insure corrective actions was taken. The findings of the investigation were also returned to the congressman or senator.

Let me share an actual situation with you. A citizen wrote to their senator that among other things they had been badly abused and humiliated while undergoing a Customs examination. They wrote that the inspector threw all their clothes out of their suitcase and made them disrobe in front of other arriving passengers. As ludicrous as that may or may not seem, I had to investigate the allegation.

I tasked a senior supervisor with that and he responded, "Sarge, you know that's all BS. Why do I have to waste my time doing this?"

He didn't get to vote on that task; he got to do it. So, the supervisor interviewed all the inspectors involved in the examination, all the inspectors working that day, the airline personnel in the area, the skycaps and anyone else who was working in our area. I was then able to give a detailed reply to the senator that no such abuse or humiliation of their constituent took place in U.S. Customs.

The senator was then able to write back to their VOTER that their office had vigorously investigated the complaint and although it was apparently unfounded, the senator had put Customs on notice that any such treatment of arriving passengers would not be tolerated. Mission accomplished for the senator who would appear to the constituent that he was fighting for the rights of one and all. There was only one problem, the senator never saw the complaint letter—it was handled by a minor staffer who prepared the reply based on our findings. The staffer would then run the letter through the senator's autopen and off it went.

In essence the senator and his staff couldn't give a rat's ass about the complaint itself; it was all about placating their constituent—the VOTER. I had many a staffer call me that he was faxing over a complaint letter and they would say, "Sarge, I know that this guy is wacko, but you know the drill. We have to send it to you like we believe it all."

Yes, I knew the drill. At my end the drill was doing an in-depth investigation regardless of how idiotic the complaint might sound. I know it drove my staff

nuts that I took these letters seriously. However, that was my job. For this particular task there aren't any short cuts. It is a lengthy and a time consuming procedure. The worst thing you can do is sloppy work, leave something out or try to
cover up something to a congressman or senator or anyone for that matter. When
dealing with an elected official, do the job once, do it right and move on to other
things.

◆   ◆   ◆

You have to develop a sense of trust with elected officials. They have to feel
comfortable in dealing with you and be able to trust you also. It's really not, however, a two way street. It's all about what you can do for them or how you can
perpetuate their image to the public, meaning the VOTER. You can have the
best relationship with a senator, but if he feels he can get more votes by crucifying
you, guess what? You will be nailed to the cross, and there's nothing you can do
about it except hope that you too will rise from the dead in three days' time.

So, be wary in all your dealings with elected or appointed officials. There is a
double standard in that you have to be honest, but they don't have to be. They
can be anything they want to be as long as the VOTERS keep them in office.
Respect the title and the office, even if you do not respect the person holding
them. Remember, hell hath no fury like a congressman or senator scorned.

◆   ◆   ◆

Hoteko's Law: *Remember this commandment: honor thy senator, congressman,
governor, alderman, elected dog catcher or appointed judge with all thy heart and all
thy might. If you don't, it could cost you your ass.*

7

The Media

It is inevitable that at some point in time someone is going to stick a microphone in your face and ask you a probing question. You had better be ready. You may receive an unexpected telephone call from a print reporter. You had better be ready. The day of *no comment* is long over, especially in law enforcement. The media and the public expect their public officials to be able to answer their questions succinctly.

Twenty-five years ago you could easily avoid a tough question from an inquiring reporter. The Chicago Police Department was classic in this respect. If, for example, they were at a dead end regarding the capture of a serial rapist, they would use their ace-in-the-hole to avoid answering any more questions. They would simply trot out some half-literate, old time captain who would look right into the camera and repeat this worn-out piece of Chicago elocution, "We ain't got no comment on dis investigation at dis time. Tank you."

With that having been said, this eloquent spokesman would quickly turn away from the media and march his beefy frame back into the safe cocoon of the police station. This doesn't work anymore. As a manager, especially in a federal law enforcement agency, you had better be ready to tell your side of the story. If you don't, someone else will tell it for you, and you might not like what they say.

◆   ◆   ◆

For the most part media interviews should be left up to the BIG PICTURE person. The only caveat to this is when the BIG PICTURE guy is a *90 percenter* which can spell disaster for the agency. Ideally a *90 percenter* should never be promoted that high up the ladder, but it happens all too frequently. They know that they shouldn't be there and you know they shouldn't be there, but nonetheless there they are.

I've seen it often; the call comes in that an investigative reporter has a hot story and is on his way over to interview the boss, the *90 percenter*. Since it's too late for him to hide or go home on sick leave, all hell breaks loose. Frantic phone calls are made out to the field in a vain attempt to get all the facts and brief the boss who should have known what was going on in his district if he was paying attention to the operation. It's all for naught. Even if this bozo has all the facts, he doesn't have the mental faculties to do verbal combat with a seasoned, cynical or shady reporter.

At best, when he is asked a probing question by the reporter, the *90 percenter* will gasp for breath, his deodorant will miserably fail, his tongue begins to stick to the roof of his mouth and he blurts out words that sound like, "Hum-in-ah, hum-in-ah, hum-in-ah."

I've witnessed this scene far too often; it's comical and sad at the same time. My advice is that if you're one of the *90 percenters* BIG PICTURE guys who really believe that *hum-in-ah* is a proper answer to a reporter's question, go ahead and keep giving interviews. You'll eventually sink yourself and damage your agency. If, however, you're intelligent enough to know what you don't know how to do, stand aside and let one of your *ten percenters* step up in front of the camera. It will be a relief for you and a win-win situation for the agency.

◆   ◆   ◆

Over my career I've been interviewed dozens upon dozens of times by the media. They ranged from junior high school newspaper journalism students to national network reporters. I willingly accepted the responsibility since most of the people I've worked for had the *hum-in-ah* syndrome, and they feared reporters more than they feared accountability.

Someone once asked me, "Sarge, why do you do it? They don't pay you enough money to be a spokesperson."

That's a fair enough question. As I've stated before, I didn't go into government for the money—I went in to serve the people. If being a spokesperson would help my agency explain to the public what it is we do and why we do it, then that is what I'd do. We did have one public affairs official who was a brilliant writer but uncomfortable in front of the microphone. It was this person who would call me from time to time to set-up media interviews. I respected this person for acknowledging their weakness and letting someone else be the spokesperson.

There are certain things you must always be cognizant of when dealing with the media, even on stories that are favorable to your agency. Many will criticize what I say, but it comes from experience. First of all, don't trust a reporter. Although they may be giving you *good* airtime or print on the subject at hand, they are waiting for you to make the yaky-yak mistake. The yaky-yak mistake is when your ego takes over. You just keep running your mouth and getting off the topic. Eventually you will say something stupid.

Mostly likely you will not even be aware of what you are saying in the course of the interview when your ego over takes your common sense. If that happens, you are then filled with such a sense of self-importance that you begin to tell your innermost thoughts to this reporter whose real motives are unknown to you. You let down your guard thinking you can trust him because he's now your friend since he's interviewing you. The momentary euphoria of having your day in the sun will soon be lost when you read what he writes after you've yaky-yaked your career into the gutter. Stay on the topic and remember that's the story he came to hear in the first place. If you do that, you won't become the story.

It is my belief that the media is interested in only one thing—ratings. A reporter is interested in only two things—a scoop and their own career. They could care less about you. It's all a game to them, but you can't let yourself become a pawn on the chess board. You have to be a knight or a bishop who has freedom of movement or you will lose the game. There are many things you can do to control the game and even the playing field.

◆   ◆   ◆

In the course of being interviewed over the telephone one time, I could hear the print reporter pounding away on their computer keyboard as I spoke. There was no way that the reporter could accurately capture all the words in my answers to his questions. It was then I learned something very important; speak slowly and stay on point.

Never having gone to journalism school, I'm only speculating that reporters are trained to ask you a question and after you reply to just stare at you and say nothing. I've had it happen and that long silence is very awkward and uncomfortable. Your first reaction is to keep talking and that's what they want. It's not only the answer to their question they seek; it's the yaky-yak nervous banter afterward that they hope you'll spill the beans on something or other that would be better left unsaid. The something or other may seem harmless to you at the time, but the media can make a mountain out of a molehill as well as take your words out of context.

To avoid this mistake, I learned to wait them out. I carefully answered their question and always used that opportunity to stay on point. What I mean by that is I would *spin* my agency's policy back into the answer in the most favorable light. If you have listened to any of the presidential debates you understand the meaning of *spin*. If the moderator asks a question on foreign policy, the candidate may totally ignore the question and answer with a point on domestic affairs. In other words he *spins* the question and answer to his strong suit.

I recall one interview where a reporter asked me a question regarding our effectiveness in discovering narcotics concealed on a person's body. I answered, "We find concealed drugs on one of four people that we search."

The reporter purposely twisted my words by saying, "So, you admit that you're wrong 75 percent of the time."

"No," I replied, "We are right one in four times. Finding drugs is a difficult job. If it were easy, we wouldn't have a drug problem in the United States. Consider this if you will, if a baseball player maintains a .250 batting average he's going to have a long and successful career. We're right one in four times."

Whatever the reporter's motive might have been, I wasn't going to let him get away with my answering we were wrong 75% of the time. If he was going to use statistics to represent his side, so was I. I wasn't going to be intimidated by him and used the opportunity to *spin* my agency's side of the story. This reporter played the game and so did I.

◆   ◆   ◆

It's very difficult to keep quiet and let the reporter be the first to speak after you've answered a question. Diane Sawyer, the dynamite co anchor of the well-respected ABC TV show, *Good Morning America*, is one of the best interviewers in the business. She has a calculated blond moonbeam gaze, coupled with her friendly almond shaped eyes, that is both disarming and lethal. I've seen her ask a simple question and listen intently to the answer while she tilts her head, locking her engaging personality right into the soul of the victim. Sawyer silently waits for some nervous yaky-yak that may open up a can of worms before she asks another question. She's the best and I always give credit where credit is due.

I've been asked how I stay calm and in control during these interviews. I reply with one word, "Fear."

Yes, fear. I readily admit I always feel fear prior to an interview. Fear is a good thing. It keeps you on edge, it keeps you sharp and it keeps you from doing stupid things. Fear makes you continuously review your subject matter so that you know it better than anyone else. Fear helps you anticipate what questions will be asked as well as the follow-up questions. Fear gives you the upper edge because it makes you prepare for what lays ahead.

Fear can be your best friend if you understand the simple fact that fear is really only respect. If you have respect for the other person's ability, you will prepare for the encounter. If you are prepared, you just might succeed. Fear signals you to pause and take stock of the situation. If you see fear as doom or as the enemy, then you cripple yourself and become a hostage to a force that will destroy you, in this case the press.

◆   ◆   ◆

I earlier stated that rule number one was not to trust a reporter. Now I want to complete that statement, don't trust a reporter NOT TO DO THEIR JOB. Remember, it's the job of the press to hold us accountable for our actions by holding our feet to the fire. I do believe that a probing press is necessary to keep government in balance, and I totally support that concept. People should know what their government is or isn't doing for them.

It is within their right to ask you deep and probing questions. You have an obligation to answer them, for if you do not, they will still go with their story—minus your input. Thus the report might not accurately represent your agency's views. Most people believe what they read, hear or see in the media. So, you've got to get your story out and hope that the press will fairly portray what it is you've actually said and not parlay your words into something that isn't. Always keep in perspective that the press plays a game, but remember that two can play.

All the best answers and policy statements can be for naught if you nervously yaky-yak. I was once called by a print journalist while I was on a TDY assignment in Canada. I was there in my job as the Customs liaison officer for the 15th Winter Olympics. I wasn't expecting a call or the question he asked. If I hadn't followed my own law against yaky-yak, I might have made a horse's ass out of myself, but worse, I could have created a situation that did not exist.

He asked me, "Sarge, are you up in Calgary because the airport isn't safe?"

I felt blindsided and the question threw me for a momentary loop. It was then I recalled seeing the newspaper headlines that morning which stated a fired security officer told a reporter that there were gigantic holes in the airport screening system that might allow a terrorist into Canada during the Winter Olympic Games. It was a hot front-page story.

I turned the tables on him as I cautiously replied, "No, I have no knowledge that the airport isn't anything but safe. Do you have any information to the contrary I should be aware of?"

He didn't answer me right away and there was this pregnant silence. I again remembered the yaky-yak part of my law and waited him out. He then discussed the headline story regarding the disgruntled worker until the end of the interview. He accurately portrayed my answer in his article in the late edition of his newspaper.

If I hadn't been thinking, I could have said something like, "Well, yes, I saw the article in the paper. I'm concerned and I'll have to look into that."

If I had let my ego take over, talking about issues that didn't involve me in my quest for self-importance, I would have really put my foot in it. Any seemingly innocent innocuous statement could have been taken out of context to create a situation that did not exist. The headlines would have screamed: *Top U.S. Customs Official Has Worries Over Calgary Airport Security*. This would have set off a bombshell of controversy, garnered me a one-way ticket back to Chicago and embarrassed U.S. Customs in Washington.

Once the toothpaste is out of the tube, it's hard to get it back in. I didn't condemn the reporter for doing his job, for he was after a story. I would have had nobody to blame for opening the can of worms except myself if I had yaky-yaked. However, I didn't, because I remembered one of Hoteko's Laws.

If I had answered, "No comment." The reporter would have gone with his follow-up story anyway without my input. He could have written that a top U.S. Customs official was in Calgary due to rumors of inadequate airport security. One part would be true, I was indeed in Canada, but for a budget meeting. If I shied away from answering because of uncertainty, he would be free to speculate as to why I was there and print his story. Remember the press WILL DO THEIR JOB; therefore, do your job and stay on point.

◆　　　◆　　　◆

Have I ever trusted the press? Yes, I have. You cannot be paranoid around the press. I received a call from a network investigative reporter once who was doing a series about smuggling at various international airports. This piece wasn't about drugs, but about Cuban cigars. I had never dealt with him before but had with others from his network.

He asked me, "Sarge, I'm doing a piece on Cuban cigar seizures that will feature the Miami Airport which is number one. Statistic wise, O'Hare is ranked on the bottom. Can you tell me why?"

I wanted to tell him the truth but was hesitant for one reason. Our HQ *90 percenters* and *stargazers* would go bonkers with my answer. These are people who respectively hide from the truth and think that every Customs enforcement program is legitimate and works well. Apparently, some HQ *stargazer* alluded to the fact that seizing Cuban cigars would accelerate the fall of Castro.

I cautiously answered him, "Pete, I'll answer your question on two conditions—that my answers are off the record and off background."

When you answer off the record, the reporter can still quote that the answer came from a high-level Customs official at O'Hare Airport, which could be traced back to me. If, however, you're off background too, they can use the material you supply but cannot indicate the source. I decided on those conditions because I wanted him to know how we operate at O'Hare, but I didn't need to put up with the idiots at HQ regarding my answers. He agreed to my conditions.

I told him, "Pete, Cuban cigars are not a priority at O'Hare. We are looking for drugs, that's our priority. If some poor schmuck buys a box of Cubans at London Heathrow because they tell him it's ok and we find the box, yes, we will seize them. But do we expend our limited resources looking for a cigar? No and we never will while I'm in charge. Drugs and drug money cause crime and misery in our inner cities. That's what we focus on."

I had to trust that he would respect my conditions. He was as good as his word. If he didn't and did use my name, so be it. I'd still have a job, but I'd have had to spend countless hours explaining to some HQ *stargazer* why his Cuban cigar program was stupid. I would have also spent hours calming a HQ *90 percenter* that he wasn't going to lose his job over my decision not to search for cigars. He respected my wishes, he got his information and I got my story out to him.

◆   ◆   ◆

As I've said about politicians, I'll say it again with the press too; you have to tell the truth and they don't. Consider the CBS *60 Minutes* episode that aired in 1997. Veteran journalist Mike Wallace relied on a memo that implicated the Customs top cop on the southern California border. It alleged that Rudy Camacho was in cahoots with a major Mexican drug cartel. The only problem was that the memo was a fake. Wallace didn't do his homework and the story caused serious damage to Camacho's reputation. About a year later they issued an apology, but only after Camacho filed a lawsuit and received a judgment against the CBS newsmagazine. I found it interesting, however, that reporter Leslie Stahl was the one apologizing. It seemed that Wallace was conveniently unavailable at that time.

Also consider the Dan Rather investigative report regarding President George W. Bush and his National Guard duty. The veteran CBS reporter ran with the piece in September 2004, just crucial weeks before a close presidential election. The story was based on a memo that cast doubt on certain portions of Bush's military service and was very damaging to the president. Once again the problem was that the memo was a fake. Rather didn't do his homework just as Wallace had not done his. What happened to both of them? Immediately nothing, although much later, Rather *retired* from his network anchor job but is still on the CBS payroll, as is Mike Wallace.

If I had used a fake memo to support a warrant for a drug arrest I think you know what would happen to me. I would be *gone,* as my good friend Chief Inspector Zoran D. Knezev would say, accentuating the word *gone* with a wide sweep of his hand, and quite possibly I could be facing criminal charges too. I certainly agree with firing any public official who commits such acts. We are, and need to be, held to a higher standard because of our position of public trust.

◆　　　◆　　　◆

The media is very powerful and their influence over the public cannot be downplayed. Pope John Paul II understood that and used it to help spread the faith. He used the media like a savvy Beltway politician and it worked for him. He played the game and used his *spin* for the greater good. We can all learn from the saintly man.

He had stated early in his pontificate, "If it doesn't happen on television, then it never happened."

◆　　　◆　　　◆

The media has a position of public trust and an obligation to report the truth. When they don't do that what happens? Usually nothing, for the media seemingly takes care of its own. There is an obvious double standard here, and there isn't anything you can do about it except to know that it exists. The press is all powerful in the game they play, but know that you can play the game too. If, however, you decide to play the game, be careful never to have an argument with anyone who controls unlimited airtime or buys ink by the barrel.

◆   ◆   ◆

Hoteko's Law: *Do your homework, know your subject, no yaky-yak and stay on point. If you don't, it's your ass on the line!*

8

The Lawyers

As a manager in a federal law enforcement agency such as U.S. Customs, you will have more exposure to lawyers than someone from the Railroad Retirement Board or the National Oceanic and Atmospheric Administration. There is more likelihood of you being directly involved in criminal cases. You have more involvement vulnerability in civil lawsuits stemming from allegations of abuse of authority. It's the nature of the beast when you're a manager whether it is in Customs, the Chicago Police Department or the rural Umatilla County Sheriff's Office in Oregon. Crime happens, suspects are arrested and people complain about police brutality. It isn't pleasant, but you need to know how to deal with lawyers.

Lawyers—you can't live with them and you can't live without them. Prosecutors are a noble bunch who seek the truth and speak for the victim. Most are underpaid and overworked. They dedicate their lives to seeking justice for the people. When they lose a case, the general statement they make to the press is, "The people have spoken and we accept the verdict."

Criminal defense attorneys are a weird breed. It seems as if every time their client is found guilty by a jury they spew out, "This is an obvious miscarriage of justice. We will appeal and prevail."

It must be something in the water in the jury room that makes those 12 people find an innocent person guilty. However, the fact remains that only 7% of guilty verdicts are ever overturned by an appellate court. I guess that juries do in fact reach the correct verdict, even though a defense attorney will indignantly cry about concerning the miscarriage of justice. It won't stop him, however, from hogging media time to gain more exposure for his practice which means $$$$.

◆   ◆   ◆

I believe a defense attorney will do anything short of murder to get his client off the hook. I'm not so sure that some of them wouldn't commit murder to obtain a not-guilty verdict. Not to judge a book by its cover, but take a good look at some of these fine chaps who defend drug smugglers, serial rapists, child murders and various and sundry other criminals who cause mayhem throughout our society.

When you speak of criminal defense lawyers, you speak of egos spelled with capital letters. Look at the famed dream team that successfully defended accused double murderer O.J. Simpson. According to many sources, the only thing that kept these fine lads together was their overzealous desire to see Simpson walk out of the courtroom a free man. If you followed the trial, you would have thought that LAPD was on trial and not the former University of Southern California Heisman trophy winner.

Apparently, the dream team believed in winning at any cost and using any means. The team consisted of Johnny Cochran, Robert L. Shapiro, F. Lee Bailey, Alan M. Dershowitz, Barry Sheck and a Mr. Nuefeld. The jury apparently disregarded the voluminous evidence that pointed at Simpson and chose to believe the supposition put forth by the dream team. That is certainly in their purview; however, the dream team disintegrated after the not-guilty verdict.

However, not all was copasetic in River City. Robert Shapiro told Barbara Walters in an interview aired after the verdict, "Not only did we play the race card; we played it from the bottom of the deck."

Shapiro went on to state that he would never try another case with Cochran nor would he ever speak to F. Lee Bailey again. You would think that these fine chaps would have formed a life-long bond after seeking the truth and obtaining a not-guilty plea. Did the dream team think Simpson was innocent? When asked that question, Cochran always answered it in measured words. Mr. Simpson has always maintained his innocence, he would say. If justice was served in that trial with that verdict, why not say so?

◆   ◆   ◆

Take a good look also at the expert witnesses for the defense that are brought in to counter the physical evidence collected by the police. These so called criminal scientists, forensic pathologists and a host of others will twist, obscure or blatantly lie on the stand to obtain the not-guilty verdict. Why? They are paid handsomely for their testimony. Money speaks in the courtroom.

You have to understand that the courtroom is a game of chess at its best. Lawyers have brilliant, logically calculating minds. It is fascinating to watch them at work whether they are the prosecutor or the defense attorney. They plot their strategy and make their moves. It all ends with a checkmate for one side or the other. Anyone who testifies in court is a pawn subject to being moved or removed from the board depending on the veracity of their testimony and their ability to withstand a blistering cross examination.

Look back at the many criminal cases where the defense expert witnesses have put on a circus-like show in the courtroom. I can recall one trial of a man accused of beating his wife to death. The prosecutor showed the jury numerous photographs of the blood splatter evidence high up on the wall that would be inconsistent with a tumble down the stairs. It was compelling evidence of a brutal assault that could have only been the result of a blow high up on the head when the victim was standing.

The defense expert witness testified that he believed the victim died as a result of a fall down the stairs. Remarkably, his testimony perfectly coincided with the defense theory. He illustrated his testimony by dramatically spitting out a concoction of catsup and water onto a white poster and empathically stating that's how the blood splatters shot up to that height up on the wall. The jury didn't buy that horse-and-pony show and convicted the person of capital murder.

There was another famous case on the West Coast in which the defense attorney was a well-known DNA expert. The DNA evidence collected by the police and presented in the court by the prosecution pointed to the fact that the guy was guilty. The defense DNA expert testified to the unreliability of DNA as if he were speaking about alchemy. Yet he makes his primary living using DNA evidence to get people out of jail, touting the exact scientific reliability of this medical miracle. One would think that identified DNA evidence is either unreliable or reliable. Either DNA testing is alchemy or it is science. In this case, however, I guess you can have your cake and eat it too. The jury bought the defense expert's testimony; hook line and sinker, the guy beat the wrap.

It's all a game to them. They will do anything to win, for winning means they get good press which, in turn, means they get more clients which means they make more money.

◆   ◆   ◆

Lawyers who file civil lawsuits are also a unique bunch. They are more digni-
fied in appearance, but if you examine their eyes you can actually see the $$
reflection clearly. When they smile, if you listen closely, you can hear the *cha-
ching* of the cash register! Yes, they're after their 33 percent of the pot, nothing
more (unless they can get it) but certainly nothing less.

They will listen to anybody who walks into their office with a so-called griev-
ance. They'll patiently listen, nod their heads in compassionate agreement and
then sue the hell out of you. I've always chuckled when one of these fine gentle-
men would say to the press, "It's not about the money at all. It's about what's
right."

It's really about all the piles of greenbacks that they can stuff into their Mark
Cross briefcases! Anytime a lawyer tells you something is for the public good,
keep your hand on your wallet because it's going to cost you money. The only
way these leeches can be paid is if you lose in court. No judgment for the plain-
tiff; no money for the attorney!

These people will go to any lengths and any means to grab the cash. I recall
one civil lawsuit that was filed in Michigan. A person was convicted of vehicular
homicide and received a lengthy jail term. Apparently, he had been driving while
intoxicated, crossed over a culvert on a divided highway and hit another vehicle
head on. The two occupants of that vehicle were killed and the convicted driver
was paralyzed for life.

While he sat in jail, being fed, having his medical needs attended to, he started
thinking about his paralyzed condition. The more he thought, and more he most
likely read about the law in the free legal library that is available to convicted fel-
ons, the more he felt he had been wronged. Finally, he contacted an attorney and
poured out his tale of woe and unjust suffering. The attorney nodded in sympa-
thetic agreement and vowed to represent this unfortunate wretch to make right
the wrong that was done to him.

This attorney filed a civil lawsuit against the estate of the people he had killed.
In that suit, this caring, compassionate attorney stated that the other couple had
some liability in that they should have seen his vehicle veer across the road and
head toward them. That the driver of the other car should have taken evasive
action that would have prevented the collision that crippled her client. She
claimed her client was owed restitution.

The convicted murderer wanted HARD COLD CASH from the estate of the deceased to compensate him for his self-inflected paralysis. He killed them and he wanted to rob their bank account. Therefore, what did the attorney want who filed the lawsuit on behalf of that plaintiff? What do you think? $$$$$$$$$$$$—that's what! Fortunately a judge dismissed the lawsuit. As famed defense attorney Mark Geragos once stated when commenting on a potential civil lawsuit, "If this isn't about money or the seeking of money, then someone is living in their own Neverland."

◆   ◆   ◆

Some of the very same advice in dealing with the media applies to dealing with lawyers. Be careful and cautious and not only stay on point, but always be to the point. Don't yaky-yak. Testifying in court or in a deposition is stressful. Remember one thing about a defense attorney or a plaintiff's lawyer; they are not your friend. No matter how affable they may be, they are out for one thing—to win the game at any cost.

Whether in court or in a deposition, count to three before answering their question and answer only the question. Don't nervously chatter. Let them ask the follow-up questions; don't provide follow-up answers to questions that haven't been asked. Make them earn their money by doing their job, and remember that their job is getting information out of you.

I was once asked in court, "Are you aware of the Customs' policy and procedures regarding personal searches?"

I answered, "Yes."

There was a long pregnant silence as the attorney waited for me to blab on. It didn't happen. He asked a question and I answered it—period. It was up to him to ask the next follow-up question on which part of that policy and procedure he was interested in having me answer. I could have gotten nervous with the silence after the question and yaky-yaked and given him an opening.

If you answer only the question asked and answer it truthfully, you do make the attorney's job more difficult, but that's what he is being paid for. You'd be surprised how little some of these fine chaps actually know about the law regulating federal agencies. It has always amazed me that they rarely ask the critical follow-up question that would lead them down the path that might indeed help their client! It's their job to help their client, not mine.

Be a competent, professional witness. Know your subject matter. Remember it's OK to be nervous when you testify and remember, fear is a good thing. It keeps you sharp, alert, on edge and prevents you from yaky-yaking. Take your time and answer one question at a time. Don't anticipate what the question may be. Let the attorney stop speaking, count to three and then answer in as few words as possible.

◆   ◆   ◆

I was subpoenaed to testify before the Chicago Police Merit Board. They were in the process of firing a police officer we had arrested for a trace amount of cocaine. I had testified as the supervisor who had field-tested the suspect substance in his criminal trial. He was found not guilty, however. The judge issued that ruling because of Class X sentencing guidelines. He felt he just couldn't send him to prison for an insignificant trace amount of cocaine.

I had no problem with that. We had done our job and it was up to the court to do their job. Well, CPD wanted to fire him and it's within their right to do so. His attorney apparently wanted to impeach the testimony of the inspectors who found the vial containing a trace amount of cocaine. He also questioned the field-testing procedure in an effort to show the board that his client, who had been found not guilty in court, in fact did not have cocaine in his possession.

I had been sequestered and when I was called into the boardroom the attorney whispered to his client, "Oh, we have Hoteko now. We're not going to get much help from him."

He was right. They didn't get much help from me at the trial since he didn't ask the right follow-up questions and I only answered what was asked. I answered those questions truthfully with as few words possible. It was not my job to help his client; it was his job to do so. Apparently, he didn't convince the board and the officer was fired.

◆   ◆   ◆

I've testified as an expert witness in two major civil cases. Testifying in court is not a pleasant experience. In civil cases the plaintiff's attorneys are after the all-mighty buck. As an expert witness you present a major hurdle between their being able to drive a Mercedes Benz or a Mercury Marquis. Their goal is to impeach your testimony by twisting your words, trying to confuse you and simply making you look like an idiot on the stand under cross examination.

This is why the U.S. Attorney's Office never asks one of the *90 percenters* to be an expert witness. The last thing they want in open court is some one answering questions with a *hum-in-ah, hum-in-ah, hum-in-ah*. This type of testimony can only lead to Uncle Sam opening his pocketbook and letting the plaintiff and his attorney reach in and grab all the bucks they can.

People will sue the U.S. government for everything and anything. If a person feels that their rights have been violated, they sue. When they file their lawsuit they start with the individual officer, or in Customs' case, an inspector, then the immediate supervisor, the chief inspector, district director, Commissioner of Customs and the Secretary of the Treasury.

They're not after the inspector; the inspector doesn't have any money so to speak. They're after the U.S. Customs Service, the federal government, which has deep pockets. I'm really surprised that their attorneys do not name the president of the United States, the secretary general of the United Nations and the pope in their action too! They want to get to who has the money and that's what it's all about—$$$$$.

In one tort claim action a person alleged that he had been subject to abusive treatment by two Customs inspectors. The U.S. government waived sovereign immunity and allowed the plaintiff's attorney to substitute the government rather than the individual inspectors. Smart move by that attorney, the government has a heck-of-a-lot more dough than the inspectors.

I was on the stand when this bozo attorney asked me, "So, Chief Hoteko, you do know what the truth cone is, don't you?"

I looked at him and then at the jury panel and answered, "No."

The attorney's eyes grew wide with befuddlement. He didn't expect this answer. I guess it threw off his entire opening line of cross examination. In fact, I thought that I heard him stammer under his breath a *hum-in-ah* or two.

At that point the U.S. Attorney objected and the judge sustained the objection. I later learned that this so-called truth cone was some kind of half-concocted theory that gave numerical weights to answers given when questioned. I still don't understand it, but it was explained to me that nobody who goes through the *truth cone scenario* can ever be telling the truth. This is why it isn't allowed in a court of law. It's all chicanery.

Now I could have fallen into a trap very easily. If I had let my ego overtake me, I could have blundered into a messy situation. Most people who are expert witnesses have an ego and do not like to admit that there is something they do not know. Being intelligent means knowing exactly what you know and knowing exactly what you do not know.

I could have fallen into a dark hole if I let my ego do the speaking, "Uh, ya, sure I know the truth cone. Sure, I know what it's all about."

With that having been said the plaintiff's attorney could have taken me apart piece by piece. I would have been twisting in the wind trying to answer something about which I had no idea just to prove to my ego that I was an expert. Remember, no yaky-yak and park your ego at the door.

The next thing that this clown tried to do was to stuff words into my mouth. To testify as an expert witness you either have to detail the level of your experience to the court by question-and-answer testimony so that they can certify that you are indeed an expert, or your qualifications can be stipulated to by both sides. Stipulation means that both sides wave the lengthy certification process and in effect agree that you know what you're talking about.

This attorney asked me a question to which I did not know the answer. I replied, "Counselor, I do not know the answer to your question."

At which he rapidly retorted, "You state that you're a so-called expert, yet you don't know anything about what you're talking about do you?"

Again, I could have let my ego speak, but I didn't know the answer to his question. It's OK for an expert not to know something; just be honest—it's the best policy. He was also trying to get under my skin, to get me mad so I would blurt out something I shouldn't be saying and that would detract from my standing with the jury.

I simply answered to him, "Counselor, those are your words, not mine."

After that I was able to gain control over the pace and content of the questioning by exerting my ability to stay calm and stay on point. When I was excused from the stand, the U.S. attorney told me that he admired the way I stood up to the cross examination. No *hum-in-ah* or yaky-yak, just honest answers to questions asked and in as few words as possible. I appreciated his compliment.

◆   ◆   ◆

You have to deal with lawyers; you can't avoid them. Attorneys are like politicians and the media—you have to tell the truth but they don't. Approach them with fear. Respect their ability to do their job, because they will do just that and at any price. Don't let them intimidate you. They play the game and so can you if you tell the truth, know your subject matter and know what you know and know what you don't know.

The really important thing to understand about lawyers, and it goes for the media too, is whether they win or lose the game, they go on to the next client or the next story to make more money. They remain essentially undamaged. They will remain callously unconcerned about the damage they do to your name and to your career. To them, the only thing that matters is winning. Remember that when you play the game.

◆   ◆   ◆

Hoteko's Law: *Be truthful. Don't be bullied by a bozo. Stay on point. Only answer the question that's asked and in as few words as possible.*

PART III
Communication

Just as most government managers shy away from media interviews, they shun any form of public speaking as if you've asked them to undergo a colonoscopy. As a *ten percenter* you have to be able to talk to and to motivate the troops. Whether in verbal or written form, if you expect someone to do something, you've got to tell them what to do and how to do it. In its simplest form, communication is direction.

Many of the *stargazers, clowns* and *wackos* spend extraordinary amounts of time and effort stroking their own egos in what they say and write. Yet, when all is said and done, what have they really accomplished? Nothing other than confusing and alienating the very people they should be leading. Hence, never say or write in 20 words what you can say or write in five words. Be direct, be concise and be brief.

9

Talk to the Troops

The major error most managers make, whether in the government or not, is the inability to communicate effectively. You really can't get people to do what you want them to do unless you tell them just what it is that you want done and how you expect them to do it. A good manager must be able to both speak and write clearly and effectively. Communication is a two-part process, and each part is interdependent on the other if the person hopes to succeed and become a *ten percenter*.

To some extent your ability to communicate comes from the early formative stages of your life. Your parents, your family and your teachers are a strong influence on the way you do or do not communicate. If you came from a family where silence was golden at the dinner table, the chances are that you will either become a voracious yaky-yaker in later life or you will become as reticent as a mob hood being grilled by the FBI.

We are all products of our environment, so if you had a parent who growled when you tried to say something at dinner, you would naturally retreat into the safety of silence. Once inside that cocoon of comfort, it is difficult to venture back into the world of having, and more importantly, expressing, an opinion. Moreover, there can be nothing more devastating that having a teacher ridicule you openly in the classroom. This kind of scar can remain painful throughout life and can cause a person to keep their mouth shut.

Thankfully most people overcome these obstacles and can effectively communicate with others. Some never do, however, and they do not belong in managing a federal agency. Yet, they are promoted up the ladder into positions where their ability to communicate is essential to the success or failure of the mission.

These hesitant, non-communicators can only succeed if they are intelligent enough to know what they don't know how to do and surround themselves with someone who knows how to write and how to rally the troops in a meeting. Unfortunately, many are either ignorant of their deficiencies or they forget to park their ego at the door, insisting that their communication capabilities equal or surpass those of Ronald Reagan, the Great Communicator.

◆   ◆   ◆

I knew a supervisor Jeb (not his real name) who insisted he was a stellar public speaker. He also considered himself a potential and bona fide future Pulitzer Prize winner. His bravado and ego, when added together, equaled a number that would have made people like Stalin and Mussolini envious. No matter what feedback he received from others regarding his deficiencies as a speaker and writer, he would just shake them off and keep on making a fool of himself.

His boss, one of the *90 percenters*, was uncomfortable giving briefings, but was a very competent writer. Ron (not his real name) had half the talents necessary to be a really good manager. Ron, for whatever reason, never tried to hone his speaking ability. He was intelligent enough, however, to know that public speaking wasn't his forte. He was satisfied doing the in-depth research and writing, but left the presentation to others. This was the main reason he'd never be a true *ten percenter*.

Ron prepared a concise briefing book and asked Jeb to give his branch's presentation of it to our new district director. It was a recipe for disaster. Jeb's ego and testosterone took control of him, he disregarded the briefing book and rambled on and on questioning why he had never been promoted to a higher level. When briefing the boss you need to use the same methodology as with the media and lawyers—be brief and stay on point. Jeb didn't do that. He made a horse's ass out of himself and out of Ron too.

Since the district director was new, he was very patient at that meeting. Afterward, however, he said to me, "Sarge, that man should never be allowed to speak in public. He's a disgrace! What's wrong with Ron, letting this idiot speak for him?"

Often first impressions are lasting impressions. As long as this new director was in Chicago, Jeb was lucky to have a job and Ron lost any chance he might have had with another promotion. Remember, when you choose someone to represent you, it's your reputation at stake. Ron understood his weakness in public speaking but made the gigantic mistake of letting a *clown* represent him. By doing so Ron also became a *clown*.

This wasn't an isolated incident with Jeb. In his quest for that next elusive promotion he joined a community service group in a vain attempt to pad his resume. A *clown* is a *clown* no matter what they do, no matter how hard they try or no matter what groups they may join. The president of that organization once said to me, "Sarge, Jeb is an embarrassment to Customs. Why do you let him speak in front of groups?"

I didn't have a good answer to that question since Jeb didn't work for me. If he did, he would never be involved in that activity. I would have used his talents where they lay best, behind the scenes in our special enforcement teams. He had a knack for smelling out the smuggler but not for public speaking.

◆   ◆   ◆

In written communication, first and foremost be brief. Too many government managers seem to become enamored with the printed word when creating a memorandum. I believe that many think they are writing a profound presidential inaugural address that will be judged by history and displayed in the National Archives. Generally these wordy nerds are the very same people who cannot utter a cohesive public word at a meeting; they hide behind their printed page.

For instance, when these bozos issue a directive, they write three paragraphs of literary gobble-de-gook to say something that can be stated in a simple sentence or two. They are bent on trying to impress everyone, especially themselves, that they are highly literate and have a complete mastery of the English language. All they succeed in doing is confusing the recipients. They also run the risk that the intent of the directive may have different meanings to different people which defeats the purpose of uniformity.

For instance, never write, *our natural resources are becoming scarce and our environment is becoming exceedingly fragile. Our dependency on foreign sources of energy is continuing to contribute to a huge trade deficit and that undermines our gross national product, which in turn causes an unfavorable impact on our economy. In an attempt to alleviate this critical situation you are hereby requested to conserve electricity by ensuring that all lighting fixtures are extinguished at the end of the normal business day.*

Use as few words as possible to convey what it is you want people to do. In doing that you limit the amount of misunderstanding that can occur with a wordy document. If your point is conserving electricity, say just that in the memo. State—*the last supervisor leaving the office will turn out the lights.*

As someone once said, "Keep it simple, stupid."

◆   ◆   ◆

Many of the same people who can write a clear and concise directive are unable to explain it to the troops at a meeting. An example is Ron, our friend Jeb's boss. Call it stage fright, a mental block or just plain fear of facing people in a room. They just can't do it. Remember fear can be your friend if you understand that it's only respect and you proceed accordingly.

I've witnessed really good technical experts who could not explain their expertise. They either become tongue-tied or when they try to speak they give out too much knowledge rather than staying on point. I believe that their intelligence is such that when they try to explain a simple thought, their mind races forward to consider all possibilities rather than a simple solution. They seem to feed off the challenge of the question. That's not bad if you're in a research institute. That mentality, however, usually leaves your question to them unanswered.

I had one computer guru tell me in response to a request for assistance, "Well Sarge, you can do this, or you can do that, or you can wait 60 seconds and try this and if you want to get really creative you might try that. But then again, try this, that and the other thing too."

He gave me numerous avenues of confusing possibilities, yet he didn't solve my problem. I then told him, "Bob, my computer is stuck. Fix it."

With that having been said, he hit two keys and my document reappeared. That's all that I wanted. In my capacity I didn't need or yearn to learn about the multitude of capabilities of the IBM System 36. He relished the all-encompassing challenge of the problem; all I sought was to finish my document. When I communicated the terse command, *just fix it,* he did. Keep it simple and to the point.

◆   ◆   ◆

I attended a training seminar in Washington, D.C., in 1991. Customs Commissioner Carol Hallett made a wise decision that all midlevel managers needed a refresher course in the fundamentals of management. At the end of the seminar each participant had to prepare a written outline and give a 15-minute verbal presentation on an elective topic using one training aid. Her point being that direct, clear and concise communication, both verbal and written, was essential to the managing the Customs mission.

Judging by the response in my class, you would have thought they were asking us to have blood drawn with a dull square needle. Many of these seasoned managers had been safely living in a communications-free cocoon. Many deemed it beneath their dignity to talk to the troops. They felt that this was a supervisor's job, not their job. Hence, an air of fear and doom invaded our classroom as each person had to prepare and present their topic.

It didn't bother me in the least. I had always considered it a top priority to talk to the troops. The topic I selected was budget sequestration. Why that? Well, in 1990 it looked as if we would actually have our first sequestered budget in history. Congress was at a budgetary impasse with the administration. Both sides of the aisle dug in their heels and refused to budge one iota from their political pork barrel spending indulgences.

The Balanced Budget and Emergency Deficit Control Act of 1985 was passed to ensure that the deficit would be gradually reduced to zero by 1990. The Act prohibited both the House and the Senate from initiating budgetary outlays that would exceed revenues by more than the proscribed deficit amount for that fiscal year. These two greedy and warring cabals felt that they, meaning their special interest groups, had suffered enough. They wanted to reload the public trough with pork barrel spending legislation that would bust the proscribed deficit limit for the FY 90.

The Act stipulated that the president could reduce or sequester certain percentages of appropriated funds in the budget that exceeded what was allowed for. A simple example would be the Customs $1 billion budget for FY 90. If that figure included outlays that exceeded revenues by 25%, the president would have the authority to sequester $250 million of our budget. That's a substantial amount of money that Customs would have to give up and would still have to be able to operate within the law.

Our anticipated scenario included cutting travel, training, equipment, promotions and filling vacancies. We still came to the conclusion that layoffs of personnel would be necessary to comply with a sequestered budget. Needless to say that didn't sit well with the troops or anybody within Customs. All holy hell broke loose when the hint of a sequestered budget hit the street.

In my presentation to the midlevel management group I related how I had handled that hot potato. I was in charge of passenger processing at O'Hare International Airport at that time. When I met with the inspectors each day during roll call, we talked about the sequestered budget issue. I was able to put to rest the wild rumors about who would and who wouldn't be laid-off if it actually came down to that action. There was a great deal of misunderstanding concerning this issue.

As the days and weeks passed, they had a very good understanding about what a sequestered budget was and how a reduction in force would be implemented. I also shared with them my opinion that congress would back down and vote a compromise budget that was in line with the Act. I explained that when push comes to shove even congress would trim some of their personal fat in order not to go to sequestration.

Why? There are over four million federal employees and many are concentrated in certain localities. There would be economic chaos if 25% of them were laid-off. They would remember that with a vengeance on Election Day. So, our stalwart representatives and senators tucked their tails between their legs and gave in. There was no sequestration that year or any year since. They simply passed a convoluted piece of legislation that boxed the Act into a legal corner where it still sits today, lonely and forgotten.

I told my midlevel management group that sharing information, even if it is not good news, is better than avoiding the subject. If people know what it is they may face, they can prepare for it. Sharing information avoids panic and wild rumors from spreading like an uninhibited cancer.

My counterpart, however, in the cargo processing area didn't share any information and did nothing to squelch the rumors. Matt (not his real name), who was the cargo chief inspector, didn't believe in talking to the troops. Either he was afraid to face them or just plain didn't care. The morale in cargo was bedrock bottom. People were morose and talking about things like selling their house because they wouldn't be able to pay the mortgage when they were laid-off. They thought it was the end of the world.

I felt greatly complimented when an inspector who worked in the cargo area came over to my shop one day to assist with some time-and-attendance records. After being there most of the day, she said to me, "Sarge, it's unbelievable the difference between here and cargo. Everyone here is upbeat and doing their jobs. They have a great attitude, and nobody is overly concerned about the sequestered budget. In cargo every one is dragging and doing as little work as possible. It's a horrible place to be right now."

◆   ◆   ◆

Have regular meetings with your troops. In Customs I had daily roll call briefings for the inspectors when I ran the passenger processing operation. In most federal agencies this would not be practical or necessary, but Customs is like a police department and a daily roll call is necessary. The briefings were conducted by a first-line supervisor who would detail assignments for the day; impart daily enforcement lookouts, current administrative matters and the sharing of other information.

I would attend the briefings as much as possible to answer questions and talk about what was happening in Customs nationwide. It was an honest, open forum that allowed the inspectors an avenue to ask questions and get some answers on a wide variety of issues. It fostered an atmosphere of inclusion rather than exclusion. I found out that people want to know about their agency. The more information they have the better they understand and accept the mission.

How long should your meetings be with the troops? Whether they are a daily roll call, a weekly get together or a monthly meeting, they should be just as long as it takes to get your points across and answer their questions. With that having been said, you do have to put a limit on the scope of the questions. You can't have a *wacko* asking you if there is any truth to the conjecture that Lee Harvey Oswald had accomplishes in Dallas in 1963.

You have to have an agenda and stick to that agenda with a reasonable period for Q and A. Never structure meetings for X amount of time, say 30 minutes. If you don't have 30 minutes of worthy material, you're just wasting everyone's time and by doing that you will defeat the purpose of inclusion. People will quickly tire of sitting around while someone is egotistically pontificating or inanely inflating the subject matter to fill the time period.

As in architecture where form follows function, in a meeting time follows the subject matter and not the other way around. By doing so, you instill a professionalism that the troops will respect. If they feel they are treated as a professional, most will act accordingly and you will see the results in their job performance. Most of the troops expect you to lead; so lead.

If, however, you lose control of the meeting by letting a *wacko* or two rant and rave about nebulous matters, you will lose the respect of the troops. Or if you let a *clown* of a supervisor ramble on and on about this and that without adhering to the agenda, that will defeat the purpose of the meeting. Lead, maintain control and stay on point.

◆   ◆   ◆

I remember when Carol Hallett, the then commissioner of Customs, came to Chicago to address a major trade association. I met her at the United Airlines terminal and escorted her to a waiting vehicle. I was there when she returned for her flight back to Washington, D.C. I asked her, "Commissioner, how did it go?"

She smiled at me and replied, "Sarge, I was flat."

I answered, "Commissioner, I think you're being too critical of yourself. You're a very good speaker. I've heard you on many occasions."

Hallett smiled at me and replied, "No, Sarge, I was flat. I know when I'm flat."

This is the sign of a true professional. Carol Hallett is one of the best public speakers I've ever heard. She's always prepared, positive and on point. The reason she is so good is that she does a self-critique after each speech. She never adopted the arrogance of many a person that she can't do any better. I learned a great deal from her honest comment to me that day about public speaking. Critique yourself each and every time you speak and learn from that experience.

◆   ◆   ◆

Hoteko's Law: *Talk to the troops. Be honest, be positive and be prepared. And critique, critique and critique.*

10

Tip-O-The-Hat

Not all communication can be in person. If you did that, you wouldn't have time to do anything else. As a manager it is essential that you connect with your troops on the issues, your expectations and what's happening in Washington. You especially need to take the time to say thank you for a job well done. An accolade from the boss goes a long, long way. When you personally put it in writing, it means that much more. I can't emphasize it enough—take the time to say thank you.

When I was reassigned to passenger processing in 1996 at O'Hare International Airport, I decided to write a weekly email newsletter to all the troops at terminal five. I entitled it, *News and Views at T 5*. I concentrated on what had occurred the previous week in my operation. I reinforced certain administrative matters, and I always tried to end the newsletter with an inspirational quote from a noted source.

One of the worst mistakes you can make is starting a newsletter and after a short period of time letting it fall into oblivion because the effort is too great. If you don't stay the course, the people will question your commitment. When they question the boss's commitment, they begin to question why it is they should be committed. It's better not to start that project rather than to initiate it and give it up after a few issues.

◆   ◆   ◆

My newsletter was only as long as it needed to be. There wasn't any set length or format. Some weeks it would be ten paragraphs and other weeks it might be only three. At first it was greeted with skepticism by the *90 percenters* who didn't like to lift a finger to do anything extra. What they were really afraid of was that if it would be a success, they might have to follow suit with a similar form of communication. To a *90 percenter* that might mean some hard work on their part.

I sent it out via email not only to my troops, but to my district and region office. Those recipients started to forward the newsletter to people on their own distribution lists. Soon hundreds upon hundreds of people were reading about what was happening in Chicago. I would get positive feedback from people as far away as Toronto, Miami, San Francisco, San Diego and other cities. Soon the big brass—district directors, regional commissioners, HQ program managers and some assistant commissioners in Washington D.C.—were reading it.

No one else had ever attempted this informal personal form of communication in Customs. At one national conference in Washington D.C., I was asked to give a presentation on my weekly newsletter to top airport managers. At another local conference our regional commissioner tasked his district directors to copy my format and communicate with their troops in a similar way.

I had more than one upset director come up to me and say, "Sarge, because of you I've got to write a newsletter!"

In making a commitment to my newsletter I was making a commitment to the troops. I decided to develop a personal writing style that was distinctively mine, fast paced, which would condense the pertinent facts into as little space as possible. I wanted people to enjoy reading the newsletter, but I also wanted them to learn. I wanted it to be a format for inclusion that would stimulate their pride in Customs and hence in themselves.

So, I created a unique form of recognition that was indigenous to my newsletter. There was the *Tip-O-The-Hat* and there was a *Doff-O-The-Hat*. If an inspector made a good narcotic seizure or any other accomplishment that was above the norm, he received the *Tip-O-The-Hat* recognition. I would detail the activity and end the paragraph by stating, a *Tip-O-The-Hat to Inspector John Doe for a job well done*. If the accomplishment was outstanding, he would receive a *Doff-O-The-Hat*. I overheard many inspectors talking about getting a *Tip* or *Doff-O-The-Hat*. They were proud of that moniker and they sought to have a *tip* or *doff* associated to their name.

◆   ◆   ◆

Here's an actual copy from late 1998—*News and Views at T 5 # 130*:
Things I know and you should know: I've said it time and time again that it's in the story. But is it really? You be the judge. The pax arrived on AF 54 from Stockholm via Paris. But she lives in London, yet she went to Stockholm to go to Paris. Yet we have two flights a day from Stockholm to ORD, yet she went to Paris to come to the Windy City.

Inspector Ray Smith sent her to secondary. She told Ray she was coming to Chicago to buy clothes. Sound Familiar? Inspector Mike Reid did the interview and bag examination. Some rolling papers were found. She avoided eye contact and her voice was quivering. She said she was here to visit a friend, Vicky. She was unemployed and her mother paid for her trip. She didn't know what Vicky did for a living and she would be staying at a hotel while in Chicago and not with Vicky. Her hand shook when she handed her documents over.

A pat down search was approved and this willful violator had almost two pounds of heroin wrapped around her body. Remember, you will find it in the story before you find it in the suitcase or in/on the body. Tip-O-The-Hat to Ray Smith, Mike Reid, Laurel Griswold and Olga Martinez on a job well done!

Rockford International Airport? What? Yep! The Greater Rockford Airport Authority is seriously going ahead with plans for an air cargo and charter air pax operation. All the Feds attended an overview session with a consultant regarding this proposal. Major stumbling blocks? You betcha! First is lack of a facility and more importantly lack of staff for all Fed entities. All Feds informed the consultant that we do not have personnel to staff their proposed facility. We'll keep you posted!

ZDK and his outbound raiders keep the pressure on! They got a great bust the other day. Almost 300 grand of drug money going to Mexico! And they arrested two willful violators to boot! ZDK and the team are keeping Chicago on the enforcement map! And this week will see HQ buying lunch for the team to honor their success. Tip-O-The-Hat to the team!

We need your input. We are forming two focus groups. One will center around our procedures when we transport and escort a passenger to the hospital for an x ray. The other is about $$$$. Equipment dollars that is! Jeanette (I call her JR) Reed has secured a large COBRA budget for us this FY. We need to get our ducks-in-a-row and submit our requests for the fiscal year! See your NTEU rep if you want to participate.

And HQ will have a group out at T 5 this week. Doing what? Another air pax survey that is! Pat (They call him the mayor of O'Hare) Noonan will coordinate.

I'll be at SOG next week. SOG? That stands for Seat of Government. And that's what the FBI's J. Edgar Hoover always called Washington D.C. I have been asked to be part of a group that will discuss the topic—Air Pax 2000. I'll keep you posted.

From the HQ TOOLKIT: Electronic Payments Replace Government Checks. Most federal payments to employees and vendors must be made electronically as of January 1, 1999. While the capability to pay employees and vendors by Electronic Funds Transfer (EFT) has been available for 15 years, only 42% of government disbursements are currently made by EFT. EFT payments give employees and vendors greater security, reliability and convenience, reduce the federal government's costs and allow *greater control over the timing of payments. Because of these advantages, the Debt Collection Improvement Act of 1996 mandates EFT for payments beginning in 1999. So what does this mean? It means you get your paycheck through EFT! I've had this for years and it works! I get my travel voucher $$$$ in days rather than weeks! Sign up!*

A big thanx is owed to our Melissa Zitowsky, Jim Luce and Vicky Diez for the outstanding job they have done with this year's Combined Federal Campaign. T 5 has a 71% participation rate and that is almost unheard of! Doff-O-The-Hat to one and all who gave almost ten grand to worthy charity causes within the CFC!

And congratulations to former Chicago and Toronto senior inspector Roland Herndon on his selection as a special agent with ATF! Roland was involved in our DARE program and did a great job while in Chicago! Roland, our loss is ATF's gain! And rumor control has it that two inspectors in Chicago have been tentatively selected by OI as special agents. Who? Dawn Gabel and Bob Gallowitch are the names I hear! And both are great selections! And each brings many years of law enforcement experience to OI! Good luck to both and we look forward to working with you!

"If you can walk, you can dance. If you can talk, you can sing." A Zimbabwean Proverb.

And now you know what I know. That's it for now. Sarge Hoteko

◆   ◆   ◆

One of the best ending quotations I found, and the one that I received the most compliments on, was from the late Booker T. Washington. It was, *"I have learned that success is to be measured not so much by the position that one has reached in life as by the obstacles which he has overcome while trying to succeed."*

Another one was by the late sportswriter Grantland Rice and was a favorite of grand slam golfer, Bobby Jones. It was, *"For when the One Great Scorer comes to write against your name; He marks—not that you won or lost—but how you played the game."*

◆   ◆   ◆

When I was reassigned to the Enforcement Branch in 1999 my replacement at T 5 dropped the newsletter. I had written 156 editions of *News and Views at T 5*. The port director then asked me to initiate a Chicago district wide newsletter. It was entitled *The Port of Chicago Lighthouse*. It was a quarterly publication of all the activity within the port, not just at T 5. As an ancillary duty I was the managing editor and I also wrote a column. The *Lighthouse* ceased publication when I retired in 2002.

◆   ◆   ◆

Hoteko's Law: *Keep everyone in the loop and let them know what you know. But, once you commit to something—stay the course.*

PART IV
Visibility

Julius Caesar conquered most of the known world because the Roman army faithfully followed him into battle. Why did they follow him knowing that in the name of victory that many of them would surely die? Caesar, like General George S. Patton, was always visible at the head of his army; that is why. I believe that there is nothing more inspirational to a soldier than seeing their commander lead them into the heart of the battle. Comb the history pages and the generals who were successful were the generals who marched into the heat of the fray with their troops.

Conversely, most of *the 90 percenter* managers I've known stayed in their office as if they'll catch the bubonic plague if they went out to see their troops. I've never really known a *ten percenter* manager that hasn't been visible to the troops. It's your job to be visible to those you lead and to those you serve. Nothing can speak more about your character and your commitment than to be on the front-line with your troops.

11

A Hoteko Production

To a large extent the federal government breeds mediocrity. In that respect we are like the Roman Catholic Church. Apparently, they drill it into their seminarians to be submissive and to be ordinary. They don't want priests to stand out; they want clones who do not question the archaic dogma of the Vatican, but will blindly follow it. I'm not saying that's wrong. You can't have thousands of rebel priests preaching strange or heretical doctrines from their pulpits each Sunday. The church seeks uniformity. Unfortunately, in the quest for uniformity to propagate the faith, they stifle creativity.

Many of the *90 percenters* in the federal government also feel that there is safety in numbers—numbers of managers who want to leave well enough alone. The *ten percenters* feel the opposite, however, and feel that we need more creative, dynamic leaders who are unafraid of taking on a challenge. The *90 percenters* actually resent those of us who take the bull by the horns and succeed.

As in the Roman Catholic Church, the *90 percenters* place enormous peer pressure on their fellow managers to be mediocre and not to rock the boat. They say the way to get ahead is to toe the line and readily accept the dogma out of the Beltway as the gospel according to St. Mark. These *90 percenters* can exert an undue influence over a newly promoted manager. If the new manager has a stiff backbone, he can cast aside the don't-rock-the-boat doctrine, but, unfortunately, I've seen good people cave in to that failed philosophy.

◆   ◆   ◆

One time my team was tasked with running an intensive enforcement effort at the passenger processing operation at terminal four in 1985. The district director made the request due to the lack of narcotic seizures at T 4. The chief, who was an affable person, was one of the *90 percenters*. He was nervous about my team coming in to his shop and what we might accomplish.

He said to me, "Sarge, I hope there isn't a big spike in activity. It would really look bad for me if you come in and start making narcotic seizures. Do you know what I mean?"

Obviously, he espoused *the don't-rock-the-boat doctrine* that is the mainstay of the *90 percenters*. They feel if no one is better than the next guy, then nobody can be criticized for not producing results. If nobody stands out, if nobody is visible, then nobody can be criticized. Again, that's like the Catholic Church, for if every priest gives droning sermons, the congregations can't complain that their parish priest is boring.

Needless to say in that short week I ran my enforcement blitz at T 4, we took over 200 pounds of marijuana off the street. I didn't cave in to the peer pressure from my fellow chief inspector not to rock his boat. I rocked his boat because it was my job to do just that and to get results.

◆   ◆   ◆

In 1990, I was assigned to the chief inspector's job in passenger processing at terminal four at O'Hare International Airport. The previous chief had a staff of 48, and when I took over the staff had been cut to 32 inspectors, but with an increased workload. Relations with the City of Chicago, the Department of Aviation and the airline managers were at a low ebb. Morale among the troops was rock bottom and narcotic interdiction activity was at zero. I had my work cut out for me.

The previous chief was considered aloof and unapproachable. He had a volatile temper if things didn't go his way. Nobody really wanted to work in that operation. All he cared about was the appearance of an operation, i.e., that the office was clean and the counters spotless. So they just went through the motions of doing the job and looking pretty. It was a shell of an organization that didn't produce results.

Shortly after I took over my *90 percenter* district director asked one of my inspectors, "How do you like working for Sarge?"

Her replied befuddled him since he wasn't a fan of my type of management. She stated, "I like working for him, because Sarge runs a tight ship. He expects a lot from us and we expect a lot from him. He's always out there for us, he's visible and he talks to us. We may not like some of the things we have to do, but he's fair across the board and we know where he stands."

Shortly after I took over, we made a two-kilogram heroin seizure while the U.S. Commissioner of Customs, Carol Hallett, was visiting my operation for a town hall meeting. It was one of the first times that a commissioner was on site when a bust went down by the numbers. That seizure was followed shortly by a record 17-pound heroin seizure! The inspectors took hundreds of pounds of drugs off streets that first year.

The previous chief cried to the assistant district director later, "We worked so hard all the years I was in charge and we got nothing. Now Sarge comes in and gets all the credit. I don't understand it."

This *90 percenter* assistant director either didn't have the heart or the gonads to tell that chief the truth about his non-visible style of management-by-fear. I used a positive approach of inclusion with the inspectors, not a negative one of exclusion. I publicly recognized good work and gave credit where credit was due. I didn't hide in my office and bully my immediate staff, but gave them their assignments and freedom to do their job without micromanaging the organization. I also spent a majority of my workday with the inspectors. It's tough standing on your feet on a concrete floor all day, but the inspectors did and I was out there with them.

One inspector said to me, "Sarge, we've never seen a chief inspector spend time out on the floor with the troops. The only time we saw the last chief was when he was in a mad tirade when something wasn't cleaned or didn't go right. This speaks well of you."

◆   ◆   ◆

The region public information officer came out to do an article about me after I was awarded the U.S. Customs Supervisor of the Year Award in 1991. She asked me, "Sarge, why do you think things have turned around here? Why are the inspectors so enthusiastic and eager about their jobs? What is it that you do that makes the operation so successful? Why do they like you?"

I answered her, "I can't answer why they like me. I do my job. I give discretion to my supervisors and I spend time with the troops. I'm out there where they can see me. Each day I try to talk to each one personally. It maybe just a "hello" or just a "how's it going today." I know the names of their wives and children. I want them to know that I care about them. I guess that they appreciate that and maybe that's why they are so enthusiastic about and successful in their jobs."

Assistant Commissioner, Charles Winwood, came out to O'Hare to present me with the Supervisor of the Year Award. I said to everyone gathered, "I'm only the custodian of this award. It really belongs to all the inspectors at terminal four; they're the ones who have done the good job. I couldn't be prouder to work with a better group of dedicated people than our inspectors here today. You can be proud of the job you do, taking drugs off the street, and one day your children will realize the importance of what you've accomplished. So, go our there and keeping doing good!"

◆　　　◆　　　◆

I made an effort to repair the serious damage to relations caused by the previous chief; I set an aggressive agenda to rebuild the bridges at O'Hare. I began to be actively involved in the airport community. I started participating in the O'Hare Managers Association Meetings, the Air Transportation Association Security Meetings and joined the O'Hare Safety Committee. I was able to bridge the gaps between Customs, the airlines and the City of Chicago. I volunteered to be the spokesperson for all the federal agencies at terminal four. I became visible to one and all at O'Hare which was good for U.S. Customs and our mission.

◆　　　◆　　　◆

Visibility comes in many shapes and forms. Not all is directly related to your job. One such instance was the practice of hosting a Christmas party for employees' children at O'Hare. I continued that tradition in 1990 and took it to another level. In addition to a party for the employees' children, we sponsored a group of needy inner city children to be our guests. I involved the inspectors in this worthy charitable effort that provided the kids with their wish-list gift, a hot meal and a picture with Santa Claus. We collected over $4,000 each December to give a day of love and hope to these deserving children. I had challenged the inspectors to give something back to their community and they responded.

The media came out in droves to cover this event for the ten years that we hosted the party. We also were able to highlight to the press and to the public that we were not just about taking drugs off the street, but we also cared about the children we were sworn to protect. Customs became visible to the community, and by doing so we received their support for our mission.

◆　　　◆　　　◆

I learned that some of my activities at T 4 upset some people. I worked hard to make Customs more visible than ever before at O'Hare. The airlines, the Chicago

Police Department, DEA, FBI, Secret Service and the Department of Aviation became avid supporters of Customs and our mission. I thought that there's nothing wrong with that. Boy, was I mistaken!

I can't recall the specific situation, but I was apparently conducting a high profile media event to give Customs more visibility. Apparently, this upset a public information officer. He cried to our district director that publicity was his job, not mine. The director calmly told him, "Cliff, this thing is bigger than you or me. It's a Hoteko production. Just stand back and let it happen."

A Hoteko production? That was novel, especially coming from this particular district director who had not been a fan of mine. I accepted that as an ultimate compliment. Was I usurping the public information officer's job? I don't know, but my job was to garner support for Customs and take drugs off the street. If, in becoming more visible was going to help, then I would become more visible. As I've said before to those *90 percenters* who occupy jobs and are not doing them, get out of the way and let the *ten percenters* run the show!

◆　　　◆　　　◆

In 1996 I was reassigned to run passenger processing at terminal five. I had been in the administrative chief's job at the district office and was glad to get back to the field. The previous chief at T 5 was a good fellow, good administrative person, but not a leader or a BIG PICTURE guy. Once again, seizure activity and morale had suffered. Just as before when I took over at T 4 in 1990, I had my work cut out for me.

I had a meeting with all my supervisors and the union steward. I had to include him since these were the years of Commissioner George Weise and Bill Clinton's reign where they had instituted a policy of partnership. I'm all for including the people; but, when Weise gave the union the right to veto management decisions, I felt that this was going too far. It felt like communism to me.

The union steward said something in that initial meeting that was interesting, he said, "Sarge, we're all glad you're back. The people are looking for you to lead. They need leadership."

Again, we started making hits. Our regional commissioner asked one of the inspectors shortly after they made a number of big heroin busts, "Why are you guys making seizures now? What's different?"

The inspector answered, "Sarge is back."

Why did he say that? I don't know except perhaps it was my reputation that had preceded me. I was perceived as a strong manager with a pro-enforcement posture that would back up his people. In reality all I ever did was to connect with the inspectors by being visible out on the terminal floor where they could see me. If they perceived that action was leading them into battle, so be it. In the end, it was the first-line supervisors and inspectors that made the narcotic seizures that made us successful, not me.

◆   ◆   ◆

Visibility is an important factor and in Customs that includes just how well you do or do not wear your uniform. From day one, my uniform was always clean and pressed and my shoes shined daily. No jewelry, shaggy long hair, pen-stained shirt pockets; just a crisp class "A" uniform. I've always given some credence that you are what people think you are. If you look like a slob, people perceive you as such and won't give you the time of day. A clean uniform projects an image of authority and order. If you sport that image, people will defer to you. Perception can indeed become reality.

On many occasions I would be able to control volatile situations because of my uniform appearance. I could get irate passengers to complete their Customs examination by just walking over and introducing myself and saying, "I'm Sarge Hoteko. Let me explain to you why you are here and what it is we need you to do."

I learned a big lesson from my boss in the army, Brigadier General Fred W. Collins. Military officers are very rank conscious and are often over-eager to let everyone around them know that they outrank the others in the room. General Collins never walked into a room and stated he was a general officer. He simply let the silver star on his shoulder speak for him. He would sit down and get down to business. His star and his uniform had stated volumes before he said one word.

◆   ◆   ◆

I can recall an incident about a year after I had taken over as chief of passenger operations in terminal four at O'Hare Airport. There were a few inspectors standing around talking in between arriving international flights. They were talking about uniform standards. Nobody saw me approaching, but I could hear the conversation.

Inspector Harold Klumpp stated, "Now you take Hoteko. Look at his uniform, even after all these years. It's immaculate. I remember the day he started with Customs in 1975. I took one look at him in his uniform and just knew he was going places."

The group broke into laughter when they saw me, and Klumpp was mortified at what he said. I told him it was a compliment and I took it as such. What that illustrated was visibility has many avenues and you need to use all of them to your advantage. Was I promoted up the ladder because I wore a good uniform? I like to think not, that it was hard work that got me to where I was. In actuality, however, wearing a good uniform didn't hurt either!

If a wearing a good uniform can help you, what does sporting a slovenly one do? We had one *clown*, try as he might, he always looked disheveled. His shirt looked like it had been ironed with a hot rock, there were food stains on his tie and his pants had never seen the inside of a dry cleaning establishment. Yet, he deluded himself into thinking he looked professional.

He had good abilities, but the visible image he portrayed worked against him. While he could be presenting the best enforcement briefing, people wouldn't be paying any attention to what he was saying. They were intently focused on his tie to see if they could identify what he had for lunch. Hence, all the hard work he did researching the briefing was lost. All the talk afterward wasn't on enforcement initiatives, but on the speculation if he had pizza, spaghetti or a taco for lunch. He always wondered why he never was promoted.

◆　　◆　　◆

Visibility, image and perception go hand-in-hand. Any time I was in front of the troops or speaking in public, I always remembered my responsibility and who I was representing. Whether I wore a uniform or a suit, I felt that I was flying the flag and carried myself in a professional manner. I felt that at that moment I was the United States Customs Service. I worked hard to project that visible image. Remember, visible images are lasting images.

◆　　◆　　◆

Hoteko's Law: *Be visible, be creative and be bold. Whatever you do, however, as Spiro Agnew once said, "Don't listen to the nattering nabobs of negativism."*

PART V
Keter Shem Tov

Keter Shem Tov is a Hebrew phrase that means *the crown of a good name*. Everyone is born with a good name. Most people carry their name throughout life with honor. There are certain situations where others may tarnish your name and you have little or no control over those actions. Generally, however, nobody can take your good name away from you except yourself by your own actions or your own words.

Here are three examples of people who foolishly lost their good names. The first two were indeed *clowns*. They were good-natured people who if they had just paid careful attention to what they were doing wouldn't have ruined their reputations. The last person is a prime example of someone who deliberately went out of his way to tarnish his name. You need to be aware of how easy it is to lose your good name.

12

Reputations by Accident

In the end all that you have in life is your good name. Whether that's fair or not, you're judged by your reputation. You can have a lifetime of achievement which can be quickly washed away with one ripple of a scandal. This ripple can be self-induced or it can be a vicious cloak of darkness cast upon you by the media, an overzealous prosecution or simply by someone trying to do you in.

Maurice Stans was Secretary of Commerce in the first Nixon administration. He was the finance chairman for the Committee to Reelect the President in 1972. Stans was indicted on charges of conspiracy, obstruction of justice and perjury along with the former Attorney General John Mitchell in connection with the Watergate scandal. Both were ultimately acquitted of those charges.

After that verdict Stans faced the press and said, "Can someone tell me how I get my good name back?"

Nobody could because you can't get your good name back once it has been dragged through the mud. Besides, he was talking to the wrong people; the press has always had a field day when it comes to mudslinging. The more mud means more print and airtime that will be devoted to keeping someone in the gutter because that sells newspapers and increases ratings. Most people, however, never face a prosecution like Stans did to lose their good name. They usually open their mouth, insert their foot and close their mouth. They do it to themselves and have no one else to blame.

As a manager you have to be aware constantly that your actions and your words will receive the utmost scrutiny all of the time. The higher you progress, the more intense is that scrutiny. It comes with the territory and you need to be aware of that and act accordingly. The problem is that many managers let their ego and delusions of grandeur do the talking. It's those loose lips that sink their ship and carries their good name down to the bottom of the sea.

◆   ◆   ◆

There was one supervisor who was always promising rewards and gifts to his inspectors if they would do the complicated tasks he was unable to do. One sign of a good manager is to surround yourself with good people who can get the job done and there's nothing wrong with that. What is wrong, however, is a manager who promises and doesn't deliver. That's the sign of a conniver.

First of all bribery is illegal and I do not condone it. A manager who promises a gift as a reward for a job well done walks a slippery slope. The reward for the employee should come in the form of their yearly evaluation or official agency recognition and not as a personal gift. With that having been said, a superior can indeed give a gift to a subordinate without violating the code of conduct as long as there are no strings attached, i.e., as a quid pro quo for doing a job.

One inspector, Randy (not his real name), had been doing complicated computer programs, reports and analysis for one supervisor, Jennings (not his real name). Randy kept a catalogue which contained a picture of an expensive item he relished on his desk. Apparently, Jennings had alluded to the fact that if Randy continued doing those complicated tasks, he would be rewarded with that item. Randy kept faithfully plugging away day by day and dreaming about his reward.

His supervisor got wind of it and confronted him by saying, "Jennings, you can't give out an expensive item to a person for doing your work. It's wrong and has the appearance of bribery and favoritism."

He replied, "No, it's not for doing those jobs. I am going to give it to him as retirement gift from me. He will get it when he retires. I am not bribing him."

The manager looked at Jennings, who was a crafty, sly fox, and knew that he was technically right about a retirement gift and said, "Well, if you promise someone something, deliver on that promise. Remember, it's your word that you give."

When Randy retired, he received a gift from Jennings, but it wasn't what he wanted. It was the shaft. Jennings had been accused in an EEO complaint of disparate treatment of minorities regarding the assignment of overtime. He was interviewed by an EEO fact-finder. Jennings, who was always chasing and never catching his next promotion, didn't want an EEO rap on his sheet. He did what any conniver without scruples would do; he gave up his trusted aide, Randy.

He told the fact-finder, "Well, Randy did it. He assigned the overtime and I just initialed the sheets. I trusted Randy and he let me down."

When Randy found out about that he was livid. Even though he was retired, he was proud of his honorable service and his impeccable record in Customs. He called Jennings and stated, "How could you do that to me after all I've done for you? I never discriminated against anyone. I always assigned the overtime to the people you told me to assign. Everyone always knew you were devious, but I never thought that you'd do this to me to save yourself!"

Jennings matter-of-factly answered, "Well, you're retired and there isn't anything they can do to you. I didn't think you would care."

To this day Randy has never again spoken to Jennings, his friend of many years. Jennings deluded himself into believing that everybody else was stupid and he was smart. Jennings thought people had forgotten that he had promised Randy that gift. He also thought nobody knew that he had given up Randy in the EEO case.

Randy wasn't the only employee that Jennings promised gifts and favors to. He gained a reputation of not being a man of his word. When he enticed new employees to do his work, the older ones would laugh and take bets on how long it would take them to see through Jennings duplicitous façade. Sadly, people finally realized that Jennings couldn't be trusted and they shunned him. His name became mud to one and all.

◆   ◆   ◆

People are funny as the statement goes. Many delude themselves into thinking, just like Jennings, that nobody sees through their façade. There was one supervisor who would do anything, kiss any behind to get ahead. He thought that he was pulling the wool over everyone's eyes. Although he fooled no one, he was always able to make a fool of himself.

Smith (not his real name) was always throwing parties at his home. Some were rather formal affairs in the evening and some were casual outdoor afternoon barbecues. He would generally invite some of his peers and the higher-ups in the agency rather than his troops and there's nothing wrong with that. If you are going to entertain, however, entertain by good service and not by being a circus *clown*. The very people whom Smith had hoped to impress, with promotions in mind, were the very people who laughed at him behind his back after the parties. The parties were more of a comedy than a social event.

One higher-up walked through the kitchen during a summer day's cookout and saw two cats on the table licking the potato salad bowl that was then carried out to the guests. One person had his wine glass cleaned by Smith using a pressure garden hose which sprayed water over other guests. Another person saw a puppy urinating on mint leaves by the garage. Shortly afterward Smith picked the same mint leaves and placed them in a pitcher of ice tea for his guests.

At one of his formal affairs a bigwig was sitting at the bar with Gregg, one of the few troopers ever to attend a dinner. Smith asked, "Greg, would you like an after-dinner drink?"

Greg asked for a cognac. Smith placed a snifter in front of him, brandished a bottle of Remy Martin VSOP and carefully poured a healthy libation into the crystal glass. He then asked the bigwig, "What can I get you?"

He shrugged his shoulders and answered, "Smith, cognac is fine."

Now you would have thought that Smith would pour a drink out of the same bottle he used for Greg. No, in an attempt to ingratiate himself to the bigwig, he reached behind him and pulled out a bottle of rare, 50-year-old Courvoisier Initiale cognac and stated with a sly smile on his devious face, "My very good friend, for you the good stuff."

Well, when Greg heard that he almost gagged, thinking that he must be drinking radiator fluid. It didn't faze Smith at all to offer the bigwig the *good stuff* while Greg was sitting next to him and drinking the *ordinary stuff*. In Smith's mind the boss deserved the best; Greg was an underling and shouldn't question being served the *ordinary stuff.*

Smith was a good-natured person. Unfortunately he was a *clown* by his own actions and words. It was obvious to those guests invited to his "elegant" soirées just what he was doing—trying to kiss as many butts as possible. Although his actions seem humorous, he lost the crown of his good name. He became the butt of everyone's jokes in the organization.

◆　　　◆　　　◆

Both Jennings and Smith were not bad people; however, in their overzealousness to succeed, they made fools of themselves. Neither would listen to any advice given regarding their conduct. If they had, they would never have tripped and fallen down so easily. Neither understood that you can gain a reputation in a day that can take you a lifetime to shed. Unfortunately, for the rest of their careers people looked upon them as *clowns,* and they had nobody to blame but themselves.

◆   ◆   ◆

Hoteko's Law: *Understand that people are intelligent and they will see through your charade if you're playing a game. Be yourself, be honest and be careful of what you say, do and promise, because people have memories.*

13

Reputations on Purpose

Believe it or not there are managers that covet a *hard ass* reputation. They firmly espouse the theory of *management by fear* (MBF) rather than management by objective (MBO). Their meaning of fear isn't respect; it is terror and that makes a big difference. They feel that their employees, especially their subordinate supervisors, should actually quake at their approaching sight or when they hear their voice over the telephone. These are the very type of managers who gave legitimate birth to the labor union movement in this country, and rightfully so.

Although I am not a psychologist or a psychiatrist, my experience with this type of cranial midget is to conclude that they have a seriously insecure personality. They were probably bullied as children rather than to have been the bully. They were most likely to have been the last child selected for an intramural basketball game in school, sitting all alone in the middle of the gym floor while all the other children snickered. Kids can be cruel to kids.

Perhaps they were constantly taunted in the school yard, "Ha, ha, there's fatty!"

Or maybe they were belittled while waiting in line for lunch, "Oh, don't get too close to him, don't touch him, he's got the cooties! The cooties, the cooties!"

These types of scars run deep and remained hidden. Children hope and wait for their day in the sun, so to speak, to get even with the world that rejected them in their youth. Even as adults they still do not garner the respect they think that they deserve. When they get home, they meekly enter the house and do whatever it is their spouse orders them to do. Their spouses dominate their home life, which reminds them of the bullying they received in their childhood. Hence, they vent their frustration in the only place available them, the workplace. It's the only avenue for them to assert their authority and be in control.

Most of the MBF managers who rant and rave can be handled. They are ignorant and display their character flaw out in the open. If, you can't stop their behavior, at least you know what to expect. If you know what to expect, you can work around them and still get your job done. It's the manager that subtly and deviously exercises MBF that will be your nemesis. He can cause you sleepless nights, especially if he is your boss.

This type of MBF manager does not rant or rave. He's too intelligent for that, so he gravitates to a more refined method of fear. Fear of the unknown, usually in the form of going after the small stuff. They take an inordinate delight in knit-picking your branch or unit apart, bit by tiny bit. They spend time on the most mundane of items in an attempt to keep you off balance so they can assert their authority and control over you.

In plain language, they sweat the small stuff. The big stuff goes over their heads since they really don't have the ability to grasp or handle complex situations. The only way they can hammer it into your head that they are the BOSS is to belittle you bit by tiny bit. They leave a trail of subtle fear behind that they hope will keep you on pins and needles until their next usually unannounced foray into your world.

◆   ◆   ◆

We had a charming fellow at our HQ office who was in charge of a sensitive operation. His critical field division had 200 inspectors and about 25 supervisors scattered in several locations across the map. Mertz (not his real name) had been in Customs for almost 20 years and had been an excellent and highly respected Customs officer. He had impeccable credentials, but on the technical side of the house, not on the operational side.

As a HQ program officer he was a whiz at analyzing problems and issues. He was a walking encyclopedia of knowledge. You could give him a complex issue and let him go to work. He would close his door and in a couple of days present you with a paper. The problem, however, was he didn't give you an answer; he gave you multiple answers to the given situation. You as the BIG PICTURE guy would appreciate this. You could review them and choose the best course of action. It was a gift to have someone like Mertz on your staff.

His inability to focus on a single solution, however, also meant Mertz wasn't a BIG PICTURE guy. He would never be able to choose the best scenario answer for the problem. In fact, he would probably choose the worst answer for the issue even though he had formulated all the answers. He had flawed judgment and reasoning abilities when it came to making a decision. Unfortunately, he always thought of himself as a BIG PICTURE guy, someone who should be in charge. He coveted a chance to be the boss.

He was extremely good in his HQ program officer's job. One day he put in for a promotion to head a critical field unit. Someone in HQ, either a *wacko* or *stargazer*, thought he could do a good job as a BIG PICTURE guy. What a mistake. First of all, he didn't have any real field experience and had never been a uniformed inspector. This is not to say that's a requirement, but usually technical people; people who do not deal with people, but only with paperwork, normally fare poorly in a uniformed management position. There are always exceptions to the rule, but Mertz wasn't one of them.

Corky McMullen once told me, "Sarge, first-line uniformed supervisory inspectors usually make the best managers in Customs. Why? They are used to dealing with people and in time-sensitive situations, as well as making decisions on the spot. They're not like auditors or import specialists who only deal with paperwork and can take a week or two to make a decision."

Corky started life in Customs as an import specialist. So his sage advice was all the more compelling. Unfortunately, the damage had been done, for Mertz was now in charge. Yet, he could have succeeded if he really applied himself, but rather than easing himself into the job, trying to learn from his seasoned subordinate supervisors, he ambled into the operation like a large cow grazing his way through the showroom at the Waterford crystal factory in Ireland. It was crash-boom-bam in short order.

Like anything else in the government, he was now in charge, and there wasn't much anybody could do about it. Never having worn a uniform, he now acted like a boy scout who miraculously found himself in the real army. He ordered every possible uniform accessory available. He would swagger into the office as if he had just liberated Bastogne on Christmas Eve in 1944. He would make surreptitious visits to his various operational sites as if he were the Inspector General of the United States Army.

He would consistently belittle his subordinate supervisors by peppering them with inane questions of which only he knew the answers. He would look down his nose at them with an unholy glee as he rudely corrected their wrong answer. Someone once described his communication ability not as talking, but as pontificating. His whole goal was to keep his subordinate staff off guard as to his comings and goings. They would be unmercifully grilled on various subjects at his whim. His was a case study of what constitutes an MBF manager.

Someone once compared him to Captain Bligh of the *HMS Bounty*. Mertz was not unlike Bligh as both believed in draconian measures to sail their ships. Mertz, who had been an excellent technical guy, turned into a Bligh when given a command position. He had ample opportunity to learn from good *ten percenters* in action at HQ and throughout the field, yet he close a Bligh as his role model. It was pure ego, an ego that he should have been intelligent enough to park at the door.

◆   ◆   ◆

There was one instance where he had unmercifully torn apart a subordinate's operation piece by piece and a HQ program officer asked him, "Mertz, why did you do that? The operation is basically in compliance; it might need a tweak here and there, but why crucify the poor fellow? And why embarrass him in front of everyone? If you're going to do that, do it in private. It serves no purpose."

Mertz began to strut around the office like Bligh pacing the quarterdeck and replied, "You don't understand. It's my operation and everyone better run it my way or they'll face the consequences. It's not open to debate. If he was embarrassed, good. It serves my purpose. I want them to be afraid of me."

Finally, after a number of years of the unnecessary turmoil he fomented, HQ realized that they had to act and act fast to stop this idiot from causing more harm. They didn't want a mutiny on the *Bounty*. A HQ *ten percenter* came up with a foolproof plan to side-door Mertz. They consolidated his operation with another one in order to remove him from his position of authority. If they had demoted him or reassigned him he would have sued. The federal government is fertile ground for lawsuits since it has deep pockets. It also has a plethora of the *90 percenter* managers who make dubious decisions that open the door to litigation. This is how HQ they avoided the mutiny that was on the horizon.

◆   ◆   ◆

Mertz was intelligent and should have known better, but he readily used his authority to run rough-shod over people. He really believed that by using fear, he would run a tight ship, just as Captain Bligh had on the *HMS Bounty*. He certainly could have learned the job from those he worked with, but he chose otherwise. Those who had once respected him and his abilities, now routinely despised him. He had willfully taken his good name and run it into the ground.

◆   ◆   ◆

Hoteko's Law: In *the government you have nothing to fear but those who man-age by fear. Know them, know their fearful ways and work around them.*

PART VI
The Real Stars

To some extent leaders are born. In my case I was able to learn leadership from a group of good people who freely shared their experiences, their philosophy and their talents. They went out of their way to help me climb the ladder. They didn't selflessly hoard their talent in fear of competition; they boldly gave me the opportunity to excel and to succeed.

I've listed some of the best of the *ten percenters* here who ran the government. They are the stars, not the *stargazers*, but like a *stargazer*, they are visionaries. Their vision is focused, however, and not predicated on a wild yearning or a cloudy pipedream. Nobody always makes the right decisions in life, but these *ten percenters,* unlike the *stargazers*, have always accepted responsibility for their actions. This alone has made them stand apart from the crowd.

14

Corky McMullen

Richard E. McMullen was known to one and all as Corky. This moniker was stuck on him early in life due to his Irish heritage. In his career with Customs, Corky moved around the country. He started in Rochester, then on to Buffalo, Los Angeles, then Chicago and back to Buffalo where he finally retired.

He started at the bottom of the ladder and worked his way up to become one of seven regional commissioners in Customs. I first met Corky when he took over the North Central region in Chicago in 1985. Our region was the largest in Customs, covering most of the northern border and included 18 states. I could sense his leadership abilities from the get-go. Much like my old boss, General Fred W. Collins, he exuded authority when he entered the room. There was no question that he was in charge.

Corky had spent a couple of years in Los Angeles as the deputy regional commissioner to Quinton Villanueva. Mike, as Villanueva preferred to be called, was a political appointee. This was a rarity in Customs. Usually only the commissioner is appointed by the president; the rest of hierarchy has always been career civil service. This is unlike other federal agencies where hefty donors to the winning political party densely populate the bureaucracy as administrators, directors, assistant directors, assistant and deputy secretaries of various departments and agencies.

Customs has indeed been lucky not to have the pestilence of a plethora of political appointees coming in every four years and *stargazing* their way into the inner workings of our agency. Although these are good-natured and well-meaning people, they get their appointments by pumping hundreds of millions of dollars into political campaigns. They expect to receive a job, a title and immortality for their largess. They all want to leave their stamp upon history by reinventing, retooling or redesigning their agency.

Unfortunately, most do not park their ego at the door and simply let the career *ten percenters* run the show. If they did, they could enjoy the ride their campaign contributions bought. Rather, they bulldoze their importance right through the heart of the agency they have sworn to uphold, protect and defend. By doing so, they screw up the works.

◆   ◆   ◆

Mike Villanueva was a good guy. He was retired LAPD. I never really learned who his political clout was, but I heard rumors that it could have ranged from President Reagan to Ed Meese, the then attorney general. He was the first and last political appointee as a regional commissioner during all my years with Customs.

Villanueva was a smart man. He knew what he didn't know and that's why he was successful. He also readily accepted Corky McMullen as his deputy, although we never before or since have had a job entitled deputy regional commissioner. It was solely created to ensure that the LA Region didn't falter under a political appointee. Mike Villanueva was a good BIG PICTURE show guy and he let Corky make everything work.

It was obviously a unique education for McMullen. He had the opportunity to run a complex region and observe a suave political appointee press the flesh effectively. Not many career bureaucrats can effectively deal with the press, the politicians and the elite moneyed class that contribute to the political process. Most stumble and fall like children learning to walk for the first time. Villanueva was to the manner born. He was a class act and flew the flag well for Customs.

I'll mention this word often when dealing with the true stars—visionary. Corky was a visionary. He was unafraid to venture into the unknown. This is not to say he was a fool who headed the ship into perilous waters, into harm's way as a *stargazer* would, but he calculated the risk of the voyage versus the results. You can't do that if all the wires in your head aren't connected in the right way.

◆   ◆   ◆

In 1986, I was reassigned to our region office as the liaison officer to the Tenth Pan American Games being held in Indianapolis, Indiana, in 1987, and the 15th Winter Olympic Games being conducted in Calgary, Alberta, Canada, in 1988. Corky's assistant regional commissioner, Jim Piatt, selected me for that awesome job. It was in those two years that I learned a great deal about leadership, direction and responsibility.

I had nearly unfettered access to McMullen and Piatt due to my responsibilities. This was unlike the other program managers in the region who had to go through a layered pyramid to get to the top. This access afforded to me a unique learning opportunity unlike any I've ever had before in my career. I was able to see the inner workings of the decision-making process that affected the entire 18-state region and many nationwide HQ programs.

Many of those HQ programs were conjured up by hapless *stargazers* and sent out to the field. They only had the slightest chance of impacting the Customs Service or of being of any real value. They were make-work projects at their best. Many of the other seven regional commissioners would just shake their heads and pass on these fruitless, inane programs to their subordinates with words like, "Well, just make it work."

That was not Corky. If a HQ program was ill-suited for the NC region, he would modify it or promulgate his own program to accomplish the intended goal. He wasn't above going right into the face of a HQ *stargazer* who was hibernating in the Beltway with a difference of opinion. I recall one incident where one program manager at our region really didn't fathom this maverick element in Mr. McMullen. He received a rude awakening.

He was on temporary duty to our region office and was hoping for a permanent promotional job. He saw that we had completely changed a HQ program and went in to see Corky. He said, "Mr. McMullen, I see where one of the program officer's rewrote an HQ directive. If we go with this, it will fly in the face of what Washington wants us to do. Should I have him change it?"

Corky looked at him and firmly stated, "Tim, this isn't headquarters; this is the North Central region and we do things differently here. Our program is better than the HQ program. Ours will actually work. Headquarters will eventually change their program and adopt our version."

That's exactly what happened. Corky's vision prevailed over the HQ *stargazer's* mystical dream and the entire Customs Service copied our program. It was a model for success as were many of the NC region initiatives during Mr. McMullen's tenure. Of the seven regional commissioners, Corky stood head and shoulders above all. Whenever a new regional commissioner was selected, Corky was usually assigned as his mentor. That was the ultimate compliment.

Tim, our hapless manager who had hoped to stay on at the region, was disappointed. He was filling in for 120 days in the vacant job he sought. This is the maximum period in a temporary duty (TDY) assignment that allows you to be paid at the higher rate. He went in to see the boss with an idea.

He said, "Mr. McMullen, my time is almost up in the TDY job. I want you to know that I've enjoyed the job, working with you and the staff at the region. I'd like to volunteer to stay in the position until the vacancy is filled without being paid at the higher rate."

With that having been said he thought that Corky would be impressed with his selfless act of doing the job without receiving the extra compensation. Mr. McMullen answered him, "Tim, I've appreciate your being here and filling in. But on Monday you report back to the district office. I'm bringing Harry in to fill the next TDY period until the position is filled. This job is not in your future."

McMullen was one of the few who had the gonads to tell someone up front they weren't getting the job. Most others, especially the *90 percenters*, would hem and haw and say something like, "Well, Tim, your time is up. You've done a great job and you stand a good chance of getting the promotion. Good luck."

They would say that when they didn't have any intention of promoting the person at all. Corky wasn't afraid to tell it like it is. People appreciate and respect honesty. It's a rare commodity in government, whether civil service or elective office. It's much easier to lie, to *speak with a lack of candor* as the FBI used to say, than to tell the truth to get yourself out of a difficult situation.

◆   ◆   ◆

I also recall one major conference being hosted by Mr. McMullen, but he had overslept. We had about one hundred people waiting for him. He was about 45 minutes late. Now he could have come into the conference room and stated that he was sorry he was late, but he had been on the telephone with the commissioner in Washington on a pressing matter. Everyone would have believed him even though it wasn't true.

This is what he said, "I'm sorry about being late. I don't really have a good reason as to why I wasn't here at 8:30. I apologize."

With that having been said, Corky got down to the business at hand. My respect grew for Mr. McMullen for being honest that day. If you consistently *speak with a lack of candor,* eventually people will find out that you are lying. Once you lose their respect and confidence your reputation snowballs downhill until it smacks into a fence and breaks apart. Corky had the courage to tell the truth and accept the consequences.

◆   ◆   ◆

McMullen also had a knack for spotting talent as do most of the *ten percenters* in the government. They do not fear intelligent and successful people as a threat to them as many *90 percenters* do. Rather they welcome them into the fold and nurture their talents for the betterment of the Service. They are also unafraid to take a chance on untested talent. I know this from firsthand experience, because they took a chance on me.

I was at HQ preparing to go to Aruba to conduct a narcotic interdiction training seminar in the late 1980's. Corky was also there for a commissioner's conference. We ran into each other during a fire drill outside on Constitution Avenue. He was leaving that evening to go back to Chicago and wanted to get together for a drink before he left.

We decided to go to the airport so he wouldn't miss his flight. We were in the American Airline's Admiral Club in the old National Airport 1930's art deco main terminal building. When we sat down he said to me, "Sarge, I want to talk to you about your future."

He proceeded to give me his evaluation of the job I had done with the Pan Am Games and the Winter Olympics. He further stated, "Sarge, this is what I envision. There is a chief inspector vacancy at the district office. I see you getting that. You proved what a good job you can do. I need a good chief inspector at the district."

Corky had given me his stamp of approval. He had brought me up to the region on a two-year TDY assignment to be his liaison officer and apparently I had met his high standards. He was upfront in telling me what the future held for me. Call it pre-selection for a vacancy or call it what you may like. The name some people had for it was—you had been ordained a McMullenite.

Corky spotted and nurtured more talent than any other regional commissioner. Actually, he did more than that when he didn't hold on to you for his own sake. He sent you back out into the field to take over operations that needed to be fixed. It was in that way he and all the *ten percenters* have made the Customs Service a better place. They unselfishly returned the good people to the field rather than hoard them for their own use. They then started the selection process over to give others a chance.

Once you earned his trust and respect, you endeavored never to betray that trust. I recall at one major conference I was with him and Jerry Padalino, who at the time was vying for a regional commissioner's job. It was late and we were having a drink when Corky began to talk to Jerry about his future. Padalino looked at me with some concern.

Corky looked at me and told him, "Jerry, its O.K. It's as if Sarge isn't here. He can be trusted."

◆   ◆   ◆

Among other things, Corky was the first to computerize a region office. He installed an IBM System 36 that revolutionized the way we did business. No more secretaries or clerks, each program officer did their own writing, typing, editing, spell checking and printing. All the documents were readily available electronically and didn't need to be manually filed. Today we take that for granted. Back in 1980, however, it took a visionary to implement that change. Soon all other regions followed suit.

He also kept a crucial narcotic interdiction program running once HQ pulled the plug. Under V.P. George Bush, the National Narcotic Border Interdiction System (NNBIS) had been established. It brought together elements of the federal government and the military to monitor electronically our borders to try and stop the flow of drugs being smuggled in. Today, Homeland Security is trying to enhance and expand that concept to secure our nation from the evil of al-Qaida. As a collateral duty, Corky was the NNBIS central region director and reported to the vice president.

Like anything in politics, once the drug war lost its public luster in 1990, nobody cared or said that they cared about it anymore. The war became passé as a political forum, but it was still red hot for the smuggling organizations who continued to make billions of illicit dollars each year. The voting public chose not to see the havoc this criminal empire was creating to our inner cities. Out of sight, out of mind was the motto.

I guess that happens when you elect a president who states, "I tried marijuana once but didn't inhale."

Corky saved part of NNBIS from being scrapped. That part was called WANTS, the West African Narcotic Tracking System. This electronic data base not only monitored African-based criminal organizations, but worldwide trafficking cartels that were smuggling their *white gold* in the form of cocaine and heroin into the United States. WANTS turned into CABINET, the Combined Agencies Border Interdict Network which was staffed by a multitude of federal law enforcement agencies, the Canadians, the British and had a liaison with the French authorities. It was like a mini INTERPOL for drugs.

CABINET proved to be one of the most effective tools in smashing a number of powerful drug cartels. Without Corky's vision and budgetary support, CABINET would have never been established. He swam against the tide when the congress and President Clinton gave only lip service to the drug war and the rampant crime it was causing in America. CABINET continues to make an impact in the silent drug war.

◆   ◆   ◆

I was ever so fortunate to have had a front row seat all those years observing Corky manage the region. Jim Piatt, his assistant commissioner, also tutored me and gave me numerous opportunities to excel. Piatt himself had been nurtured by McMullen when they were together in LA. Corky saw the potential in the then district chief inspector and brought him to the LA region office and then on to Chicago. Later Jim Piatt became the regional commissioner in Houston. They both selflessly shared their experiences with me, the new kid on the block.

◆   ◆   ◆

Hoteko's Law: *Customs is a better place because of Corky McMullen and the army of McMullenites that he nurtured throughout his career.*

15

Sam Banks

Sam Banks began his career with Customs in the early 1970's in San Francisco as a uniformed inspector after a stint in the army. He had graduated from Georgetown University's School of Foreign Service. One of his contemporaries at GU was President Clinton. Sam would have been a big success in private industry, but he chose government. He chose to serve the people for the greater good.

Like a good general, Sam never forgot what it was like to be in the trenches as a trooper. It is, actually, a rarity among the top brass to actually talk with, and not talk down to the troops. Sam always had time or made time to talk with the troops. It was that philosophy that endeared him to one and all in Customs throughout his career.

When Sam retired he had served four years as the deputy commissioner and nearly a year as acting commissioner of Customs. There wasn't a finer, more deserving person to occupy the two highest offices in Customs than Sam Banks. He had not only earned the respect of the agency, but was widely admired throughout the federal government and was held in high esteem on Capitol Hill.

I had the pleasure of knowing Sam for nearly 20 years. Although I never worked directly for him, I came into personal contact with him dozens of times each year, either in Washington, Chicago or at major conferences throughout the country. Sam was ever the diplomat. He always carried himself with a compassionate dignity that was permeated with an honest, down-to-earth sincerity.

◆　　　◆　　　◆

Sam Banks was in the Senior Executive Service (SES) in the federal government. Positions in the government are broken down by pay grades. At one point in time the breakdown was as such; GS (general schedule) 1 through 12, GM (general management) 13 through 15, and then the SES with equivalent pay grades 16 through 18.

I was in the GM pay grade as a midlevel manager, which is a notch above the majority of the government, but not a notch below the royalty of an SES rank. The theory was an SESer could go from one agency to another and be an effective manager. Somewhat like a general officer in the military that could go from an artillery command to an intelligence posting.

Actually, it didn't really work that way. You couldn't take an SES from Agriculture who had been on the devastating Golden Nematode pestilence program and plop him over to IRS to ride roughshod over their highly intricate delinquent corporate depletion allowance (DCDA) program. I'm sure that the *stargazer* who developed the SES program had good intentions, but, it was doomed to failure when a hoard of *90 percenters* were able to wiggle their way into the SES ranks.

Many in the SES ranks did consider themselves royalty. They were the cream of the crop in the federal government just as general officers are considered so in the military. It was usually the *90 percenters* who tricked their way into the SES program that fancied and propagated their own crown. They disdainfully distanced themselves from anyone who wasn't SES as unworthy. The *ten percenters* like Sam Banks never did that. They carried themselves with a simple dignity that spoke volumes about their true character.

◆   ◆   ◆

I was in HQ as a member of a small team put together by Assistant Commissioner Chuck Winwood when I encountered Sam one day. We were tasked with conducting extensive research on a project; *the Inspector of the Future*. This was during Clinton's first term when Al Gore was blissfully trying to reinvent the government. Our object was to ascertain whether Customs actually would need inspectors to function in the 21st century or should there be an entirely new position created within the agency.

Sam was the acting deputy commissioner at the time. Mike Lane, the deputy, had been reassigned to Gore's Treasury reinvention dream team. We asked Sam to meet with us, since we needed to ask him questions, share his expertise and get his opinion on the future of the inspector position. As the deputy, he was responsible for the day-to-day operation of the entire US Customs Service. His time was at a premium, but he was gracious enough to meet with our team.

Our base of operations was located in the old Interstate Commerce Commission Building that is adjacent to the then Customs HQ on Constitution Avenue. In between the ICC and Customs is the Mellon Treasury Auditorium. Below there is a basement walkway that connects the two buildings and a public cafeteria. We had a break and I was headed there to get a cup of coffee before our session with Sam.

As I was going through that underground walkway, Sam Banks was hurriedly coming from the Customs building and heading to our conference room. He saw me and said, "Sarge, am I late for the meeting?"

"No," I answered him and continued, "We're on a short break and I was going to get some coffee."

Sam could have gone on to the conference room to talk with Tom Hardy, our team leader from Portland, Oregon, or called his office to catch up on business. He didn't do that, but instead said, "Sarge, I'll go with you and buy you a cup."

With that said we got our coffee and sat down and talked for about ten minutes. That was a class act. He didn't have to spend the time with me but he did. Sam never made you feel uncomfortable or uneasy due to his rank. He had the unique ability to relate one-on-one with you. He never forgot what it was like to be in the trenches.

◆   ◆   ◆

When William Von Raab was commissioner, Customs had strained relations up on Capitol Hill. Von Raab was a wealthy lawyer whose family were top Republican Party contributors and that's how he became commissioner. He was extremely brilliant but had a certain irritating edge to his personality. Von Raab was blunt and straight spoken on issues. This approach had apparently alienated many members of Congress who are used to being treated as prima donnas.

It was that kind of alienation that could cost Customs precious dollars or manpower positions in our yearly appropriate budget. As I've stated before, if you want to succeed in the federal government never tick-off a member of Congress. Kiss their derriere not once, but every time you meet them. Hell hath no fury like a member scorned and a member scorned never forgets. He just gets even.

So, anytime that Customs needed an increase appropriation or they summoned the commissioner, we generally sent Sam Banks in his place. Sam was well-respected by both sides of the aisle, and he worked hard to keep that reputation. He was honest and forthcoming and knew how delicately to kiss the various committee chairmen's rings. Sam was our savior up on Capitol Hill.

◆   ◆   ◆

Sam never abused his authority nor did he expect you to abuse your authority for him. I remember the many times when Sam was in Chicago ready to fly back to the Beltway. The normal standard operating procedure (SOP) for people at his level was for us to obtain a first-class upgrade on their return flight. I came across many a disgruntled SES manager who let me know of their displeasure when they were not given that first class boarding pass. Each airline had its own policy on upgrading passengers. Some were very liberal in responding to requests. Some, however, would tell you upfront that they only upgraded those who paid for the upgrade with cash or mileage.

One *90 percenter* in particular was so upset at being seated in coach that he got off the aircraft prior to departure and lectured the gate agent by saying, "Do you know who I am? Do you know who Sarge Hoteko is? The first-class section is empty. Why can't I sit up front?"

Needless to say that was embarrassing for everyone concerned. Sam never asked for an upgrade and never accepted one either in Chicago. He didn't want to put you on the spot or cause a problem. He remembered what it was like to be in your position and didn't want to make your life more difficult.

Another instance I recall was when Sam was the assistant commissioner. He had been on the road and hadn't seen his then nine-year-old daughter in almost ten days. He asked to use my telephone to call her. I told him the FTS (federal telephone service) wide-area access code to use for the call. He wouldn't use it. That would have put me on the hook to explain a lengthy long distance call to a private number to our budget officer.

Instead he took out his own credit card and told me, "Sarge, this is a personal call. I'll pay for it. Thanks, anyway."

◆   ◆   ◆

Sam received the highest recognition that a career federal employee could hope to achieve. President George H. W. Bush personally presented Sam with the Distinguished Government Excellence Award. Sam served as our deputy for four years during the near disastrous reign of Clinton appointee George Weise. Many credit him with holding Customs together during that tumultuous time. Sam was the acting commissioner for almost a year until the senate confirmed

NYPD's Ray Kelly in Clinton's second term. Sam Banks retired on February 2, 1999.

I often told him when we met, "Sam, each time I see you, you renew my faith in government service. It's because of people like you at the top that I keep going in spite of all the obstacles in the way. Thank you."

When Sam Banks retired we all lost a good person, a talented *ten percenter* who flew the flag well. I admired the way he dealt with issues. I admired the way he represented Customs. I admired the way he talked with the troops. I admired the way he would take time out of his day for the little people. I admired his integrity. I learned a higher level of decency from Sam Banks and for that I'm eternally grateful.

It had been stated that Omar Bradley was the GI's general during World War II. More than one person had fondly stated to me, "Sam Banks is the inspectors' commissioner."

◆   ◆   ◆

Hoteko's Law: *Never forget what it's like to be in the trenches; never forget the little people and always take the higher road.*

16

Bob Trotter

Another of the stellar stars was Bob Trotter. He started life as a uniformed inspector in Chicago. Trotter was a graduate of Western Illinois University. Like Sam Banks, Bob learned the job from the bottom up. Like Sam also, Bob was a military veteran having served in the US Navy. I had worked closely with him until he left Chicago for a promotion in St. Louis.

Trotter was also an active member of the National Customs Service Association, a predecessor of National Treasury Employees Union (NTEU). Bob was a great advocate of protecting employees' rights and insuring that the union contract was adhered to by management. Apparently this bothered a number of the managers in Customs at O'Hare International Airport. It actually cost Bob a personal friendship he had developed with a close colleague, John (not his real name), who had been promoted into the management ranks.

When he filed a grievance on behalf of a member, John took it so personally that he wouldn't talk to Bob at all. In fact, he ordered his wife to have no further contact with Bob's wife who was a very good friend. Now granted there are few people who would take a grievance that personal, but they do exist and the consequences can be painful.

With that having been said, Bob did pursue the action and was successful. The damage was done with John. Trotter never held it against John nor did he bad-mouth him behind his back. He just continued to do his Customs and his union job professionally. It took many years before John would even acknowledge Bob, let alone actually talk to him again. They eventually buried the hatchet and once again became friends.

Bob's conduct throughout this incident was indicative of his unbiased demeanor and exemplary character that he has displayed throughout his career. Bob ended up in Washington, then Houston and back to Washington as an assistant commissioner. Like Sam, Trotter never forgot what it was like in the trenches; he never forgot the little people and he never took things personally.

◆   ◆   ◆

I recall one visit that Bob made to Chicago when I was the chief inspector at O'Hare Airport's terminal five. We were all seated around my conference table—my boss, the port director and several mucky-mucks from our region office. Everyone was eager not only to please Bob, but to curry his favor. One of the panicky *90 percenter* mucky-mucks even conducted a rehearsal for the briefing. He didn't trust that his people actually knew their jobs. He was also afraid of what they might say to Trotter about the operation and perhaps about him.

When it came to my turn around the table I broke ranks with the mucky-mucks and asked, "Bob, you've been an inspector, you know what goes on in passenger processing, what do you really want to know?"

There were a few audible gasps at the long table. I had violated the unwritten rule of using his first name. I also broke the precedent of not immediately launching into the humdrum statistical data contained in the carefully prepared over-heads, charts and graphs. I had learned long ago when to use proper names, however, and when to use familiar names. I also learned that by being assertive you can intimidate the *90 percenter* mucky-mucks who were forever afraid of their own shadows.

Trotter smiled and said, "Sarge, just tell me what I really need to know and nothing more. I get hit with all kinds of information and data that's useful to my staff, but it's meaningless to me in my position. Just tell me the short nuts and bolts of what I need to know about your operation—nothing more and nothing less."

◆   ◆   ◆

Anyone who's familiar with the Beltway knows what a pressure cooker Washington can be. It consumes not only your time, but your personal life. There aren't enough hours in the day to get a job done, especially at an assistant commissioner's level. That's why time management is as crucial as is the management of information you receive. You can easily become inundated with statistics, analysis, projections, proposed regulations, operations and audits. This entire battalion of information can overload your cranial capacity until your head begins to circle and burn out like Robby the Robot in the 1950's sci-fi thriller, *Forbidden Planet.*

This usually happens to the hapless Beltway *90 percenters*, the ones afraid of their own shadow. They are so insecure that they feel they have to know everything and if they don't, they'll be sent off to a dusty, barren southern border crossing in California or New Mexico. These people memorize the inane statistics. They lose sleep over the endless graphs and pie charts they encumber their staff to prepare. They are so overwhelmed with basically useless information that they miss the entire BIG PICTURE and actually fail in their jobs.

Many HQ *90 percenters* concentrate on the superficial and attempt to hide behind meaningless statistics. When you give them a barrage of BS, they absorb it as the truth. Unfortunately, this method also works for them on other fellow *90 percenters* and *stargazers*. Just ask one of these hapless chaps a real operational question, however, and you will undoubtedly get a *hum-in-ah, hum-in-ah, hum-in-ah* answer, because they are clueless about the real world. They desperately seek refuge in the comfort and safety of meaningless statistics in which the Beltway's other *90 percenters* and *stargazers* choose to reside.

◆   ◆   ◆

A prime example of what useless data can do to a person happened in one of the debates between Ronald Reagan and Walter Mondale during the 1988 presidential election. Reagan's staff crammed so much inane data into the Gipper's head that he was babbling. No one really understood what it was he was trying to say. Perhaps the only people who were impressed with his attempt at remembering inane statistics were the Beltway *90 percenters* who believe that the more data you know, the smarter you are.

The president doesn't need to know that BS. He doesn't need to know the nuts and bolts of what trivial economic factors drive the consumer price index (CPI). The president only needs to rely on his staff to brief him on the key points. An example could be as to why rents are higher. He might need to know in which of the 87 statistical areas rents have been raised. He doesn't need to know which of the 50,000 surveyed landlords are charging more rent that month. All he needs to know is that rents have gone up. He can then ask questions based on that information. He only needs to know the key points and not that John Smith in Omaha raised the rents in his six flat by $20.00 a month.

Needless to say at the next debate, Reagan was his old, comfortable self. The Great Communicator did what he does best. He talked to the American people as the confident leader he was and not the micromanager his staff had tried to make him. By concentrating on the BIG PICTURE he reassured the people that he was in charge. On Election Day they overwhelmingly reelected the Gipper!

◆   ◆   ◆

What I learned from Trotter was to glean only the basic information necessary to get the job done and not be a micromanager of useless data. He also taught me how to concentrate on what's legitimate and dispense with the rest as quickly as possible. This advice included on how to deal with an MBO, a management by objective.

The MBO was the in-thing during the1980's in the federal government; this was before the Clinton era of reinvention supplanted them. These gadgets, as I call them, were seized upon as if they were holy manna floating down from the heavens as the hapless, lost *90 percenters* roamed the Beltway searching for the Promised Land. They saw salvation in an MBO and they faithfully tasked the field with creating more and more MBOs to appease the gods, in their case the HQ *stargazers* whom they served.

Trotter gave me some sage advice when he said, "Sarge, the beautiful thing about an MBO is that you get to write up your own objectives. So you write up simple goals that can be easily accomplished. The more MBOs you propose, the merrier HQ will be. But you have to throw in a couple of doosies to impress the big brass. That's where you can get into trouble if you're not careful. Remember, the great thing is that even if you don't meet the objective at the end of the year you can state in your final evaluation that whatever it is you achieved was really the objective you meant to achieve in the first place. Even if it isn't what you stated in the beginning of the year with your MBO. I know that sounds like double talk, but it works."

Bob Trotter realized that you certainly had to submit a number of MBOs to appease the HQ *90 percenters* who were trying to appease the HQ *stargazers* each fiscal year. In theory the MBO should work and give you a road map to success. The problem was that many HQ *stargazers* expected unrealistic goals. Rather than fight with them, the *ten percenters* like Trotter, whipped up a couple of MBOs each year with gigantic superhuman goals to please those *stargazers*, knowing full well that the actual goals of could not be achieved without the use of smoke and mirrors.

The majority of MBOs that were submitted in the late 1980s were very easy to achieve. Unfortunately they didn't improve the agency one bit. They were all eyewash in the same vain that sheer numbers of objectives submitted theoretically measured a manager's ability. A manager's yearly evaluation then depended on the number of successful MBOs achieved within that rating period. It was a stupid HQ game played by the idiotic *stargazers* and *90 percenters* alike.

Trotter didn't waste any more time than was necessary on this waste of time. HQ MBOs were nothing more than busy-work projects. Unfortunately, because they were *hot*, everyone climbed aboard the bandwagon and extolled their virtues. All Trotter did was state in his MBOs that he would accomplish goals A, B and C. If at the end of the year he hadn't accomplished A, B and C, he simply wrote in the evaluation that although he expected to accomplish A, B and C, he actually meant to accomplished goals X, Y and Z.

He had failed the MBO, but the *90 percenters* were too afraid to tell the *stargazers* because they were too enthralled in their own universe and they didn't realize they had been hoodwinked. Was it all smoke and mirrors? Perhaps. I like to think of it as a good wide end run around the defense across the goal line that result in six points on the scoreboard for Trotter.

In private industry an MBO is a valuable tool. Why? Because in private industry you actually have a product that's produced, marketed and sold at a profit. The manager of the final assembly process in the shoe factory has an MBO to increase the quality control of the product to reduce the number of rejects. If he meets the objective, it means greater profit for the company. Not so in government where there isn't an end-run profitable product but a service rendered instead.

Some will argue that a service rendered is an end-run product and that's true in private industry, but not always so in government. If you are unhappy with your cell phone provider because of poor service, you can easily switch to a competitor. In government if you are not happy with the service you are receiving from Customs or the IRS, where do you go? Nowhere, there isn't another Customs Service or IRS to switch too. This is another one of the big differences between the private and public sector. An MBO works in the shoe factory and rarely proves to be of value in the government.

◆   ◆   ◆

So, by spending as little time as possible on a useless MBO or trying to absorb inane statistics simply to impress others, Trotter could concentrate on accomplishing the true goals of the Customs Service. He could then spend time on programs that could take drugs off the street, shut down money-laundering operations, enforce trademark/copyright laws, insure the proper classification of importations, enhance the collection of revenue and enforce the vast 400 laws of the 40 different agencies we are tasked with at the border. I learned that this *ten percenter's* way was a better way.

◆   ◆   ◆

Hoteko's Law: *Don't clog your brain with useless information. Know what's legitimate and what's not in order to spend your time wisely.*

17

Bernie Tarte

Bernie Tarte was one of the first people in Customs whom I came to admire and respect and whom I wanted to emulate. He was a senior inspector in the days when that title actually meant something. In 1969, Miles Ambrose, the then commissioner of Customs, created that position. President Nixon had pressed Congress to authorize more funds to expand the war on drugs. In order to more effectively implement the expanded effort, Ambrose decided to elevate 10 percent of the inspector workforce into the new position of senior inspector.

The new seniors would provide hands-on leadership for the other 90 percent in field. They would be an extension of the manager who usually was responsible for about 30 inspectors. Under this plan a supervisor would now have three seniors to help him direct the efforts of his team. They would be onsite and each would be responsible for about eight to nine inspectors at their work station.

In 1969, Customs was an agency with a dismal record of providing promotional opportunities. Inspectors viewed the new senior position as a godsend and something that was badly needed to revitalize all the efforts of the agencies in the drug war. In order however to implement the promotions quickly, Ambrose chose to select that 10 percent by strict seniority. This method usually results in the wrong people being promoted. Rarely does longevity equal leadership ability. In Chicago, however we were lucky; almost all those selected were among the best qualified inspectors. Bernie Tarte was the best of the lot in 1969.

◆　　　◆　　　◆

In 2001, Judge Robert Bonner, the commissioner appointed by Bush number 43, decided to increase the journeyman pay grade for all inspectors from a GS 9 to a GS 11. Since 1969, the GS 11 pay grade was exclusively reserved for senior inspectors. He did this in an attempt to eliminate the pay disparity between inspectors and municipal police officers and federal special agents. If you wear a badge and carry a gun, you are generally going to work where they offer the best salary and benefits.

The attrition rate for Customs inspectors was abysmal. We were spending tens of thousands of dollars to recruit, conduct a background investigation, train and equip a newly hired inspector only to lose him to another agency or police department within three to five years. By the time he was able to perform his job at the journeyman level, he was gone and we had to start all over again. Multiply that by the hundreds of inspectors who left each year and it was becoming a serious, reoccurring crisis situation. We had to do something to stop the bleeding.

Of course, not everyone felt that way. I can recall a conversation I had with the head of our human resources department. This was before Bonner had made the sweeping change and upgraded every inspector. I told her, "We will always be able to hire good, qualified people. Our issue is being able to retain them. When they leave, we do give them an exit interview. The most resounding repetitive statement we get is not that they dislike Customs; on the contrary, they like the agency and work we do. It's a pay issue. When a City of Chicago police officer can make nearly $70,000 a year after only five years on the job, and they are only making $50,000 after that the same time period, something's wrong."

This *stargazer* vehemently disagreed and stated, "Well, I'd rather have them for those three or five years and get some good work out of them before they leave. We can hire other qualified people and train them to take their place. We have good people at the academy where they take pride in training the new recruits. You obviously don't see the big picture as we see it at headquarters."

I should have been tactful and nodded in agreement, but I went ahead and said, "I don't agree with that. I guess in your field you want to keep training new people and that's fine. However, once they leave the academy, you're finished with them. Look at it from a field perspective. Let me say it this way: I'm the coach of the Chicago Bears. It takes a good three years or so to train a green quarterback so he knows the plays, his offensive line and the other team's defense. It's an ugly period of time. He's going to be sacked, intercepted and demoralized. But at the end of that time period he'll have gained his confidence and finally start being a productive quarterback and winning games.

"But if I'm given a new quarterback after each three-year period, I'm starting all over again and so is the whole team. We start losing ballgames again and the productivity goes to zero. It's the same with new inspectors; it takes those three to five years before they really know what they're doing. Once they're at that level when they can really contribute to the Customs mission, they leave. I have to tell you that your type of mindset just to let them leave and hire new people is wrong and it's detrimental to the agency."

Obviously that didn't sit well with her. She did the same thing that another assistant commissioner did when we were discussing the newly elected President Clinton's National Performance Review (NPR) initiative to change the federal government. Clinton had tasked Al Gore with the job under the guise of a book entitled *Reinventing the Government*, by David Osborne and Ted Gaebler. Mike Lane, our deputy commissioner at the time, was detailed to the NPR.

This assistant commissioner, another HQ *stargazer, yes-man* and a weak-kneed *90 percenter,* said to me with a giddy smile on his face, "Sarge, Mike Lane has just read a good book. He wants everyone to read it. It's called *Reengineering the Corporation.*"

I looked at him in disbelief. Here we go again, I thought; retooling so we could start reengineering before we had finished reinventing anything. It was so typical of the HQ *90 percenters* to grasp whole-heartily onto whatever was currently being preached inside the Beltway. If someone in a position of authority reads something and makes a comment, it's amazing how quickly people hop on the bandwagon without knowing where the wagon is headed.

I sarcastically replied to him, "We never seem to stay the course on important issues. We go halfway and then someone has an epiphany, and we change course in the middle of the stream. Every time we do that we lose credibility. Well, I certainly hope that Mike Lane doesn't pick up a copy of *Das Kapital* or *Mein Kampf* in the near future."

He looked at me in the same disdainful way as did the human resources director and asked me the very same question, "Can I have your name?"

I did better than that. I gave each one my business card so they would have the spelling correct. I wasn't afraid to tell them the truth, and I refused to be intimidated by their *yes-men* positions. I had violated one of my basic laws, keep you mouth shut on both these occasions. Since I had learned a refined sarcasm from Bernie Tarte and this wouldn't be the last time in my career that I would let loose with a pointed volley. Whether that's right, wrong or indifferent; nobody's perfect. At times you have to say it like it is, but you have to be able to accept the consequences too.

◆   ◆   ◆

So, with a stroke of the pen, Bonner upgraded nearly 4,000 inspectors in an attempt to address the retention issue. As in physics 101, for every action there's a reaction and there was one here too. He had ticked-off the 2,000 inspectors who had gone through the lengthy competitive promotional process to obtain the coveted senior inspector rank. They were a bunch of unhappy campers and I didn't blame them at all.

What Bonner did was right, for the upgrade was necessary and needed, but he didn't finish the job. He should have then upgraded those who had previously been competitively promoted to next higher grade, a GS 12. This action would have allowed them to retain the senior inspector title and would have kept them in a leadership position.

Bonner ended up with every inspector being a senior inspector and that negated what Ambrose had instituted in 1969 with the use of senior inspectors as team leaders. Now there wasn't an incentive for anyone to take on a leadership role. Why should they when everyone was making the same amount of money?

If you expect people to lead, you have to pay them more, plain and simple. You can't run an effective police department if everyone is a sergeant; you need patrol officers who are directed by a shift commander. You can't have a crack platoon of soldiers if everyone is a sergeant; you need privates who are directed by their squad leader. As I've stated, he did the right thing, but he didn't stay the course and finish the job. He created a humongous mess for management in Customs that still exists today.

◆   ◆   ◆

I first met Bernie when I was assigned as a rookie inspector to his cargo station at the now defunct Flying Tigers Airlines. Tarte was a World War II navy veteran, a pilot. What I learned from him I used throughout the rest of my career. It helped to make me successful. Bernie began my education to help me understand the federal government and its strange ways.

I remember what he said to me that first day, "Hoteko, here's some advice. Learn the job the right way. Don't look for shortcuts. Learn the regulations and do it the right way. Too many of the new people just want to learn the easy way of doing it. Don't be one of them. Learn it the right way. If you do that, you will know what you can shortcut and what you can't shortcut. If you learn it the right way, nobody can ever kick you in the butt."

Tarte was neat and orderly in both his uniform and the meticulous way he ran his cargo station. Everything was properly and timely filed. He had a great relationship with the airline personnel, Custom House brokers and cartage drivers which gave him the opportunity to do a better job. The government thrives on paperwork and at many of the cargo stations the paperwork was a mess at best. Airway bills and manifests were crammed into folders holding the general aircraft declaration of the arriving international flight. It was a mishmash of paperwork that would make a seasoned auditor cringe.

Tarte's files, however, were in perfect order. Each time he attached an airway bill showing the disposition of a cleared importation, he would remove the staple holding all the paperwork to the general aircraft declaration, neatly arrange all the bills and then fasten them with a single staple—neat and orderly. You could easily retrieve a file and instantly know the disposition of an importation. This was in the days before computerization of records.

Another thing I learned from Tarte was a healthy skepticism. I recall talking to him about someone who was promoted, "Bernie, I'm glad that John was promoted, for he's a nice guy."

Bernie looked at me with his wise, knowledgeable eyes that had a way of narrowing into your soul and he said, "Sarge, they're all nice guys. I hate when someone says that! Ya, he's a nice guy. He goes along with anything anybody says, he never wanted to learn the job. He always took the easy way out. Ya, he's a nice guy, but he's incompetent!"

Bernie was right. John was incompetent but was promoted anyway because he knew somebody and they pushed for him regardless of his inability to do the job. I guess that's when I first started formulating my theory that 90 percent of those in government were only along for the ride; it was the *ten percenters* who ran the show, people like Bernie Tarte. Even though he never received the promotions he deserved, he kept running a first-class show.

◆   ◆   ◆

Even though there was a considerable age difference, Tarte made me feel comfortable. He was able to relate to people because of his down-to-earth common sense. It was just that ability and that common sense that made many managers leery of him and actually intimidated by him. He had what they didn't possess, for he had confidence and he wasn't afraid to state his case when he knew he was right.

One day a *90 percenter* supervisor, one who wore his ego on his collar in the form of his rank, barged into Tarte's work station at United Airlines. He was newly promoted and from out of town. He had heard about Tarte and his reputation. He boasted to those fearful supervisors that he knew how to handle him and would take him down a notch or three.

Without saying a word to Bernie, he went right to the file cabinet and began to audit the files. After a bit he said to Tarte, "Why aren't all these manifests closed out? What have you been doing! I want to know why they're not closed."

He was referring to foreign merchandise shipments that had been imported on a United Airlines flight and were still in their warehouse waiting for Customs clearance. This bright, astute fellow had come from Detroit, which at the time was a mostly land border crossing. They didn't have many international flights. He had no idea that he was heading straight for a Bernie Tarte ambush since he didn't know manure from shoe polish regarding international air shipments. He put his foot in his mouth and would now pay the consequence.

Tarte narrowed those wizened eyes, smiled his broad sly smile and said, "Well Bob, if you can get the Customs brokers and importers to submit their entry documents, I'll examine, release and post the findings to close out those manifests. I can't do anything until then or until the merchandise is sitting on the dock over 30 days. Then I can send the shipments to the government warehouse and close out the manifest. They still have time to file their entry documents, so I have to wait. That's in the regulations. Bob, you know the regulations, don't you?"

Mr. Detroit know-it-all left Tarte's station that day with his tail between his legs. Had he learned his job in the first place he wouldn't have had egg on his face. Had he sat down with Tarte and asked him to explain how his station worked, he would have learned a great deal from one of the best. He didn't do that because he didn't park his ego at the door. Mr. Detroit continued to exhibit the same idiotic behavior with others. It only stopped when he transferred to Miami to leave Customs for DEA. Our gain, but DEA's loss.

◆   ◆   ◆

Bernie Tarte was part of what NBC newsman Tom Brokaw called the greatest generation of Americans. They were proud to serve their country whether in war or in peace. This generation of Americans learned how to work as a team. They learned that they needed to depend on one another to survive and to get the job done. They learned who to trust and they trusted them. They learned who was a fool and they didn't suffer fools easily.

Bernie made me feel proud to be in U.S. Customs and to serve. I learned volumes from Tarte that you could never learn in a book. I learned the job the right way, and I learned that nobody could ever take that away from me. A rookie couldn't have had a better mentor or teacher at a more critical time in his career. A *Doff-O-The-Hat* to Bernie Tarte!

◆   ◆   ◆

Hoteko's Law: *Learn the job the right way and if you do, nobody can ever intimidate you because you'll know you're right.*

18

Mary Rose Loney

I first met Mary Rose Loney when Mayor Richard M. Daley appointed her the 1st Deputy Commissioner of Aviation for the City of Chicago. It was an unusual appointment since Mary Rose wasn't born, bred or raised in the *city that works*. She wasn't a resident of the city; let living in the powerful 11th ward. This was the then home of the mayor and his late father Hizzoner Richard J. Daley, more affectionately know as Da Boss. To say the least, she was an outsider appointed to a position normally afforded only to a well-connected insider.

O'Hare International Airport is considered the crown jewel in city employment. It has safe, plentiful free parking, and easy public transportation access and also offers innumerable advancement opportunities. The airport's top managers all come with letters of recommendation from clout-heavy ward committeemen, cigar smoking aldermen, crafty state representatives and slick state senators. It's not an easy place to get a job.

In 1978, political scientist Milton Rakove wrote an exposé on Chicago politics entitled, *We Don't Want Nobody Nobody Sent.* It was an interesting study on how people actually obtained employment with the City of Chicago. It basically stated if you didn't have that all important letter of recommendation from somebody who was somebody; i.e., a ward committeeman or alderman, you wouldn't be hired—period.

In 1972, a federal district court judge issued what became known as the Shakman Decree. In essence this order prohibits political hiring and firing for non-policy making jobs in Chicago. It meant that the janitor sweeping the floor at City Hall can't be fired if a new mayor takes office. It protects the people who do the real work in the city. The decree, however, still allowed the hiring and firing of key policy-making managers, such as the commissioner of aviation and the plethora of deputies and assistants that go with that job. There are several hundred such plum patronage jobs within city agencies. They are sought after and fought for as if one was trying to steal the pot of gold at the end of the rainbow.

◆   ◆   ◆

Mary Rose Loney came to Chicago from San Jose, California, where she was the assistant director of aviation. Richie Daley had been elected mayor in 1989, and he selected her as the 1st deputy commissioner of aviation. She was thoroughly qualified, having worked at various other major airports and carried the coveted AAE behind her name: accredited-airport-executive. She was a breath of fresh air at O'Hare.

So why did Daley pick her? She was an outsider that nobody had sent to City Hall. She didn't have the coveted letter of recommendation from a cigar-smoking alderman or fat-cat ward committeeman. It was a plum job that many loyal democrats were not only salivating over, but I really believe many would have killed for. How did she get the job? I have no idea, and neither did many of the insiders. She was an unknown factor and they didn't like it one bit.

She left in 1992 to go down to Dallas, Texas. In 1996 when Daley's former chief of staff, Dave Mosena, left the aviation commissioner's job and headed to the lucrative post of CEO at the Museum of Science and Industry, the greedy ward committeemen and portly aldermen had again been chomping at the bit to get their own boy into the top job at O'Hare. Once again Daley confounded his friends and enemies, however, by naming an outsider commissioner. He asked Mary Rose Loney to come back to run the world's busiest airport.

◆   ◆   ◆

Peter Drucker, the management guru, had stated that at crucial times in the life of a corporation a key person is brought in and that person is able to turn the company around. It happened at GM when they brought in a young lawyer from the DuPont Company named Alfred Sloan who saved the car maker from ruin. I believe Mary Rose Loney came back to O'Hare at a critical time in the airport's history. Daley had made the right choice. The airport needed new direction and new leadership, and most importantly it needed someone who would look the political machine in the eye and not blink when it came to contracts.

In the four years she was at the helm, Mary Rose accomplished numerous difficult tasks. The biggest task she had to overcome was a clout heavy political machine that had an iron clamp on all the contracts at O'Hare. Contracts mean money and money speaks in political circles. This is why the boys from the 11th ward wanted one of their own in the commissioner's job.

There are two types of government dollars in Chicago, the first being city contracts for city services and the second one being O'Hare contracts. O'Hare contracts translated out to BIG BUCKS. An example is if a city office needed to be painted it might cost $200, but at O'Hare you could easily add 25% to that amount. I've often heard of that referred to as the O'Hare factor from those in the know. That's how valuable O'Hare dollars are to contractors and that's why contractors pump BIG BUCKS into a politician's campaign fund. Money buys access, and access means contracts. That's the Chicago way.

Mary Rose unhesitatingly put these contracts out on the street, meaning she allowed fair competition which translated out to lower operating costs to the airport. Since this didn't sit well with the contractors and the boys in the powerful 11th Ward, they were out to do her in. Why? Because by allowing fair competition for contracts it meant that the days of a wink and a nod were over. The boys no longer had unfettered access to the O'Hare pot of gold.

She ran the airport system the way it should be run and had never been run before. Cost overruns for airport construction projects had been as normal as an after-school child snitching delicious treats out of the cookie jar before supper. It was an accepted cost of doing business at O'Hare. As in the old adage, go along to get along. Don't question, just sign on the dotted line with a wink and nod.

Prior to her coming on board, the cost overrun at O'Hare's state of the art international terminal five was approximately in excess $200 million. Even by O'Hare dollars that was a lot of BIG BUCKS. The extra cost would come out of the passengers' pockets in the form of user fees. One department of aviation assistant commissioner told me he thought the overrun was more like $500 million. A wink and nod, sign on the dotted line and everybody's happy.

Mary Rose was a *ten percenter*. She realized the political situation she was in. Fortunately, she was able to find a good number of city employees who really believed that city government should be clean and aboveboard. Until she came along they could only practice the Chicago way of government which is not good government. If they didn't go along, they would be going along, down the road of unemployed.

Mary Rose was a realist, as are all *ten percenters*, in that she didn't waste a lot of time on those *90 percenters* she knew she couldn't get rid of. She buried them where they could do the least harm. Most didn't mind that at all since they were only around for the free ride of government employment. Her salvation was the good *ten percenters* who relished the fact that they were now working with a true professional and not some dimwitted ward heeler who barely knew the difference between a carnival carousel and a baggage carousel.

She had been able to achieve some monumental accomplishments, thanks to her good team. I'll list two minor ones that continue to have an impact on the passengers at O'Hare today. They were bold visionary concepts that in the scheme of things could have easily gone unnoticed in the hectic world of a major airport. To many they would not have been a priority, but Mary Rose found time for them and once implemented, they were copied by practically every major airport in the country.

One of her accomplishments might seem minor in nature to you. Anyone, however, who travels through airports on business or pleasure can only love her for what she did at O'Hare. She negotiated a price-value contract with food vendors that prohibited them from ripping off passengers. If a famous Chicago hot dog with all the fixings was selling for two bucks just a mile from the airport, the food vendor in the terminal couldn't extract four bucks from a hungry passenger waiting for his next flight. All that he could charge was 10 percent more than the fair price on the street. The contract also brought in local noted restaurants so passengers could have a choice of more than a hamburger for a meal. In other words she brought good food at reasonable prices into O'Hare.

She also championed the idea of having electronic cardiac defibrillators installed in our terminals. O'Hare Airport was the very first in the nation to do so under her leadership. She bought the defibrillators and also arranged the necessary first-aid training for airport employees in the use of these life-saving devices. I personally witnessed a defibrillator save a passenger's life in terminal five after he collapsed of cardiac arrest.

Easily these two achievements might have never seen the light of day under a political hack commissioner unless he thought a good friend of his could get the contract and would be able to generate some substantial cost overruns. With Mary Rose, the day of the wink and a nod was over, at least while she was at the helm

In spite of all she faced, including the fact that many didn't like her because she was a woman in charge, she succeeded in being one of the best who ever ran the world's busiest airport. I was always impressed with her professional demeanor at meetings and events. She continuously displayed a positive attitude and looked forward to the challenge of running O'Hare.

Mary Rose Loney was always looking to turn corners, to do things better, more efficiently and more effectively. She met problems head on, regardless of the political consequences, and she had the courage to do the right thing. In 1999, the City Club of Chicago named her Citizen of the Year. I was proud to have known her, to have worked with her and to have learned from her. When she left O'Hare Airport in 2000, she left it a better place than she found it, and that's all you can ask of anyone.

◆   ◆   ◆

Mayor Daley would have been all the wiser had he continued to make appointments to city government like Ms. Loney. Unfortunately, he didn't and all one has to do is look back at scandal after scandal in city government under his leadership because the mayor didn't stay the course. Instead he chose to surround himself with people who had less ability and were less than honorable. Some even had larceny in their hearts. Unfortunately, they were somebody that somebody sent, and apparently that was the most important criteria the mayor used for their selection to those key positions.

One might argue that Daley can't be everywhere and everyplace watching the city till. The mayor is a good *ten percenter*. Just look at Chicago before 1989 and then afterward to see the wonders he's worked for the city. He will be remembered, however, for his failures to end the endless scandal after scandal in government because of one major issue. He made the key mistake many a good *ten percenter*, including myself, have made, he chose his friends rather than the best people for the job. When you do that, you have to accept the consequences because you're only as good as those you place around you.

◆   ◆   ◆

Hoteko's Law: *In the face of adversity have the courage to place your convictions up front, in such a way that you can face yourself in the mirror and not be shocked at what you see.*

PART VII
Obstacles

Obstacles and external factors are alike and yet they are different. Actually, both can be used to your advantage as tools to run your agency more effectively. They differ in the fact that you will be dealing with obstacles on a day-to-day basis, whereas external factors only pop up from time to time.

If you approach obstacles with fear or respect, with honesty and fairness, they will no longer be a boulder on the road to success. Conversely, if you refuse to see the obstacles, they will hit you smack dab in the face. Once that happens you have only yourself to blame when you stumble and fall.

19

Unions

As a manager you will have to deal with labor unions. Outside of the federal government unions have a real bite; they can strike and shut down production. Federal employees cannot do that; they are expressly forbidden by law to strike. Just ask any member of the Professional Air Traffic Controllers Organization (PATCO) what happened to them when they either foolishly or stupidly engaged in an illegal walkout in 1981. Ronald Reagan fired them by the thousands, as well he should have for violating the law.

With that having been said, labor unions do play a role in the federal government, and you as a manager have to understand how they work. In Customs we had to deal with the National Treasury Employees Union (NTEU) that was heavily dominated by elected IRS employees in their national office. IRS is one of the largest federal employers next to the Pentagon.

IRS is also one of the worst managed agencies in the government. By the early 1990's, IRS was unresponsive not only to its employees and the public, but to the deities up on Capitol Hill and that is blasphemy. Management and the employees were continually at loggerheads over the most mundane issues. Union grievances were filed by the barrel and unfair labor practices (ULP) were the normal follow-up activity. IRS was almost at a standstill, something had to be done to save the sinking revenue ship. So, congress stepped in during the Clinton administration and basically re-wrote the agency's charter.

Why was that draconian measure necessary? In my estimation it was because managers and the NTEU refused to park their egos at the door. Once you're not speaking with each other on the issues, you begin to speak at issues. Each side then makes public statements accusing the other of not bargaining in good faith. From there the rhetoric heats up and the mudslinging becomes vicious. This doesn't solve anything. It's been my experience that when you draw a line in the sand, it's awfully difficult to back down; so never draw the line in the first place if you can help it.

◆   ◆   ◆

Labor unions in general were an outgrowth of repressive management practices in private industry. All one has to do is to look at the coal miners situation at the turn of the century. Look at how John. L. Lewis fought to correct their iniquities in pay, benefits, and most importantly unsafe working conditions. Lewis, who headed the United Mine Workers of America (UMWA), was a tireless champion of the working class. He was the founding father of the Congress of Industrial Organizations (CIO) which merged with the American Federation of Labor (AFL) in 1955 to create the behemoth AFL-CIO. Today that giant conglomerate represents over 13 million voting union members and it is perhaps the most powerful lobbying machine up on Capitol Hill.

The federal unions were an outgrowth of too many *wackos*, *stargazers* and just plain idiots that as managers were making dictatorial decisions that were just plainly repressive in nature. Those managers forgot where they came from. They never parked their ego at the door. They would fight with any and all employees who attempted to disagree with there actions. They adopted the usually fatal us-versus-them attitude and that's not healthy for anybody.

To be an effective manager, you must understand that there are some issues that require a fight; however, you must choose your fights wisely. Not every issue requires an adversarial relationship. Most issues can be resolved in an open meeting where opinions are solicited, facts analyzed and a common conclusion reached by mutual agreement. Don't think that because you're a manager you should have all the answers. At times there's wisdom in numbers.

◆   ◆   ◆

The IRS leadership in the NTEU brought about a very adversarial relationship to Customs and our ability to deal with negotiable issues. The IRS NTEU officials adopted a hard-line in-your-face approach because that is the only thing that seems to work at the IRS. It's that type of mindset that you have to be aware of and work around if you want to be able to resolve issues without frivolous grievances or cumbersome ULP actions being filed daily.

In my 20-plus years of being a manager I had very very few union actions filed against me, and when I did I was able to resolve them informally at the step one stage. How was I able to do that? Simply by listening to their grievance, parking my ego at the door and using common sense. Being an antagonist is akin to shooting yourself in the foot. You gain nothing but pain from the experience.

I have to admit that it's tough to keep your cool when a union representative is purposely baiting you in an effort to get you to say something that you'll later regret. They apparently learn those tactics from the IRS NTEU training officials who apparently coach the union representatives to utilize the highly aggressive tactics of criminal defense lawyers. Don't take the bait, keep your cool and stay on point.

Most grievances are filed because some supervisor working for you violated part of the union contract, plain and simple. The first-line supervisor in Customs has the toughest job since he's on the scene and has to make quick decisions on the spot that he'll have to live or die with. I know, I've been there and done that. The mistake usually occurs when a supervisor doesn't think through his thought and makes a decision on the spur of the moment.

It quickly escalates when the NTEU representative gets right in his face and says something like, "You're wrong. You can't do that!"

Nobody likes to hear they're wrong or to hear that in an upper decibel vocal range. I've found that the NTEU stewards generally are more knowledgeable than most managers when it comes to interpreting the union contract. When I've been told I was wrong, that an issue was in violation, I generally asked the steward to show it to me in the contract. This approach worked much more quickly than if I looked it up. If they were right, and they were at times, I would change my decision.

I've never had a problem doing that if I was wrong. Remember, park your ego at the door and don't take union actions personally. Since its business, treat it that way. Most grievances are petty matters that really don't amount to a hill of beans to you or the agency, but they carry enormous heavy baggage for the person who feels he has been wronged. If you can lift that burden, make a wrong right, you will gain respect and that will help you to accomplish the mission.

◆　　　◆　　　◆

What do federal unions bring to the table and to their membership? Relatively nothing in terms of what counts; being able to negotiate pay raises, benefits and the ever-present ability to strike if they don't get what they want. All federal pay raises are determined by the president and the congress, not the unions. I can recall one year under Reagan when we received ZERO—no pay raises, or cost of living allowance in federal parlance. There was nothing that the NTEU could do about it for their membership.

Prior to the Clinton administration, unions could represent an employee in adverse disciplinary matters, and they could negotiate certain work conditions. What they couldn't negotiate was types, pay grades and numbers of employees assigned to work locations. Management retained that vital right of workload assignment in order to maintain control over the operation for which they were responsible.

In 1993, however, under Clinton's union/management partnership initiative, they were granted the right to have their say on just what type of employee, at what pay grade, got to do what job and just how many of them were necessary to do that function. This opened Pandora's Box and the resulting plague spread like a wildfire that nearly destroyed the federal government.

The union had a field day determining just where they wanted to place their friends and members. They based everything on seniority. Seniority has its place when it comes to choosing vacation periods, it has a certain weighted value in the promotional process and it definitely has a place when and if a reduction-in-force is necessary to determine who stays and who goes.

Seniority, however, should have absolutely no place in determining who gets what job, in what numbers and in what locations. This is management's right since management is solely responsible for achieving or failing to achieve the mission and goals of the agency. Management's head is on the chopping block, not the union's head. If the NTEU had to shoulder that burden equally, I would be in support of their right to have a voice in the assignment of work. Unfortunately, the union under Clinton's partnership didn't have to bear that burden of responsibility or accountability.

I had one conversation with the local NTEU president regarding seniority being the sole criteria for job placement. I told him, "Jack, you have an obligation to your entire membership to see that each and every person is able to be considered for a specific job. Using the seniority rule, we are not able to consider otherwise equally qualified inspectors for critical positions. It ties our hands and we are stuck with some of the senior people who are only able to perform just enough work to keep from getting fired. As a manager I'm left on the hook for getting the job done, while I'm not able to choose the proper resources to do that job. You just shrug your shoulders and walk away from it all. You practice a policy of exclusion and not of total member inclusion."

Jack answered me with the familiar crossed-over look of a *wacko* in his eyes, "Sarge, you don't understand. Seniority has to play the major role. We have a lot of inspectors out there who have been carrying their bucket of water for years on end and they should be able to pick and choose where they want to work. That's the way it needs to work."

It was a futile conversation in two respects. First of all I had to accept seniority as the rule since Clinton's partnership dictated it. Secondly, I should have known better than to argue with a *wacko*. I did, however, have the final say as I told him, "Ya, Jack, they've been carrying that bucket all these years but it's been an empty bucket. They had a free ride."

◆   ◆   ◆

To further illustrate the stupidity of Clinton's partnership was the internal squabbling among NTEU members regarding the jobs they could bid for via the seniority route. I had a position in my passenger processing operation that required someone to be very computer savvy. We had an elaborate computer system that was linked to our HQ and all the associated agencies enforcement data bases. Like any complex system it required weekly if not at times daily monitoring and maintenance.

In private industry we would have hired a local area network (LAN) administrator. We did have one, but he was responsible for multiple work locations which meant we would be lucky to see him once a month. If the system went down we would have to page him and hope he could get to the airport to get us up and running again. I created a position in my branch, from existing manpower resources, in which a person would be able to spend at least 50 percent of their time monitoring the system and keeping us online.

I was fortunate enough to have a senior inspector who was interested in computer systems and was willing to take on that extra job. Some inspectors saw this job as a cushy deal. Well, under partnership I had to put the job out for bid under the seniority rule. The person doing the job was a union steward, but the person who bid for the job and had more seniority was also a union officer. Unfortunately, he was a computer illiterate, but under partnership rules I had to give him the job to Blutto (not his real name).

The union steward who was doing a good job as the LAN administrator came to me and complained. He said, "Sarge, Blutto told me that he only put in for the job to take it away from me. He said he thought it was funny that you were forced to select him even though you had told him he wasn't qualified for the job. He admitted to me he can't do the job. Can't you do something about it?"

I told him, "Paul, there isn't anything I can do about it. The partnership agreement requires that I give him the job."

The computer illiterate fellow, however, couldn't do the job. It was way over his head. He was also a firearms instructor and a very good one at that. When I was away on a TDY (temporary duty) assignment, he convinced the supervisor in charge of the firearms program to let him go on a 120-day TDY assignment to our academy in Georgia. He was gloating about how he would be gone and would not have to deal with computers or me.

How wrong he was, because this was a fight worth fighting. I came back a week before he was scheduled to leave and I learned about his ruse. I then informed the supervisor in charge of the firearms program, a sad sack *90 percenter* in Chicago, that he didn't have the authority to authorize one of my inspectors to go on a TDY assignment. I called the director of the academy and explained the situation. He was livid that the wool had been pulled over his eyes and canceled the TDY.

I then approached our computer illiterate fellow and asked to talk to him in private. He was smiling like the cat who swallowed the canary until he heard me say, "Your TDY is canceled."

He gulped. His mouth and jaw jabbered, open and closed, but no words immediately came out, he finally uttered, "You can't do that."

"Oh yes, I can and I did. You're not going. You're staying here as the LAN administrator come hell or high water." I retorted.

When he realized I had called his bluff and had cancelled his TDY assignment. He quickly traded jobs to get away from the computer system. We were then able to get someone in who knew what he was doing. I guess he thought it was a game; he could bump his buddy out and then fly to sunny Georgia while I fretted about our computer system. It didn't work because I didn't let him get away with it. If a weak-kneed *90 percenter* had been in my job, our fine fellow probably would be laughing at Customs and sipping a cold beer in sunny Georgia while our computer system crashed.

Unfortunately he wasn't the only one doing that. There were many other people who bumped people out of their jobs just because they could and because they thought it was funny. They, like our friend, did it to see how management would react to seeing a competent employee bumped out of their job by an incompetent. That was the Clinton partnership.

◆   ◆   ◆

How did this abortion of partnership come about? Well, nearly every federal union backed the Arkansas governor when he defeated George H.W. Bush in 1992. Strangely, one of the first things Clinton did was to block the full implementation of the Federal Employees Pay Comparability Act of 1990. This was certainly an odd way to pay back the loyalty of all those union members who helped elect him. Clinton, however, had something up his sleeve to placate the federal unions after robbing their members of the lawful pay increases due to them.

The purpose behind the FEPCA was to steadily raise the pay of federal workers until they reached parity with their counterparts in private industry. The initial parity lag that was cited by congress was a 32 percent deficit in the pay of a federal government employee versus his private industry counterpart. This is a tremendous chasm and you would think that the federal union leaders would have howled when it was canceled. Indeed they did and Clinton being ever the astute politician appealed to their gigantic egos and offered them something even better than money—**power**.

So, they sold out their membership for power, the power they always wanted but were never able to achieve. The Clinton people called it a labor-management partnership and it became effective under Executive Order 12871 signed in 1993. In effect it set up a co-management structure that included union partners in the total decision making process. This was akin to how the Soviets (councils) ruled Russia after the Bolshevik revolution.

It created a living nightmare at Customs. Under the near disastrous reign of the People's Commissar of Customs, George Weise, we adopted a five-year plan entitled, People, Processes and Partnership. This plan was written by a coalition of union and management *wackos* and *stargazers*. Apparently, the NTEU no longer cared about pay parity for its members. Their leadership now basked in the glory of finally obtaining *all power to the people*. Marx, Lenin and Stalin would have been proud of Weise and his revolution!

◆   ◆   ◆

I'm not against inclusion when it comes to problem solving. I've stated two heads are better than one when looking at an issue. What E.O. 12871 didn't do was assign responsibility and accountability to the union. They were able to vote on issues, programs and directives; yet if any of these failed, it was management's fault. Most importantly, they got to have their say on types, grades and numbers. They had the best of both worlds, power in the decision making process and a blanketed hold-harmless certificate in their pocket against failure and blame. For them it was a win-win situation as touted in the Interest Based Negotiation (IBN) process the Customs adopted under Commissar Weise's regime. This process was subverted by power-mad union leaders. Nearly every issue that was discussed between labor and management always came down to a very sexy catchphrase—*the quality of life*.

Under IBN rules they were able to balance how *the quality of life* would affect an inspector if management wanted to implement a program, change shift hours, or to reassign personnel to where they were critically needed. They were able to undercut our ability, the ability of the *ten percenters* to run the show effectively and accomplish the mission with that single phrase. To say they abused it would be the truth.

I'd like to illustrate how a union took this to the umpteenth degree. In the Border Patrol, management saw the need to reassign patrol agents to a certain area along the Mexican border. They wanted to do this to combat the flood of illegal aliens entering the country in a very desolate, remote region. Their union balked at management's proposal of sending border patrol agents into that area on 90-day temporary duty assignments to stop the illegal crossings.

What was their basis for not agreeing to the TDY assignments? It was the *quality of life issue*. They stated to management, in partnership council meetings, that in this remote town the TDY agents would be living in, they wouldn't have access to a dry cleaner shop. Without a dry cleaner the patrol agents couldn't get their custom fitted uniform shirts stiffly starched and pressed. This would detract from their morale and affect their *quality of life*.

Sound ludicrous? Yes, but it really happened. The true issue was that these patrol agents didn't want to spend 90 days in that hellhole region of a desert filled with blowing tumble weeds, venomous rattlesnakes and dangerous illegal aliens crossing in the dark of night. They successfully exercised a partnership council veto invoking the IBN *quality of life* issue to keep their members from having to wash and iron their own shirts in a laundromat.

◆   ◆   ◆

Thankfully labor-management councils have mostly disappeared after Clinton left town. Those of us who were forced to put up with partnership soviets or councils did so at the risk of our own sanity. As one senior manager vented to our port director during that time period, "Customs takes this partnership much too far." He illustrated his point by showing a two-inch gap between his right thumb and index finger.

Customs was a lead agency in implementing E.O. 12871. The People's Commissar, George Weise, was a firm proponent of partnership councils. The scared-of-their-own-shadow *90 percenters* immediately jumped on his band wagon, especially in Chicago. We had branch partnership councils, port partnership councils, regional partnership councils and national partnership councils. We wasted more time in these silly sessions that lasted for hours on end and achieved little good if anything.

Thank the good lord that Weise left Customs in Clinton's second administration before he really killed management's ability to achieve the mission. He was replaced by the no-nonsense former NYPD commissioner Ray Kelly. This retired Marine Corps colonel had the guts and fortitude to begin the emasculation of the councils and return the management of the agency to the *ten percenters*. Without Kelly we just might have fallen apart at the seams as did the IRS.

I firmly believe that there is a place for federal labor unions in the traditional atmosphere of bargaining across the table on those issues deemed negotiable. This is a healthy concept and each side can have their honest say and not be locked into an IBN that's dominated by the ubiquitous *quality of life issue*. It's in this traditional setting that quality compromise can be achieved by labor and management. Just as life is a give-and-take scenario, so are labor negotiations and not a one-way street as they were under Clinton's partnership.

◆　　　◆　　　◆

Unions are another area where government differs vastly from private industry. Let's go back to our shoe factory. We have a very senior union employee who is very competent attaching rubber heels on the shoes as they come his way on the assembly line. He has no other skills or education, but one day he decides that he wants to work in the accounting department rectifying incoming monetary balances versus shoes shipped to distributors.

Do you think that the factory manager would allow him to bid on that job and to give him the job because he's the most senior man applying? I don't think so. If that were to happen it wouldn't be long before the coffers would be empty and the factory bankrupt. Yet, under Clinton's union partnership in the government we were forced to do just that. We were forced to give a job to a senior employee just because he wanted it and because he was the most senior applicant, although he wasn't qualified. Managing in the federal government is different than managing in private industry.

◆   ◆   ◆

Hoteko's Law: *Always negotiate in good faith, park your ego at the door and choose your fights wisely.*

20

EEO

The statutes enforced by the Equal Employment Opportunity Commission make it illegal to discriminate against employees or applicants for employment on the bases of race, color, religion, sex, national origin, disability, or age. Title VII of the Civil Rights Act of 1964 formed the basis under which discrimination was defined. Anyone filing or participating in an EEO complaint is protected from retaliation for having filed or participated in such actions.

With that having been said, you as a manager need to be aware of your responsibilities regarding discriminatory practices. If you are informed of, discover or just become aware of a potential EEO violation, you as a manager are required to take immediate action. You cannot turn a blind eye. If you do so, you will be held personally liable for not taking the proper action. It can cost you your job and money from your pocketbook.

Is that fair? Life's not fair, but as a manager you are held to a higher standard. It's plain and simple and it comes with the territory. Are all EEO complaints valid? No, but each complaint has to be handled according to EEOC guidelines, and failure to do so can cost you your job. Is that a harsh penalty? Yes, as well as it should be. It is your job to enforce the law, not to violate it.

◆　　◆　　◆

I believe that the majority of EEO complaints are resolved at the first level when a fact finder is assigned to sort out the facts. At some point in time in your career you will be involved in this process. In fact, you yourself may be the subject of an EEO complaint one day. This is why you have to use caution in your words, actions, and deeds.

There is a cardinal rule regarding behavior as it applies to EEO matters; it isn't what you find offensive, it's what someone else finds offensive. This is the standard by which complaints are judged. You might think a joke is funny, but someone in earshot might take offense at the content of the joke. So rather than laughing at the story, you have to take action. Just what does that mean? Fire the person telling the joke? No.

It can be as simple as saying to that person, "Although you may find the story you've just told to be amusing, there are others who may find it offensive. I suggest that you no longer tell that story to anyone. Do you understand what I'm saying?"

Is that the end of your responsibility as a manager? No. You have to also say, "I want you to know that I'm going to notate my talking with you informally on this subject. I know that you will not repeat this type of behavior."

Usually that will do it. The person is put on notice and most will not repeat their behavior. You must then notate your conversation and their response. You can do it on your calendar, personal diary or any other means at your disposal. You do this so if someone else reports the incident to an EEO officer you can verify the fact that you took immediate corrective action as a manager.

◆   ◆   ◆

You also have to be very careful in the way you handle potential EEO complaints. I've always asked the person alleging the complaint if they wanted me to report it immediately to the EEO officer or would they want me to intervene in an attempt to resolve the issue. Not many managers do this, especially the *90 percenters* who will use any excuse to pass the work on to someone else, in this case an EEO officer.

I had one situation where a person alleged another employee, Norton (not his real name), was harassing her. I asked Lolly (not her real name) what the issue was and she replied, "Every time that Norton talks to me he looks at my breasts and that makes me feel uncomfortable."

Lolly had a long history of complaining about anything and everything. In fact, because she was a thorn in the side of most of the supervisors, many managers would not have given her complaint any credence because of her propensity to complain. You can't let personal feelings cloud your professional judgment. You have to do the right thing.

I took immediate action and asked her, "Do you want me to report this to the EEO officer right now or do you want me to talk to Norton and try and resolve the issue?"

This was a very sensitive matter and handled the wrong way could easily blow up. She gave me her permission to try and handle it at my level. I also asked her if she felt comfortable meeting with Norton in my office, the three of us together, or would she rather I talk to him one on one. She preferred the one-on-one approach. She also stated I could use her name when talking to Norton. This is usually a key indicator that the complaint may indeed have merit.

I approached Norton and took him to a private place. I said, "Norton, I'm going to level with you and I want you to think a while before you answer me. I have an allegation that when you speak to females you don't look at them, but at their breasts."

He didn't immediately answer, but his face turned red. He then said, "Oh, you must mean Lolly."

I still didn't affirm that it was Lolly, but said, "I'm not going to talk about names right now. I want you to know such an allegation is serious, I take it seriously. It can constitute sexual harassment and it's unprofessional too."

His face got a deeper shade of crimson as he replied, "Lolly's just trying to intimidate me and she's trying to intimidate you by making a complaint. She doesn't like some of the things I'm doing in the union and she's trying to get back at me. She's trying to make a sucker out of you too."

I didn't bite on his bait regarding my being a stooge. This type of baiting is usually a ploy to make the manager angry at the complainant to turn the tables. Instead, I spelled out the consequences of his actions and our ability to resolve the issue informally if he agreed to correct his behavior. He reluctantly accepted my approach and agreed to cease the offensive behavior. I then informed Lolly of that fact.

I also had to ask her if she was satisfied with my informal approach or did she still want me to report this to the EEO officer. She answered, "Sarge, I feel comfortable with your actions. Let's see if he really corrects his behavior."

What I did next was to notate all those conversations with a copy to the EEO officer to cover that my actions were in immediate response to her request. Sound like a lot of work? Sure, but that's your job as a manager. You have to try and informally resolve issues before they become a *federal case*. Once a fact finder or investigator is assigned you're talking about hours and hours of paperwork.

Was Norton really looking at her breasts or was it a case of intimidation? I don't know. Norton was the local NTEU chapter president and was at odds with Lolly on a number of internal union issues. I didn't let that be a factor in my decision to take immediate action. If you keep it professional, and not personal, you will have made the right decision.

I learned that employees respect you much more when you take personal action rather than making a telephone call to the EEO officer and bucking it upstairs. It's not easy to handle EEO situations, since they require utmost tact and extreme diplomacy. Understand that some EEO matters must be handled by fact finders or official investigators, due to their serious or complex nature. When in doubt, call the EEO officer for advice.

◆   ◆   ◆

I had once had an informal allegation concerning sex and race brought to the attention of a fact finder. The alleged complaint was that I had selected two males to go on a TDY training assignment to Mexico and did not consider any females for the assignment. The EEO fact finder called me for an appointment to begin the process. She was amazed that I agreed to see her the next workday and thanked me for the rapid response. Most of the *90 percenter* managers would delay and delay and cancel meetings in fear that they had indeed done something wrong or in hope it would all just go away.

When we met, she started out by saying, "Sarge, I've worked with you for a long time. In fact, you were the one who encouraged me to apply for an inspector's job when I was your clerk. I've been thinking about this allegation because it bothers me. I know you so well and I've never seen you discriminate against anyone. You've always been fair across the board."

I started to thank her for saying that when she continued, "But there was that one time, about ten years ago when you were expecting visitors from headquarters. You asked me to make coffee. You didn't ask any of the men; you asked me. That got me to thinking that maybe you do discriminate against women as stated in the allegation."

I looked at her and calmly stated, "Sandy, I really don't recall that incident. But let me say this: Is my entire career, my life to be judged by my having asked you to make coffee ten years ago? Is that a factor to consider when making your judgment? Is that fair?"

I went on to answer the allegation. I informed Sandy of the selection process and the fact that no females had applied for the TDY assignment. I certainly couldn't consider or select a female if none had applied. I further stated that I had selected a Hispanic male, because he could speak Spanish and an African-American male for the TDY assignment to Mexico because he was a seasoned instructor. She wasn't aware of these facts. She then recommended to the EEO officer that the allegation was unfounded and no follow-up action was necessary.

It wasn't pleasant going through the process, of basically being called a sexist and racist, but I didn't let it get to be personal. I kept it professional. I didn't have anything to hide because I hadn't broken the law on discrimination. I went through the process and it worked. The allegation was deemed unfounded. As a manager you will have many days such as this in your career. Don't avoid them, but meet them head-on.

◆   ◆   ◆

I've testified, under oath, in formal EEO hearings in many cases brought against the Customs Service. Whether or not I thought that the complaints were frivolous or not, I testified truthfully and professionally. I can't recall one case in which I was a witness for the government that we lost. Hearings and complaints are time-consuming for everyone involved.

Do some people abuse the system? Absolutely, and there's nothing you can do about it. I knew one person who filed over 40 EEO actions against Customs in a ten-year period and never won one of them. Did that dissuade him? Nope, he just kept filing more which involved more fact finders.

One mistake I've seen managers make is trying to talk someone out of an EEO complaint by coyly stating to a third party, "You know, George has filed a lot of EEO cases and I'm hot he has filed one against me. The guy's bananas! There's a promotion coming up and I won't promote him unless he, well, drops the case."

We have had many such *clowns* try to, via the grapevine, keep people from filing actions. Remember, that's retaliation and that's against the law. The only thing this veiled threat will result in is actually getting George his promotion because that *clown* thought he could intimidate him from filing an EEO action. Once an action is filed, let the system run its course without your comments.

Yes, people knowingly abuse the system but that doesn't mean we should scrap the system. It's there to protect all people and ensure a level playing field when it comes to employment or application for employment. As cumbersome as it seems, the system has to be allowed to operate if it is to have a chance to work.

◆   ◆   ◆

As I've stated before, lawyers will do anything to win a case. EEO lawyers are no different than criminal defense attorneys. They all want to win and most will do anything to gain a favorable judgment for their client. To them it's a game. It's not a pretty picture, but that's life. You just have to accept it, do your best and keep it professional.

Is EEO an obstacle? Yes and no. Yes, in that EEO actions will take an enormous amount of your time, your supervisors' time and employees' time away from the job. Yet you still have to get the job done. That becomes an obstacle for you as a manager to figure out how to get the work done with numerous people missing from the worksite. You have to learn to work around that.

No, in that the EEOC is at times the only avenue of recourse people have to correct situations that are plainly wrong. Providing a system that can address these issues is not an obstacle, but an opportunity to insure an equal playing field. You as a manager owe that to those with whom you work.

◆   ◆   ◆

Hoteko's Law: *If you see a wrong, do the right thing and take immediate action. Be sure to take notes, don't take it personally and always remain a professional.*

21

Friends

Your friends can be the most difficult obstacle to overcome in your career. Friends take on a different meaning when you're the boss. It is only natural to want to take care of those who have taken care of you over the years. You have to be careful, however. Once you are a boss, some of your friends may attempt to use you in your new position of authority for their own gain. If they do, it will be at your expense.

It's hard to say no to a friend, someone with whom you have built up a trust while you were equals on the job. Again, all one has to do is look at city government in Chicago. Mayor Richard M. Daley put scores of "friends" into key city management positions. He knew them and he trusted them. These "friends" then reached out to their "friends" and that enabled them to obtain fat city contracts solely because of their connections.

This became a vicious cycle of "friends" feeding off "friends" with a wink and a nod. It bred a cult of personalities that only allowed those who were "friends" of "friends" to fish in the lucrative pond of BIG BUCK city contracts to the exclusion of fair competition. The results were a devastating and exorbitant drain on the budget. It's the citizens who ultimately pay for the pork barrel contracts in the form of rising property taxes, exorbitant user fees and reduced city services.

These "friends" began to think of city contracts as a birthright, an entitlement due them with a wink and a nod. These "friends" of "friends" were not doing Daley any good; in fact, they were bringing shame upon the mayor and his government by their seemingly insatiable greed. They took advantage of Daley who had trusted them and had placed them in key positions. Unfortunately, apparently Daley felt comfortable with these "friends" running his government with the old wink and a nod mentality.

Yet, Daley had only himself to blame when they failed him. When you limit competition for key positions only to those who live in the city of Chicago, especially the clout heavy 11th Ward, you are asking for trouble. Daley chose to run the city as did his father and all those before him. He chose the clout heavy *we don't want nobody nobody sent* form of government. We only want the "friends" our "friends" sent.

If Daley had broadened the employment pool outside of the city, as he did when he appointed Mary Rose Loney the aviation chief, he could have avoided the endless scandals his "friends" created. When you depend on the recommendation of a political ward committee man or alderman as the sole criteria for a city management position, you are doomed to failure. Why? Because the ward committeeman or alderman only gives his nod of approval to someone who dumps cash into his political fund. There isn't any discussion of qualifications, education or experience. The only qualification seems to be BIG BUCKS.

Until Chicago stamps out political patronage and expands their pool of hiring, scandal after scandal will continue to dominate the headlines. The "friends" of the "friends" will greedily be sticking their hands out and asking for their share of the loot. They will fill their pockets with the old *wink and a nod*. Nobody will deny them because they don't want to upset the ward committeeman or alderman who sponsored that thief for a job or contract. They fear that their own sponsored appointee or clout heavy contractor might be cut out of the pot of gold in retribution if they object.

I'm confident that Daley has never personally benefited from a contract or a job placement. When you tolerate scandal after scandal, however, people begin to believe where there's smoke there is fire. If the "friends" with whom you surround yourself with are in cahoots with a bunch of crooks or are plainly incompetent, you get to wear that title too. Yes, your friends can do you in.

◆   ◆   ◆

People react in different ways to their friends when they are promoted. Some think to the manner they were born and immediately adopt a regal air of pompous self-worth that makes them all the more intolerable to everyone. These are the people who can't wait to tell you how much better they are than you. Others, especially the *90 percenters*, shun their friends. They hibernate in their office where no one, not even their friends, can find them. There are also those who can't wait to order you to do the job they never did themselves, telling you how important that task has now become, especially since they can have someone else do it.

There was one person who worked for the Department of the Agriculture at O'Hare Airport. Jack (not his real name) always played cards with others in between arriving international flights. When he was promoted, he told his group, "Just because I'm now a supervisor doesn't mean that we can't be friends, but, I won't tolerate card playing during the downtime and I'd prefer that you call me Mr. Smith from now on. Other than that we can be friends."

Rule of the thumb is to be yourself, don't forget where you came from and park your ego at the door. Don't turn your back on your friends, but don't give them complete access to your office either. Give them the same assignment sequence you give to others as that relates to good, bad and indifferent tasks. Evaluate their talents as you would evaluate everyone's talents. If you do this, you will grow into the job the right way, keep your friends and gain the respect of many.

If someone was a *wacko*, a *yes man* or a *stargazer*, however, they will certainly remain one as a manager. I believe in the old adage that a leopard can't change its spots, although I have witnessed some people who were *wackos* as inspectors become really effective managers. It's rare, but there are exceptions to the rule. Unfortunately, it's been my experience that *wackos, yes men* and *stargazers* become more of a *wacko*, more of a *yes man* and more of a *stargazer* when they are promoted. Whatever restraints they may have had are suddenly lifted, and they quickly reach their true potential of being an idiot.

◆   ◆   ◆

There will be a great tendency on your part to surround yourself with people you know. That's only a natural animal instinct in a jungle survival setting which is akin to being the new boss. If you study lions and their behavior within their pride, you will see the tendency of the leader to associate more with old cronies than the younger beasts.

I call it the comfort factor. A good friend of mine who didn't receive a promotion he thought he deserved had a meeting with the selecting official to ask why. He was told, "Well, I know that you're qualified, but I just feel more comfortable with Jim. I've known Jim a long time and we're friends. I feel I can work better with Jim."

This is exactly the wrong answer. Comfort isn't an objective term; it's very subjective. You cannot quantify comfort the way you can quantify verbal, writing or analytical abilities. If you use the term "comfort factor" you are inviting a grievance from the employee who was not selected. He will win that grievance because comfort is very subjective and in the eye of the beholder.

Avoid surrounding yourself only with your friends because you feel comfortable. What you will be doing is alienating most of the other capable employees who most likely will do a better job for you if given the opportunity to excel. The comfort factor breeds an aura of favoritism that will surely reap a harvest of poor morale and unattained goals. When comfort factor lulls you into a false sense of security, you risk the possibility of having a staff filled with eager, smiling *yes men*.

◆   ◆   ◆

There also is a natural tendency to turn a blind eye to what a friend is or isn't doing because he is just that, a friend. You will not be doing anyone a favor if you get a friend promoted to a job he cannot do. The agency suffers and the people whom he works with will suffer. He himself will also suffer when the pressure grows too great to produce results and he cannot meet those expectations.

I had a friend who called me and said, "Sarge, can you do me a favor? I'm putting in for a criminal investigator's job. We go back a long way and I'd like to use you as a reference."

This person was a good technical inspector, but had some serious inter-personnel relationship skill problems with people. Being a criminal investigator requires delicate tact when dealing with people, violators, judges, attorneys and prosecutors. Not everyone can do this job well. The person asking for the recommendation was one who would be marginal at best.

The easy way out would have been to tell him, "Sure, put me down. I'll give you a great recommendation."

This is just what most of the weak-kneed *90 percenter* managers would do. They would recommend the person for the job knowing they would fall flat on their face. They do that because they are afraid to tell the truth. I've also witnessed some *sandbagger* managers give lip service to the person, telling them they would push for them to get the job. They then gleefully bury them in the recommendation stage preventing them from getting the job.

They would later commiserate with the person saying, "I wonder who did you in?"

One thing that separates the *ten percenters* from these creatures is their honor in telling the truth even though it may hurt. I told this friend, "No. I can't do that. You're a good inspector, a good technical guy on the regulations, but you continue to have problems in dealing with people. I'd have to be honest and tell the selecting official just that if you use me as a reference."

Callous? Perhaps it was, but *ten percenters* look at it this way: you are not doing the person any good to push them for a job they can't do and the agency will suffer too. It's your word of honor also that is at stake too, for once you lose your credibility you're finished. Nobody is going to believe you anymore. Once you've lost your good name where do you go to get it back? Remember, Keter Shem Tov.

◆   ◆   ◆

People will be watching just what you do or don't do with your friends. If you treat them as you treat others, fair across the board, you're going to be OK. If, however, you give them preferential treatment, watch out. As a manager you hold a responsibility to the agency to put the right people in the right jobs. Don't put your friends in a job they can't do. Get the right person in there who can do the job.

I can recall one situation where a person sued Customs over a promotion. He stated that he didn't get the job because of cronyism and favoritism. I had to testify in that hearing. His attorney tried his best to intimidate me, but it didn't work.

His attorney asked me, "Chief Hoteko, do you know Lanny Jones?"

Jones (not his real name) was the person we selected over the plaintiff. I answered, "Yes."

"Is he your friend?"

I answered, "Yes."

"Isn't it true that the only reason you recommended him for the position because he was your friend?" The attorney hammered at me.

"No," I replied, "I recommended him because he was the best qualified candidate for the job."

All the evidentiary records submitted proved Jones was a superior selection over the other fellow. He had outstanding evaluations, numerous awards and recognitions. He had volunteered for difficult assignments that the other fellow avoided like the plague. Had Jones's only qualification been being my friend, we would have lost the case. I recommended him because he was indeed the best candidate for the job and not because he was my friend.

◆   ◆   ◆

Be aware of those who are always saying that they are your friend. I knew one person who stated, "Ned, don't worry about anything. I'll never name you in any of my lawsuits. You are my friend forever. You can count on that."

Well, whenever Jordan (not his real name) had been passed over for promotions and command positions, and he sued Customs in various formats. He stated it was ethnic discrimination, age discrimination and the like. The one thing he never considered was his own competence level. This *clown* was incapable of being in charge. He blamed everyone and everything except himself.

Needless to say Jordan did name Ned (not his real name) in his next lawsuit. He did that even though Ned had always carried him, did his technical work and corrected all his mistakes. When push came to shove, Jordan was ready to sacrifice his loyal friend's reputation in a lawsuit in a futile attempt to gain a promotion he didn't deserve. With friends like Jordan, Ned didn't need any enemies. Yes, your friends can do you in.

◆   ◆   ◆

Hoteko's Law: *You won't do your friends any good by putting them into jobs they can't handle, and if you do, be prepared to pay the price.*

22

Your Ego

Just as your friends can do you in, your ego can do you in too. An ego is a good thing, but, too much of a good thing isn't good at all. According to the dictionary an ego is defined as: *a person's thinking, feeling, and willing, and distinguishing itself from the selves of others and from objects of thought.* I guess in essence you could say your ego is your public persona for better or for worse. It's what makes you stand apart from the crowd and shine or it can make you stink.

Most of the *ten percenters* I knew had gigantic egos. They harnessed that formidable power, however, to work to their advantage. Most of the horses' asses I knew had gigantic egos that let their mouth write a check that their pocketbook couldn't cash. As the saying goes: There's a fine line between genius and insanity. The same can be said for a good and a bad ego.

I was alternately accused of having a huge ego that teetered on being, arrogant, intimidating, compassionate, and confident as a leader. You can take your pick because the perception of an ego is in the eye of the beholder or the ear of the listener. Remember that to most people, however, perception becomes reality. To lead, you not only have to have internal confidence, you have to display an aura of public confidence that will fill a room with electric enthusiasm. A properly developed ego feeds your confidence level and that bolsters your ability to lead.

An ego also allows you to know when to go forward, when to back down and when to listen quietly to others in any given situation. This is the critical difference between a good ego and a bad ego. A good ego keeps the avenues of communication open so that you can evaluate the opinions of others prior to making an important decision. A good ego lends that air of confidence to those around you and removes any inhibitions they may have in following your lead.

A pompous ego, on the other hand, is one that is nurtured by delusions of grandeur and will easily cripple you. As the old saying goes: *Wise men say only fools rush in.* This is what happens when *wacko* or *stargazer* managers couple their flaws with a mal ego. They don't listen to anyone but their own ego, which is usually fortified by the vast army of *yes men* around them. They thrive on the false accolades of the *yes men* to the point they think that they are invincible and the end-all of knowledge.

When they do not tolerate a difference of opinion, those around them back off to keep in the good graces of the boss. This creates an atmosphere of fear, of a management by fear (MBF), that dooms any decision they make to failure. These are the very people who should park their ego at the door when negotiating union contracts, issuing discipline to employees or making major decisions. Unfortunately, they don't do that and who suffers? Everybody suffers, especially the agency, because its mission and goals will never be achieved at the optimum levels.

◆   ◆   ◆

I recall one supervisor—let's call him Rex (not his real name)—who had a gigantic ego which was also fragile and insecure. He had the deserved reputation of being unapproachable on any and all issues. His philosophy was one of the *divine right of kings*. He really believed that supervisors and managers could do no wrong and employees should never dare to question their decisions.

He was a *90 percenter* who actually had value to the agency as an analyst, but not a supervisor. He headed up a small analytical unit that was very successful in working with the Chicago Police Department and other federal agencies in researching drug smuggling organizations. This intelligence provided valuable information that led to many arrests and the crippling of some major drug cartels.

Unfortunately, he was a near disaster when he was supervising areas of our regular operations. One day he was responsible for overtime assignments at O'Hare Airport. Customs inspectors work long hours. The average workday can be 12 to 14 hours. They are adequately compensated for their time, but as a manager I was always sensitive to the physical and mental strain of working a consistent 60-hour week. I remembered: *Never forget what it's like to be in the trenches.*

Rex never knew what it was like in the trenches since he was promoted at a very early stage in his career with the help from an uncle. He was kept sheltered by a group of close friends. There were those times, however, when we had to use him in regular operations. Then it seemed he went out of his way to alienate the troops and whatever decision he made was the wrong one.

In one instance he piled on numerous cargo overtime assignments on one inspector for no apparent reason. These overtime assignments required the inspector to drive to various airline cargo stations to examine and clear foreign imported merchandise. Some of these stations were 15 to 20 minutes apart and some of the shipments required detailed examinations to insure they met complicated quota/visa textile requirements or in-depth examinations for narcotics.

This particular evening he assigned an inspector to eight examinations in a two-hour period, a full double work load over the normal overtime assignment policy. The inspector complained to him that this was unfair, both to him and to the Customs brokers requesting the assignments. He further stated he wouldn't be able to do proper examinations because he wouldn't have the time necessary.

The inspector asked, "Rex, why do I have to do eight examinations in the two-hour period?"

Rex looked down at him and his lower lip quivered as he stated, "Because I said so." With that Rex turned his back and walked away.

He couldn't stand being questioned about his decisions. Rather than parking his ego at the door and listening to the merit of the question, he barked out an idiotic response and then ran away. The ramifications of these types of actions cause seismic waves that batter and strain good employee/management relations. It gives legitimate birth to union grievances and unfair labor practices too.

◆   ◆   ◆

I was selected to take on many tough jobs in my career. Apparently, people felt confident that I could deliver a product that others couldn't. When I was at our region office, I was tasked with being the U.S. Customs liaison officer to both the 10th Pan American games in Indianapolis and the 15th Winter Olympic Games in Calgary, Canada. I had to select and train dozens of inspectors and detail them to these two cities to supplement our staff at those locations.

These were good TDY assignments for the inspectors. They required, however, diplomacy and tact in dealing with the throngs of spectators and the thousands of arriving athletes. The TDY inspectors would enjoy comfortable hotel rooms and have some free time in which to enjoy the events. In essence it was a good deal for one and all. All I asked was that they didn't disgrace Customs with rude or undesirable behavior.

At the end of the training sessions I closed with these remarks, "You've all been hand-picked to represent the Customs Service at these historic athletic events. Not many people get an opportunity to fly the flag in a proud manner when the athletes arrive and the foreign visitors come to in to see them compete.

"You'll be witnessing history. I expect you to conduct yourself in an exemplary manner both on the job and off duty. I won't tolerate anything less. If you fail to do so, you'll be gone so fast you won't know what happened. I'll put you on the next flight back to your duty station. You won't even have time to pack. I'll send your clothes back to you on a later flight. I want to be perfectly clear about this. Is there anyone who doesn't understand what I'm saying?"

In the Calgary audience that day was Lenny Friedman, our regional director of internal affairs. He had conducted the integrity training for the inspectors. Unbeknownst to me when he got back to the office he talked with Corky McMullen, our regional commissioner who had selected me for this job.

He said, "Corky, I've never seen anything like it. When Sarge said those words you could have cut the room with a knife. It was that quiet and that chilly. Everyone was listening and everyone understood their obligation. I've near heard a manager lay it on the line like that! It was great. We need more like him."

I used my ego to boost my confidence and that translated into a formidable leadership aura that enabled me to get that point across in the manner I did. I didn't ask them to do anything that I wouldn't do. There was no double standard for managers and I held myself to the very same high standards. I was upfront, honest and led by example.

◆   ◆   ◆

Many years ago we had a district director in Chicago who I will call Herman (not his real name). Herman was a brilliant person, definitely a *ten percenter* who got the mission accomplished. He ran the district with an iron, but cohesive, hand. Not many people liked Herman; in fact, some hated him, many feared him and most avoided him if possible. Herman had a big "good" ego that allowed him to lead effectively, but unfortunately he had a large "bad" ego that tended to belittle people unnecessarily.

The first time I met him I was escorted into his spacious corner office on the second floor of the Customs House in downtown Chicago. I knew something was wrong when I sat down on a broad couch in front of his desk, for it felt like I was sitting on the floor. Apparently he had all the furniture legs cut down so he would be at eye level with anyone in the room. Since Herman was about five feet tall, apparently his height bothered him and that insecurity fed his "bad" ego.

He would hold weekly staff meetings with his key managers. Since Herman ran a tight ship, all his meetings had a focused vision and were not rambling ad hoc sessions. Toward the end of each meeting he would go around the table and ask each manager what was new in their area, what problems they were having or what they could foresee.

At one such session he told the passenger branch chief, "Conrad, I've noticed numerous errors and delays in the processing of overtime pay assignments. This is a critical area and we can't afford to be time delinquent. It's a black mark against the entire district when we fall short of expectations. We can't have that kind of shoddy work going on anywhere."

Needless to say Conrad was embarrassed in front of his peers. He spent the rest of that week looking into the problem area and correcting it. At the very next meeting when it came his time to speak, he proudly told Herman, "I've looked into that problem and I've had two supervisors working with the payroll clerk to ensure that the assignments are processed timely. You won't see any more error reports from my shop."

Conrad sat back and expected a well-deserved accolade for fixing the problem. Instead, Herman looked at him and casually lit a small cigar (this is in the days one could smoke themselves to death in office buildings) and said to the entire group, "This is a good example of wasted time. We have more important priorities. If we lag in that area, we lag in it. It's no big deal. Conrad, you have more serious issues in passenger processing. You really need to prioritize your issues and that goes for everyone here. Anyone else have any questions or issues regarding their operations?"

Needless to say the room was stone cold silent. None of the assembled managers dared say anything for fear of being cut to ribbons. What Herman had done was to stifle totally any valuable input that his managers may have had. Nobody likes to be embarrassed, especially in public. Hence, from that meeting on nobody had anything to say when he would go around the table. He killed any creativity or healthy criticism that might have improved his operation.

So, why did he do that? Herman had the broad-based good, confident ego that's required to be successful as a leader. He did it because the dark side of his ego took over. It crept up without his knowing it. Once it was out, it was too late and the damage was done. It was his bad ego that drove him down the road that hurt his operation.

◆   ◆   ◆

Most of the *ten percenters* have a good and bad ego; they know that and usually they balance it out. Their percentages of good ego usually overwhelms the bad portion by a large margin. It's this that allows them to make good, solid decisions at critical times. The *90 percenters* on the other hand are oblivious to the good/bad ego complex. They ignore this phenomenon. They then subsequently panic in the decision-making process and make stupid mistakes, or they just let the bad side take over and cause undue havoc among the troops.

You have to be cognizant of the good and dark side of that seemingly nebulous entity called your ego. I've always paused when I felt a euphoric feeling start to take over. I would stand back and think: Why is this feeling of masterful superiority taking hold of my soul? It was in those instances that I knew I had to park my ego at the door before making a decision.

Use your ego as a sword to lead the troops into battle and not as an axe at the chopping block. The *ten percenters* always drove their ego. They remained in control. The *90 percenters* and others would let their ego do the driving. They were never in control and that usually resulted in a run away truck careening down the side of a mountain.

◆   ◆   ◆

Hoteko's Law: *Your ego can be your best asset or it can be your worst enemy. The choice is yours—choose wisely.*

PART VIII
Know When To Go

Quit while you are on top. The much beloved late Johnny Carson, host of the *Tonight Show* for 30 years said it best when he left the award winning TV program in 1992, "I've been lucky. I found something I enjoyed doing and was able to do it all my life."

If you're so lucky, go out on your terms with class and dignity as Carson did. People will then always remember you for the good you've done. Overstay your welcome and people will begin to resent your being in their house. Any good that you may have done will be overshadowed by your lingering at the dinner table when everyone else has left.

One baseball Hall of Famer stayed a season too long. It was pitiful to watch this once graceful athlete stumble while rounding the bases or when futilely chasing fly balls in the outfield. Although the fans and sportswriters were kind and didn't jeer this aging icon, people shook their heads and wondered why he stayed so long.

23

Those Who Knew

Hedda Hopper once said, "It's better to leave the party early rather than be swept out with the trash."

Associate Justice Potter Stewart stated upon his perceived early retirement from the Supreme Court, "It's better to leave too soon than to stay too long."

These were two vastly different people with diverse careers in opposite fields of endeavor. Yet, each one gave sage advice: *Know when to go*. When I joined the federal government, I had a career plan of retiring when I was 55 years old after 30 years of service. Thirty years is a long time to do one thing and to try to do that one thing well. If after that time period you haven't accomplished your goals, you never will. Enough is enough and it's time to go.

The majority of the *ten percenters* have abided by the 30-year rule and retired. Why? Because they have succeeded in accomplishing their goals. They are disciplined people and they look forward either to pursuing other goals outside of government or to just enjoying retirement. They also have the type of ego that lets them close up the shutters and walk away knowing they gave it their best. They don't have anything to prove to anyone, since their accomplishments quietly speak for themselves.

◆　　◆　　◆

To be able to retire you have to satisfy three elements;

1. Have your financial house in order.

2. Mentally be able to accept retirement.

3. Have an active plan for your retirement years.

The first is obvious. If you have a huge mortgage on your home, if you still have children going into college or if you have ZERO in your financial portfolio—don't retire. The second is a bit more difficult in that you have to gear your-self toward that day when you walk out of the door for that last time. The moment you cross that threshold you go from being somebody to being nobody. This is where ego comes into play. If you possess a good healthy confident ego, you can do just that—walk away without looking back.

To prepare for that day, you do have to start a couple years before D Day. This is how I approached that last day. A number of years before my D Day I reflected on the success I had in my career up to that point. I then developed a three-year plan toward retirement. I geared that plan toward new goals I wanted to accomplish before I retired. Doing so gave me a purpose and it put me on a timetable to achieve those goals.

This mindset helped me to focus on the narrowing path of opportunity to see my goals to completion. It helped to reinforce the fact that I had only so much time left until that final day. This mindset also eased the fact that the final day was looming, however, by choice and not happenstance. It was the inevitability of being pushed out the door that seems to be the only way the *90 percenters* retire.

The last element is the most difficult: *Finding a life after your career.* You just can't go home and sit in a chair; if you do that, you'll die young. You have to have a reason to get out of bed in the morning. Your purpose after you retire can be noble; you can volunteer your time to a service organization that helps others. It can be financial; you can now use you talents and knowledge to earn more money than you could in government. It can totally selfish; you can now take a low-paying job with certain benefits, perhaps as a starter at a golf course that allows you to play golf for free.

You've earned the right to do one or all three of the above. The point is you have to have something to do whether you are 55 or 85 years old. Don't wait until the last day, but formulate a plan for retirement. Make it a dynamic plan in which you can switch gears when needed. Think ahead especially where health or financial issues may crop up and have a plan to deal with them too. The ideal plan is to have a plan.

◆   ◆   ◆

I was having lunch with a good friend who had already retired, Norm Gunn. We were joined by Bernie Tarte, one of the *ten percenters*, who had 40 years on the job at that time. Norm had been retired over a year at that time.

Bernie said to him, "Norm, what do you do with yourself? Do you just sit in the house? I'm not going to retire. I'm having too much fun here. I don't know why anybody would retire."

Norm explained that he and his wife were traveling and he was playing more golf. Bernie still didn't understand it. Why? Although Tarte was financially secure, he hadn't started thinking about that last day nor did he have a plan regarding his life after retirement. He met one of the three Hoteko requirements for retirement, but he simply refused to plan or think about that possibility. This was an unusual attitude for a *ten percenter*, especially someone of Bernie's caliber.

Sometimes it takes a good old kick in the pants to get the brain thinking. In Bernie's case it was money. In 1988, the government was going to place a five-year moratorium on a civil service employee's ability to request a lump sum repayment of his 7 percent payroll contribution into the retirement fund. This anomaly in the law allowed you to get back what you put in the fund and still draw a pension. It was a good deal. Congress, however, decided to temporarily close the loop hole.

To be able to take advantage of the cash payout you had to retire that year or wait five years and hope congress would let the provision sunset and not make it permanent. Bernie, being the wise person he was, knew he couldn't wait, because you can't trust congress and he was right. They did permanently end the lump sum payout in 1993. It's a good thing that Bernie didn't wait to pull the pin and retire.

About a year later Norm, Bernie and I went out for lunch. I asked Bernie how he was doing. He smiled that bright, warm smile of his and said, "Sarge, it's great. I'm spending more time with my grandchildren. I'm having a ball taking them to places I took my two sons as boys. If I had known it was this good, I'd have retired long ago."

Yes, if Bernie had had a plan and had mentally prepared, he would have realized that there is life after the United States Customs Service. Thankfully he enjoyed more than a decade of happy retirement with his family before he died. Some wait way too long and never have the joy of experiencing the sunset years of their life. They either don't think far enough ahead, or they just don't think at all. Perhaps they are afraid of the road that lies ahead. If you have a road map, you'll get to where you're going.

◆   ◆   ◆

Another one of the *ten percenters*, Henry Ristic, had the best planning of all. Henry and I were uniformed inspectors together. He was not only a friend, but a mentor as well. Corky McMullen, recognizing his talent, had plucked him up right away from our district office when he took over our region. Henry was a very prolific program manager and was our first director of Canadian preclearance operations, where he was responsible for over 160 inspectors assigned to six Canadian airports. Henry ran a first-class show.

Henry took advantage of an early retirement option being offered. So in 1998 at age 50, he pulled the pin. Prior to that, he was also operating a small business, an art and frame store. People were envious of Henry and his success in that enterprise. These *90 percenters* didn't realize or couldn't understand that to be a success Henry had to work evenings and weekends in his small shop after putting in 40 hours for Customs.

Ristic had a plan in hand and when the opportunity arose for early retirement he was ready. Henry was always thinking ahead, and that is why he was so successful in Customs. He looked to the future. After he retired, he also accepted a part-time consulting job with an aviation group in Canada and, not surprisingly, was very successful there too.

◆   ◆   ◆

Not very many of the *ten percenters* I knew were ever pushed out of government or buried in mundane jobs that stifled their mental abilities which would eventually force them out the door. They had their goals and plans and they took advantage of the opportunities afforded to them. They left on their own terms with their heads held high. When they closed up the shutters and walked away, they never looked back with regret. They had their day in the sun and they left Customs a better place.

Knowing when to leave is the most difficult career decision you will ever have to make. It not only impacts you, but it impacts the government. Many overstay their welcome and that usually proves to be disastrous in many ways. One example is by staying too long you keep the door closed to promotions for deserving people. All the time and effort that had been expended nurturing the next generation of *ten percenter* managers will have been wasted.

If you decide to stay ten years longer till you're 65, the next generation will be eligible to retire when you do and most will do exactly that—retire. Many of them will have been demoralized because you stayed as long as you did and in effect kept them out of a job. They will never have had the opportunity to excel and make their mark on the agency. That's a huge loss for the government.

◆　　　◆　　　◆

At one retirement function I heard a *90 percenter* say, "I wasn't ready to retire but my health dictated that I had to go. I wasn't mentally able to get ready for this big move. All of a sudden I was a nobody on Monday morning. I still can't believe it. I really don't know what to do with myself."

This fellow was one of the good *90 percenters* in that he didn't have an evil bone in his body. Unfortunately, he was in a BIG PICTURE job that he couldn't handle very well. His agency suffered through his benign, leaderless management style that bred an entire generation of so-so *90 percenters* to follow in his wake. Had it not been for the health issue he would have hung on and on while his branch slowly spun down and down until it would have eventually hit rock bottom. Fortunately a good *ten percenter*, from another agency was appointed to take his place. This was the only salvation that could have saved that branch from ruin.

◆　　　◆　　　◆

When you leave, it's your reputation and accomplishments that will be remembered. If you haven't accomplished anything or were uniformly viewed as an idiot, well, that's how history will remember you and there's nothing you can do about it. What's done is done.

A sad example is President Bill Clinton. He had the opportunity and had the ability really to impact America when he was elected in 1992. What happened? Nothing. He wasted that golden opportunity to make this country a better place. Few people are ever given a chance to impact upon history. So what do people remember about Clinton? Most likely Monica Lewinsky, his embarrassing impeachment by the House and ultimate acquittal in the Senate trial.

Clinton fell into the trap that many people, even some of the best *ten percenters* do; when he got to the top he relaxed. Rather than continue to work hard and do their best, some people just sit back to enjoy the free ride. That's what happened to Clinton. He had a personal, jolly good time being president and enjoyed the perks of the office.

He traveled, he socialized and apparently he womanized. Where was the substantial legislation he promised, like health care and social security reform? You can't party your way through eight years in the presidency and still have substance. He will spend the rest of his life in a futile attempt of trying to rewrite history. Remember, what's done is done and you can't change it. So, do good while you have the opportunity to do some good.

◆   ◆   ◆

I was going to a holiday luncheon at the airport about two years after I retired. In the parking lot I ran into a new Customs and Border Protection officer I had never known when I was on the job. When we got on the elevator together and I asked, "How long have you been with CBP?"

"About two years," he replied and added, "I know who you are, and you're Sarge."

I asked him, "How do you know me?"

"I've seen your picture and people still talk about you," he answered.

"I see," I laughingly replied and continued, "Now I know why my ears have been burning. I won't put you on the spot. You don't have to tell me what they are saying about me."

He smiled and honestly answered, "It's mostly good. A lot of people would like to have you back. They really miss you."

To me that was an ultimate compliment. He could have lied and stated everyone loved me and that I was the greatest. He didn't do that. He didn't even have to mention what he did say about me, but he told me that most of them thought well of me, but not all of them. In life that's a reality, not everybody is going to like you. The difference between an intelligent person and someone who suffers from delusions of grandeur is knowing that not everyone will like you and accepting that fact.

◆   ◆   ◆

Hoteko's Law: *Do good while you can. Have a plan, have a timetable, so when the time comes you can walk out the door with your head held high on your terms and with dignity.*

24

Those Who Didn't Know

Prior to Jimmy Carter's presidency all federal employees had to retire at age 70, no matter what. There was one notable exception, however, and it took an annual act of congress to keep him on the payroll. That person was J. Edgar Hoover. He worked until the day he dropped dead at the age of 77. Lyndon Johnson and then Richard Nixon pushed congress to keep him on. Why? It's mere speculation, but the conventional wisdom was that Hoover had the goods on nearly everybody within the Beltway.

No congressman, senator or president wanted to push the envelope to see if Hoover really had the goods on them or not. It was easier for them to cave in and keep the old man in office. Hoover was found dead in his pajamas, sprawled out on his bedroom floor, on the morning of May, 2, 1972. At first there was jubilation across Washington.

The jubilation was quickly replaced, however, by a rampant fear because nobody knew what would happen to the director's personal files, the files with all the goodies. His office was immediately sealed and quarantined. Nobody really knows what happened to those files or if indeed they ever existed. Apparently the secrets died with the director and everyone breathed a sigh of relief.

Upon hearing of Hoover's death, Nixon supposedly remarked to Bob Haldeman, "So, the old cocksucker is finally dead."

◆　　　◆　　　◆

Hoover was a classic example of a *ten percenter* who didn't know when to let go and leave. He had transformed the old corrupt Bureau of Investigation into the finest professional law enforcement agency in the world. He accomplished that based on the force of his personality, i.e., his confidence, his good ego. He used that to curry the favor of congress to get the necessary appropriations to fund the FBI into the crime-busting machine it is today.

Had Hoover gone out in 1965, when he was 70, I believe he would have been remembered more as a true patriot rather than an aging demagogue. By staying on, he stumbled into the Vietnam War protests, the disastrous Chicago Democratic Convention, and beginnings of Watergate. Hoover would have been long retired and would have distanced himself from these immolating events in history. By staying on, however, he came to symbolize what was wrong with America which helped galvanize the antiwar, antigovernment movement. Since it also gave the protesters a personal target, that, in turn, also tarnished his beloved FBI.

Had Hoover left in 1965, another person would have had the opportunity to improve the FBI and take it to another level. By his staying on, that eliminated any possibility of positive growth was eliminated which actually stagnated the Bureau. It was a lose-lose situation. All the good that Hoover had done prior to 1965, was wiped away by the events that unfolded in those seven years until his death in 1972.

If Hoover had gone out on his own accord in 1965, the FBI wouldn't have had to suffer through the chaotic aftermath in the wake of his sudden death. There could have been an orderly transition that would have not disrupted and stained the FBI. Unfortunately, that didn't happen. After Hoover's death Nixon was rushed into naming L. Patrick Gray for the job. Gray was inept at best, continuously stumbling until he was finally fired.

The legacy that Hoover had hoped to build never happened. Instead of being remembered as the person who transformed the old corrupt Bureau of Investigation into the present FBI, he's remembered as a defiant, entrenched bureaucrat who abused power and didn't know when to let go. His was sad legacy that was summed up in what Nixon supposedly stated, "So, the old cocksucker is finally dead."

◆   ◆   ◆

You have to know when to go. There was a supervisor in a major Customs district, Seymour (not his real name) who stayed too long. Few people could equal his enforcement record, and like Hoover he should have left on a high note. Like Hoover, his mal ego took possession of his soul and he stayed on and on and on. He didn't know when to let go.

The longer he stayed, the less effective he became at his job. He had to be unceremoniously moved and given a created job where he could do little harm or damage to the agency. The amazing thing is that he didn't see or want to see what was happening to him. He couldn't keep up with the high technology, let alone the simple computer programs that managers are required to know.

He became more and more dependant on key employees to do his work. This isn't a bad thing; remember a good manager is one who surrounds himself with good people who can get the job done. The only problem was with the programs he had his subordinates perform. They required restricted access that was only available to select managers. For these employees to complete the programs he had to allow them access to his computer system, which was an internal security violation.

When this integrity issue hit him smack in the face, he was suspended for a week. That might not sound too bad to some, but to someone who was very proud of his career it was devastating to Seymour. He decided he wasn't going to take it lying down. He struck back and struck back with fury. He filed an EEO lawsuit against the managers who suspended him and against the agency.

He claimed that he was suspended because of age discrimination. I suppose in one respect he was right, but not in the legal aspect. It's aging and the diminishing mental faculties that come with that process that cause a person not to be able to perform or to grasp new technologies. Most intelligent people accept the aging process, certainly the *ten percenters* do, and they quietly remove themselves from harms way. They retire before they embarrass themselves.

Unfortunately, people like Hoover and Seymour begin to live in their own fantasy world. They surround themselves with willing supplicants, the scores of *yes men*, who continue to praise their every movement and decision. This reinforces their mal ego. They constantly relive the glory days of their past as if that's all it takes to be successful in the future.

They become so in love with themselves that little if anything else matters. They actually begin not to care for the people around them, the very people who keep them propped up. They begin to use people in the worst possible way and when one person is not longer useful, they discard him like trash.

It becomes a classic example of a sociopath. One employee remarked, "It's really sad about Seymour. It used to be fun working for him. He was a good enforcement supervisor, but now nobody wants to deal with him. It's a repressive atmosphere. It's all about him and what we can do for him. He doesn't care about us or Customs anymore. He's so bitter. It's all about him."

In his lawsuit Seymour blamed everyone else for his suspension except himself. He refused to acknowledge the fact that he illegally allowed the employee to access the restricted system. The employee had fully cooperated with internal affairs during the investigation. Even when confronted with this evidence, and the detailed computer records, he still refused to believe that his suspension was based on anything other than discrimination.

This stubborn refusal to accept personal blame accelerated his decline. He was dumped into another do-nothing job. I suppose they thought he'd retire, but they miscalculated his resolve. He began a cat-and-mouse game of baiting his managers to allegedly violate another one of his civil rights. Then he could launch another vicious lawsuit. He was determined to win. But win what?

There would be no victors in this fight. Everyone would lose, he would lose, the employees would lose and so would Customs. He saw himself as a champion of employee's rights. He basked in the self-imposed glow of David fighting Goliath. He actually believed he was uniformly respected for his challenge to authority.

It was exactly the opposite. People laughed at him behind his back as he spent thousands and thousands of dollars unsuccessfully suing the government. He told a fellow manager, "The people love me. They look up to me because I am fighting Customs for the little people. They call me a champion."

The manager shook his head and bluntly told him, "Seymour, they don't call you a champion. They call you a chump behind your back."

Seymour is still on the job and still suing the government. His office is full of fading old mementos from the glory days of a long-ago past. Next to well-earned accolades are silly political letters from senators and presidents cheaply framed and haphazardly nailed to his wall. Alongside of them are large photographs of himself, another sign of a sociopath.

It's as if the big brass will look at these cheap trinkets and decide they better let him have his way or the president will fire them. Anybody who's ever been suckered into sending in a political donation gets these types of photographs signed with an autopen. He actually believes that the president has signed his picture personally. Sociopaths live in a deluded world.

He also practiced the politics of intimidation. Seymour once told the EEO investigator assigned to one of his frivolous cases, pointing to a batch letter signed with an autopen, "You know that if I don't like your findings in my complaint, I'll go straight to the White House."

◆   ◆   ◆

I believe that many people can keep going into their 80s and doing their jobs very well. I also believe that is the exception and not the rule. In our private industry shoe factory, if an 80-year old can no longer do his job, he's *retired*.

Plain and simple, if you can't do your job on the shoe assembly line you jeopardize the entire operation. You're gone, out the door, whether your 38 or 88 years old. Not so in government where non-productive people are allowed to go on and on, regardless of whether or not they can do their job.

That's why Carter was wrong to sign the legislation abolishing the mandatory retirement age. You have to help people from harming themselves and the government, as in Hoover and Seymour's cases. Had Seymour retired earlier, he, like Hoover, would have been talked about as a true legend and not as a bona fide buffoon. It's a sad ending to what had been a grand career.

When Seymour retires, if death doesn't take him first, people will probably say, "Well, the old cocksucker finally retired."

◆   ◆   ◆

Hoteko's Law: *When you stay too long you are no longer a functioning cog in the wheel of government. You become a crack in the wheel that will not only derail the wagon, but will derail you too.*

PART IX
The Self-Immolation Syndrome

There are people out there that would like nothing better than to do you in. Know that, understand that and deal with it. Understand that your worst enemy, however, can be lurking within you. We all harbor a haven for some demons within our soul. If you understand that and keep those demons in check, you won't self-destruct.

I've seen people self-destruct for various reasons: Their self indulgent behavior, their inability to maintain self-control or their inability to exercise common sense. Some self-destructed early in their career and some near the end. Some were on top of the heap and some were on the bottom of the ladder. They all shared one common trait, however, they were headed for destruction and there wasn't anything anybody could do about it except themselves. They let the demons take control and by doing that, they did themselves in.

25

A Watchdog Destructs

Customs like all federal agencies has a department of internal affairs. This organization solely exists to keep the agency clean. In Customs, more so than other agencies, this is critical due to the law enforcement and national security nature of the mission. You would think that only those people with impeccable credentials would be chosen to be guardians of the kingdom. Unfortunately, that's not always the case.

Internal affairs special agents are often referred to as watchdogs or headhunters with a daunting responsibility. Consider the fact that Customs alone has over 14,000 employees across the United States, and most have access to very sensitive, highly classified information that impacts on national security. Each year dozens upon dozens of employees are busted by the headhunters for breaking the faith and violating the law.

Some are arrested for taking bribes from drug smuggling organizations, some are busted for being in collusion with unscrupulous importers and others are handcuffed because they were pocketing money out of the till, or stealing a computer or spending hours on a sex hotline at government expense. In most cases IA does an outstanding job keeping the agency clean. Unfortunately, there have been numerous situations where they doggedly continued an investigation without due cause, and that stubbornness has in fact harmed innocent employees.

So, who watches the watchdogs? Nobody and that's not good for anybody. IA agents form a bond that at times is an unholy union of a secret, closed society. The police are often accused of maintaining a *blue wall of silence* when it comes to ratting out a possibly corrupt officer. In IA they seem to have adopted the motto: *I can't do any wrong because I'm above you.*

They acquire the mindset of a holy crusader: That their function is to cleanse Customs of any and all evil. They see their mission as a holy war against corruption, and I'm not saying that's bad in itself, but when the IA agent breaks the law to arrest a corrupt employee, he's no better than the guy he slaps the cuffs on.

Legally they are answerable to the Commissioner of Customs and the Treasury Department Inspector General, but in fact there is little, if any, oversight on their investigations. They're allowed a free rein and are expected to haul in the bad guy before he does real harm to the agency. It's this Wild West cowboy attitude that fosters an air of invincibility among the headhunters that makes them feel they are immune to the law themselves.

◆   ◆   ◆

Let's take the case of Herman Lupperini (not his real name). Herman started out in Customs as head of the internal audit branch on the east coast. Internal audit is one of the two branches within internal affairs, the other being internal security. Audit is responsible to ensure that Customs revenues are properly deposited and that internal control procedures are followed. The internal security branch are the guys who bust the corrupt employees.

Herman then was promoted to head of internal affairs in a major southern seaport city. Then he was the responsible official for both audit and security in one of the most vulnerable gateway cities into the United States. This is a city where a number of employees are arrested each year for crimes ranging from plain theft to assisting Colombian drug cartels in plying their trade. From that IA job he became one of nine regional commissioners at a very young age. He was on the fast track and he loved it.

When Herman hit the big time with a promotion to commissioner in one of the most complex regions within Customs, he was now on cloud nine. The very first thing he did when he got to that Midwestern city was to ask a chief inspector to initiate a meeting with the mayor. He had apparently been use to hobnobbing with the social and political elite in the last city where he had been assigned. In that small metropolis he was considered a big fish. In his new city, however, federal regional commissioners are a dime a dozen and the mayor there didn't waste time on anyone who couldn't get out the democratic vote.

His request was refused, so his ego made him ask for a plaque from the mayor's office. He was determined to get some kind of recognition from the mayor. He bugged the chief inspector unmercifully about getting that piece of brass and wood. He told him, "Conrad, I need to know the size of the plaque so I know how much wall space to leave open in my office around my other plaques."

He then created a monthly newsletter entitled *The Majestic Message*. This in itself was good since employees thrive on information regarding their agency. The only problem was that it became known as the *Lupperini Gazette*. The reason being it featured articles and dozen of pictures of him as he regally traveled around the 18-state region. People laughed at it as just a personal PR rag that promoted Herman's big ego.

Apparently, Lupperini got himself into a little trouble while transitioning to the new city. He had pushed the envelope and applied for continued reduced partial per diem payments beyond what was normally allowed. The government grants one housing hunting trip and 30 days of subsistence allowance on any given move. Anything more than that comes out of your own pocket whether that's fair or not.

Herman applied for and received continuous reduced daily payments beyond the 30-day period. Some *wacko* in HQ had approved it. This supplemental allowance then came into question and was referred to the Controller General's office which eventually ruled that it was illegal. Everyone should have known better, especially Herman, who had a financial audit background with his extensive stints in internal affairs.

Included in that decision was the stipulation that Lupperini repay the government for all those partial payments he had received. It totaled just under $10,000. Not to worry, Herman got a crony in HQ to nominate him for a Meritorious Service Award, which he did receive. Along with that reward was a check in the amount of $10,000. All Lupperini had to do was sign it over to the government and he was off the hook. He had skated on this one, but the lesson would remain unlearned. Lupperini had his eyes on bigger and better things.

Herman put in for a position as the Customs attaché in a glamorous foreign city. This was a prestigious diplomatic assignment usually reserved for a senior special agent (a criminal investigator), since the main duties were being a liaison with the police and INTERPOL. The problem was that Lupperini wasn't a criminal investigator, but that didn't stop him from applying.

Some HQ crony, perhaps a *90 percenter* or a *clown* or a *wacko,* selected him for the position. They sent him to the three-month special agent's training course at the Federal Law Enforcement Training Center (FLETC) in Glynco, Georgia. He had to pass the course in order to become a special agent and hence qualify for the promotion he had already been given. Needless to say, his selection as the attaché was uniformly denounced by numerous special agents who thought they had earned the right to that job by their hard investigative work and not their HQ connections.

Because of the protests you would think that Herman would play the game, go to class, study and keep a low profile especially in face of his unpopular selection. No, Lupperini was flying high and he rubbed it in their faces at FLETC. He attended about half of the classes, leaving to make "official" telephone calls to HQ or so he stated. His HQ clout and IA background was strong enough that they passed him anyway. He now had the coveted gold-plated special agent's badge and was on his way to Europe. He also had the black covered diplomatic passport that stated: *the bearer is on an assignment abroad as the U.S. Customs attaché to the United States embassy in……*

His air of invincibility was now so strong that Lupperini felt he could do anything he wanted. That contagious attitude grew-and-grew on his wife too. At a major conference of European Customs attachés his wife rather rudely demanded of their HQ assistant commissioner, "When are we going to get a new car. The Chevrolet we have is four years old. Herman is the attaché and should be driving something new and more presentable. I want a new car!"

The Customs attaché offices are subjected to internal audits once a year to ensure that they are complying with programs, policies and procedures. Herman lobbied for and was assigned to audit the attaché offices in Bangkok, Hong Kong and Tokyo. This was a plum assignment and usually reserved for only senior attaches and not the newly assigned. Herman touted his internal affairs audit background as sound credentials for the assignment. Again, a HQ *stargazer* or perhaps a *wacko* crony pulled the strings and Lupperini was on his way to the exotic Far East.

Apparently all Herman did was spend his time buying gold jewelry for himself and his wife. He spent a minimum amount of time actually doing any useful audits. Of course, those offices being audited rolled out the red carpet. They willingly drove Herman to all the gold markets he wanted and they got him a "police" discount to boot. They were only too glad to get him out of the office where he might actually find discrepancies that would drop their HQ efficiency rating.

Herman was happier than a fat pig rolling around in manure. He happily stuffed his pockets with gold chains, bracelets, pendants and rings. His air of super invincibility was so strong that he never saw what was coming. Remember, he took a coveted attaché job away from a deserving special agent. Common sense would dictate that perhaps one of the investigators assigned to Hong Kong or Bangkok offices, or one of the guys driving him to the gold bazaars might have put in for the job Lupperini had hijacked.

Herman was flying back home the long way through the United States ostensibly to brief the assistant commissioner in Washington on his audit assignment. On the ten hour flight from Tokyo to LAX, Herman had more than enough time to fill out his Customs Declaration properly. Being from internal affairs for a large portion of his career, he surely knew the regulations regarding the penalty for failure to declare foreign merchandise purchased abroad.

When a person is flying high, not so much as in an airplane, but in a self-concocted cocoon of invincibility they really don't make good decisions. Why? Because they are now living in the Neverland of their own created self-invincibility. That is a certain recipe for disaster and in the end run they will have nobody to blame but themselves when things go wrong.

Herman got off the long, tedious Tokyo flight and immediately badged his way to the front of the Immigration line. The Customs Code of Conduct states that any employee who uses or attempts to use their position of authority to circumvent any and all legal processes is in violation of the Code and subject to disciplinary action. That seems plain and simple. Don't use your badge to get out of a traffic ticket, to gain free entry into a baseball game or to barge to the head of the line. Wait your turn.

Not Herman, he apparently cast aside his IA background as a keeper of the faith. He blatantly went to the front of the line, got his passport stamped and headed to the luggage carrousel to get his bags. While he was waiting, a Customs inspector approached him and asked for his declaration saying, "How much are you declaring in gifts purchased or received abroad?"

Lupperini looked down his large, angular Roman nose at this peon invading his space, flipped open his credentials and retorted, "Nothing, I'm not over my exemption. I'm a Customs attaché. Did you know that?"

The inspector asked Lupperini again to verify that he hadn't purchased anything abroad and Herman replied in a condescending manner, "I already told you that I didn't buy anything over my exemption. Do you understand that?"

The Customs allowance at that time was $400 per person. Herman had knowingly lied to the inspector since his gold bonanza was in the neighborhood of ten grand. Once he had retrieved his bags he was taken to a secondary examination area and once again asked to confirm his oral and written declaration which he did. After that he was allowed to leave.

Now you would think that a normal bright person would have thought something was up. Wouldn't you? If someone were to ask me twice about something that I was trying to hide, I would immediately think that the jig was up. At that point in time a reasonable person would fess up and say something like, "Oh, I'm glad you asked me that question. I was confused. It's been a long flight and I'm very tired. Let me see, oh, yes, I did purchase more than my exemption. Actually I bought gold jewelry valued at about $10,000."

If you say that, you're off the hook, but not Herman. Even after they escorted him back into Customs from the outside lobby, he stonewalled the inspector. He again told him that his purchases were within his allowance. His air of super invincibility and his past IA connections apparently provided the testosterone to keep on lying. Herman was betting he could intimidate the inspector. What Herman didn't know was that he was toast.

Apparently his accommodating hosts in Bangkok and Hong Kong had faxed copies of his gold jewelry receipts to internal affairs stateside with a cautionary note that Lupperini might not declare his purchases. They set him up big time and he didn't have an inkling of what was happening. They had been out to do him in.

IA had to act on the tip, but they didn't want to see Herman fall unnecessarily. So, they instructed Customs at LAX Airport to give him at least three opportunities to amend his declaration. I can only surmise that they hoped that he would catch on that he was being set up and amend his declaration. Then Herman could pay his duty and be on his way. Stupidly Herman didn't do that and apparently ended up being forced to retire as part of a plea bargain agreement with the government rather than stand trial.

◆   ◆   ◆

High-flying Herman had been shot down by his own idiotic sense of super invincibility. It was a classic case of self-immolation as if he poured gasoline over his head and lit the match. Lupperini was destined for destruction by his excessive appetite for recognition and material possessions, aided by his royal air of arrogance. He had nobody to blame but himself.

Herman Lupperini was a talented, smart person who could have had a long and brilliant career with Customs had he played by the rules. Instead he chose to break the very rules he had been sworn to uphold in internal affairs. Everything he had worked for was gone in a flash because he thought he was smarter than anyone else. His air of super invincibility turned out to be his albatross of defeat.

◆   ◆   ◆

Hoteko's Law: *If you're sworn to uphold the law, if you're sworn to see that others uphold the law, then do just that; abide by the law yourself and anything that happens will be OK.*

26

A Gross Abuse of Authority

Self-immolation comes in many shapes, sizes and forms. Not every downfall is based on career enhancement, money or a raw grab for power. Some is based on sex. Sex on the job has been the downfall of many a manager, including the 42nd President of the United States. Sex and the job mix as well as oil and water, especially if you're a manager and the person you're pursuing, or who is pursuing you, is a subordinate employee. Playing that game is akin to lighting a match to check for a gas leak. Eventually there will be a giant explosion.

The worst case scenario, however, is secret sex on the job which spells trouble with a capital T. Corky McMullen once told me, "Sarge, never say or do anything that you wouldn't do in public. Whatever it is you do, people will find out. So, if you can't say or do it in public, then you have to ask yourself why are you saying or doing it at all. Nothing stays secret on the job for long. People will find out."

◆   ◆   ◆

The most despicable person is the manager who preys on young, vulnerable victims, especially people who are working as college interns in the hope of gaining a federal law enforcement position. This brings us to our next friend, John P. Wilson (not his real name).

Brother Wilson was in charge of all criminal investigations in a large Customs region. I call him Brother because many people often accused him of being a blowhard, not unlike a street corner preacher. Wilson had a windy story or lengthy anecdote about any given situation. He loved nothing better than to hold court and pontificate over his chosen topic of the day. He was a bore, but he was the boss and people played up to him.

He had been a very successful investigator who worked his way up the ladder in Customs. Wilson had moved around the country, in various positions of increasing authority from a dusty southern border to Los Angeles and the big city. He was a good *ten percenter* at his peak of his career when he drove off the mountain. His secret life did him in.

The end came for him on a Friday afternoon. A Hollywood director couldn't have filmed a better script. Two senior internal affairs investigators from the Treasury Department's Inspector General (IG) came to see him. They were then escorted into his office sometime after 3 p.m. and they closed the door. Nobody really gave it much thought; Brother Wilson was always receiving various law enforcement types from many different agencies. At 5 p.m. the visitors were still behind closed doors with Wilson.

Everyone went home that Friday and enjoyed a good weekend. On Monday morning the regional commissioner told the staff, "John had a heart attack over the weekend. He's in intensive care and he can't take telephone calls."

It wasn't until a day later that some of the truth started leaking out. Apparently the two IA headhunters had confronted Wilson on Friday by saying something like this, "Mr. Wilson, you're the subject of an IG internal affairs investigation regarding allegations that you have engaged in sexual relations on numerous occasions with interns. This is a serious violation of the code of conduct."

They further went on to tell him, "We'll be back on Monday morning to continue the investigation and to take a sworn statement from you at that time."

That's a time-tested IA tactic. Let the guy you are investigating know you're investigating him and let him sweat it out over the weekend before you question him. I've seen it happen to numerous people. They fret, they sweat and they don't sleep. All they do is worry about the upcoming encounter with the headhunters. By Monday morning they are a babbling wreck and will readily confess to anything, even to having shot President Kennedy in Dallas if so accused.

Monday, however, never came for Brother Wilson and IA. He went home that Friday evening and promptly had a heart attack and was hospitalized. Did he actually have a heart attack? I don't know. What I do know is numerous people throughout history when confronted with adversarial situations, either by the press or the cops, have indeed closeted themselves in the intensive care unit where nobody could get at them. It's only a stalling tactic since they can't permanently reside in the hospital, but it does buy them some time.

◆   ◆   ◆

Perhaps one of the most famous people to have a sudden heart attack was a special advisor to President Johnson named Walter Jenkins. On October 7, 1964, after working long hours at the White House and attending a cocktail party hosted by *Newsweek*, Jenkins walked a couple of blocks to the YMCA on G Street. There he apparently participated in some type of an illicit sexual act with a retired soldier. Unfortunately for him, they were observed by two Washington D.C. undercover cops who had staked out the men's room at the Y because of numerous complaints of seedy encounters.

They arrested both men, allowed each to post a small cash bond and assigned them a court date. The next day a local newspaper reporter went to Metro Police HQ and looked over the arrest blotter. He saw a name that caught his attention—it was a Walter Wilson Jenkins arrested on a morals charge. He did further research and was able to discern that the same Walter Wilson Jenkins had been previously arrested on a similar morals charge and had forfeited his cash bond rather than contest the charge in court.

Wondering if this was the same Walter Jenkins who was a top aide to the president, he called him at the White House. The rest was history. Apparently Wilson hung up the telephone, went home and had a heart attack. He was hospitalized in the intensive care unit and was unavailable to answer any reporters' questions. Again, he was just buying time. In the end he had to admit he had been arrested on those charges. Wilson subsequently resigned. Secret lives never stay secret for long.

President Johnson had stated when learning of the arrest, "That telephone call was like a knife going through my heart."

◆   ◆   ◆

Apparently our Brother Wilson was having raucous sex with young interns. All were over the legal age so there wasn't any possibility of criminal statutory rape charges. All of them were males. So, how did the case break? One of his conquests, Lee (not his real name) had gone from being an intern to being a criminal investigator and by all standards was a good one. He was the one who let the cat out of the bag.

Lee had gotten into an accident in his assigned government vehicle. When you have an accident, there is an accident review board that convenes to evaluate the facts to see if there was any negligence involved. They determined that Lee was grossly negligent and imposed a stiff 30-day suspension. He appealed the harsh disciplinary action. The ultimate deciding official was his "friend," John P. Wilson.

For whatever reason Brother Wilson upheld the suspension. Perhaps the facts were so blatant that he couldn't reverse it. You would have thought he'd have protected Lee to keep him quiet. You'd also have thought Lee would have kept his mouth shut to spare himself embarrassment, but he didn't. He was hot that Wilson didn't take care of him and reverse the suspension. So, in a huff he went to internal affairs and ratted out Wilson.

The interviewing IA agent was flabbergasted when Lee spilled out his graphic tale of intern sex on the road. At one point the IA agent said to Lee, "He did what to you? You let him do that to you?!?"

Apparently Brother Wilson would take interns on the road with him to conferences or when he made official visits to the various field offices. He claimed it was a good for their internship to be exposed to how Customs is managed. He never flew and always drove. He never booked hotel rooms in advance but picked one out at random when they reached their destination. The funny thing was that the hotel always seemed to have only a single room left for the night. So, conveniently he and the intern would just have to *bunk* together.

He'd tell the unsuspecting kid something like this, "You don't mind being in the same room, do you? It's just like being in college, being in a dorm room for the night."

None of them apparently minded. Since they were still in college and doing an internship, they didn't think it strange. The next thing he'd do after dinner, when they were back in the room, was to take out a bottle of Jameson's Irish whiskey. Wilson always traveled with a bottle of Ireland's best. He'd pour two health shots.

Wilson would hand one to the intern and say, "Let's have a short one before we go to bed. It will help you sleep better."

What was the kid to do? Nothing, but sip the whiskey unless he wanted Wilson to think he was a wimp. The problem was that one led to another and another. Meanwhile, Brother Wilson would spew out old war stories about drug raids as they downed shot after shot until the kid was near the inebriation stage. Once the effects of the whiskey took over, Wilson would apparently make his move on the intern.

In the morning he would say something like this to the kid, "Boy, I don't know about you, but I drank more than I thought last night. I don't remember a thing. My mind is blank."

Those words coming from a guy who had the authority to give you a full-time law enforcement job after your internship were a powerful form of suggestion. Apparently, the interns began to think perhaps what had happened didn't actually happen, if they could remember anything it at all. That is the power of a powerful suggestion from a powerful person. Apparently, he did this for years and nobody ever raised a complaint until Lee spoke up.

◆　　　◆　　　◆

Nobody ever suspected him; nobody saw any sign that he was a sexual predator using his official position to seduce impressionable interns. He was an extremely adept predator, carefully choosing his prey. Apparently after each successful seduction he became more brazen and took more chances. He pushed the envelope. He began to think he was invulnerable and would never be found out. How wrong he was.

Once more of the story leaked out within Customs, someone then apparently leaked it to the media, and there was a feeding frenzy to get at the facts and to get Wilson. One NBC investigative reporter was relentless in his pursuit of Wilson. All the notoriety and the ensuing reports substantially embarrassed Wilson and Customs across the country.

Various other federal agents called up their Customs counterparts and laughingly asked, "So, tell me, how did you get your job? Just what did you have to do or have done to you to qualify to be an investigator in Customs?"

◆　　　◆　　　◆

What happened to Brother Wilson? After his heart attack he never returned to the job and quietly retired. Apparently the two IG headhunters royally screwed up the case and he wasn't prosecuted or disciplined. Many people thought that they did this on purpose to protect him. To this day he has stated numerous times that he was set up by people who didn't like him because he was a tough boss and that they planted the false stories in the press about him.

Self denial? Perhaps, I don't know. What I do know is that Wilson shot himself in the foot with his own shameful actions that he apparently couldn't control, in situations with interns that mandated he control those actions. It was only a matter of time until he self-immolated. In the end Wilson had nobody to blame but himself. His career ended in a fireball of infamy.

◆   ◆   ◆

Hoteko's Law: *If you have sex on the brain and on the job, you're going to slide down a slippery slope and slam into the wall of self-destruction.*

27

When Nobody Likes You

In the government as in private industry, people who are personable and well liked seem to get away with things that people who are mean-spirited and disliked cannot get away with doing. Whether that's fair or not doesn't matter; that's life. People also have a tendency, when given an opportunity, to rat out those people who have gone out of their way to make their lives difficult. I guess that's only human nature. The government, however, conveniently provides a relatively easy cloak-and-dagger way of doing that—by use of a wire.

This is another one of the differences between government and private industry. In government there are always some who are willing to wear a wire to do someone else in. A wire or recording device has been used for many years to trap and convict criminals. The device can be worn on a person, placed in an office or spliced into your telephone line. A court order is necessary if you want to use the evidence gathered on the wire in a criminal case. Internal affairs investigators have routinely used a wire when conducting non-criminal investigations if they suspect an employee of breaking or bending the rules.

There is no more devastating situation than to be called into the headhunter's office and told you're the subject of an IA investigation, as evidenced in the previous chapter. While you sit there, they smile and then they press the play button on the recorder and you hear your own words incriminating yourself. I've known it to happen to several people. IA holds enormous sway over who they investigate and how they investigate them. They say all investigations are conducted impartially. That's, however, is a bucket of hogwash.

If IA is predisposed to like you, the job you've done and the assistance you've given to them in the past, they'll conduct a superficial investigation into any allegations against you. If the facts uncovered show that you are guilty, you pay the price; there's no getting out of that. What they will not do, however, is dig so deep into the earth to find the buried facts that would really do you in. They will only look on the surface and if the facts aren't readily visible, you walk home free. I've seen that happen.

On the other hand, if there is an allegation against you and you've always been a horse's ass with IA, well, they're going to get you. They do take those things personally even when they should keep it on a professional level. They have all the investigative tools at their disposal to do you in if they so choose. Whether this is right, wrong or indifferent, it's life. When IA strikes, they always strike back with a vengeance.

◆   ◆   ◆

Take the case of Morgan (not his real name). Morgan was a chief inspector who was universally disliked by most people. As an inspector he compiled an excellent enforcement record but had a temperament problem when dealing with sensitive situations. He should have never been promoted into management due to his failings. His temperament was such that at times he couldn't speak when confronted by others and would either yell at people or abruptly turn and walk away.

That's a big no-no as a supervisor and especially as a chief inspector. In those management positions you have to have the ability to mediate situations between two opposing factions in a rational manner. Morgan couldn't do this, which was a problem. It got to the point where nobody wanted to deal with him, not the employees, his fellow managers or any of the top brass. Everyone avoided him if at all possible. It was akin to walking on eggshells when he was around.

Morgan was also opinionated to the point of being abrasive. It was his way or no way but life's not like that. You have to be able to compromise at times to get the job done, but not Morgan. He also had an inferiority complex that he wore on his sleeve. If there was anybody who contradicted him or had a different opinion, Morgan would immediately shoot him down. Apparently, he felt threatened by anyone who seemed to have more knowledge than he did on any given subject.

Morgan didn't like IA and would publicly ridicule the headhunters whenever he could. Well, there is a saying that your chickens always come home to roost. They did so with Morgan, except when they came home to roost they weren't chickens. They were predatory internal affairs chicken hawks and they were looking for his blood!

Morgan committed the same sin that many people do in both government and industry; they do personal work on the firm's time. Usually nobody really cares unless it excessively affects your job or you're using a disproportionate amount of the company's assets or your utilizing company employees to get your personal project completed. That's what Morgan was doing. He was using an inspector to type the equivalent of a 300-hundred page personal research paper on government time.

The first person to notice something askew was an eccentric employee who was a self-taught computer guru. He had also assisted IA on a number of sensitive cases. By doing so he had incurred the wrath of Morgan, who belittled this poor soul for being a so-called IA snitch. Well, Cyril (not his real name) was not only eccentric but was also quite paranoid and extremely sensitive to any and all criticism. He didn't take kindly to Morgan's harsh and very public comments.

Cyril was also the LAN (local area network) administrator for the Customs computer system at Morgan's worksite. It was his job to see that the system was up and running and all necessary upgrades were installed. He also had oversight to insure that people weren't abusing the system by accessing outside data sources such as pornographic websites and chat rooms or doing some day trading on company time.

He tried to put aside his negative feelings for Morgan and do the right thing. He told him, "Morgan, I see that you're doing quite a bit of personal non-government related work on the computer system. I'm the LAN administrator and I need to tell you not to do that. It's a violation."

Now a normal rational person, when confronted with that information would say something like, "Wow, I didn't realize I was doing that much. I guess it just slipped my mind. What do I need to do now? I surely don't want to violate the rules. Can you help me?"

If that was said, the situation would have been resolved. It would have been over. But Morgan viciously snapped back, "Cyril, I'm a chief inspector and I can do whatever I like. It's none of your business. You stay out of my business or you're headed for trouble! Do you understand?"

You bet Cyril understood. He went right to IA and told them what Morgan was doing. The headhunters licked their chops, for this was just what they needed as an excuse to get back at Morgan who had been badmouthing them for years. They not only wanted to get back at Morgan, they wanted to nail him to the cross. What they needed was someone to cooperate with them so they could officially crucify Morgan.

They found that someone in a hapless soul named Mel (not his real name). Mel was a nice guy and good inspector but had the indelible imprint of a *90 percenter* stamped over his wide forehead. As much as he would try and as much as he coveted it, Mel would never become a manager in his own right. Mel would do whatever it was that you asked of him in hopes of ingratiating himself to you in hopes of being promoted. To say that he was vulnerable to suggestion was an understatement.

Morgan had also witnessed this ambitious trait in Mel and had used him to type the rough draft of whatever it was he had been writing into the computer. Mel eagerly complied and spent numerous hours tediously transcribing the hand-written manuscript into Word Perfect. Cyril told IA what Mel was doing. They found their undercover guy they would use to get Morgan.

Late one evening as Mel was laboring away on the research paper project, IA closed in on him. To use a movie cliché from the *Godfather*, they offered him a deal he couldn't turn down. They used the time-tested tactic of not too subtly informing him that he would be fired if he didn't agree to help them out.

They told him, "Mel, you've been doing non-government work for Morgan using the Customs computer system for weeks now. You've also been collecting hundreds of dollars in overtime pay for doing it. You know that's against the code of conduct and the first offense is a suspension of 30 days to removal and the second offense is removal. We have you under surveillance committing two offenses."

Mel pleaded, "I was only following orders of the chief inspector. I didn't think I was doing anything wrong."

He used the same argument the Field Marshal Wilhelm Keitel used during the Nuremburg war crimes trials. It didn't work for Keitel, for he was hanged, and it didn't work for poor Mel. IA answered back, "Mel, you're toast."

Well, Mel was like a fish out of water. His mouth gasped up and down as he saw his career going down the drain. What else could he do? There was nothing to do except cooperate with these devious headhunters. He agreed to wear a wire and entrap Morgan. They coached this simple country boy from central Illinois on what to say to Morgan regarding the writing project.

It worked; they not only got an earful on the wire, but were able to get evidence of an attempted bribe. Morgan had become somewhat suspicious after Cyril confronted him about the illegal use of the computer system. He was cagey and he tried to cover his tracks. Late one evening as Mel was pounding out more pages he approached him and engaged in some small talk.

Morgan then said, "Mel, I know that I can trust you and I want you to know that I appreciate what you're doing for me. I want you to have dinner on me tonight."

With that having been said he apparently put a 50-dollar bill in Mel's front pocket. That act sealed Morgan's fate. Any hope he had of escaping disciplinary action was gone when he inserted that greenback into Mel's pocket. An argument could be that Morgan was only giving Mel a gift, which is allowed under the code of conduct. When taken in the totality of circumstances, however, a reasonable and prudent person would come to the conclusion it was a bribe.

About a month or so later Morgan wrote an email and sent it off to the district director at 4:59 p.m. on a Friday. It wasn't viewed until the following Monday morning. The message contained what can only be described as a final *swan song*. Morgan had suddenly decided to take advantage of an early retirement option and leave the government.

The message was weird to say the least. It directed Customs to move rapidly on his retirement request, and any and all questions regarding the request should be made in writing and sent to his home. It was obvious that he didn't want any personal contact with anyone. He had turned in his ID, gun, keys and other items to a lone trusted employee on Friday. Usually, these items are turned over to your supervisor on your final day. Normally, they have a cake and coffee session to be followed by a small party. Morgan had neither.

When word of Morgan's sudden *retirement* rippled through the Customs' office people were happy. In fact, one inspector played a CD recording of *Ding Dong the Witch is Dead!* There was no love lost. People were glad he was gone. No tears were shed. It was a sad way to end a career.

Morgan had done it to himself. Had he been open, friendly and honest with people, nobody would have worked with IA to do him in. He was just the opposite; he was arrogant and mean-spirited. Morgan had often gone out of his way to reprimand and belittle employees. He had no friends. Nobody liked him.

There wasn't any attempt by the top brass to intercede with IA to plead that Morgan had committed a minor mistake but should be given a second chance. IA also could have easily concluded that the investigation was solely an administrative matter. That would have allowed management the option of a giving Morgan a minor slap on the wrist. They didn't do that. Morgan had fostered an oppressive atmosphere of ill will. That fierce wind created the gush of oxygen that fed the fire that consumed him.

◆   ◆   ◆

Hoteko's Law: *If you reach out to people, people will reach out to you. If you meet people half way, they will help you. If you go out of your way to scorn people, they will eventually walk that long mile to do you in.*

PART X
Things I've Learned Along the Way

Everyone in their career has picked up bits and pieces of knowledge that have helped or hurt them along the way. For each of these laws I've learned, please understand that I came by them because at one point or another I violated them and suffered the consequences. I learned from those mistakes as I learned from observing the success of *ten percenters*. I took what I learned, adapted it, constantly evaluated it, updated it and made every attempt to have these laws govern my actions as a manager.

I also learned something about lunch from President Richard M. Nixon. What I learned from this *ten percenter* formulated a philosophy about personal management rather than a basis of where to go at noon. This created a mindset that instilled the importance of time management and that helped me to keep the ship on course.

I've also learned the differences between government and private industry. Some are drastic, some are humorous and some are downright idiotic. I learned that the difficulties the *ten percenters* overcome while managing government positions make them stand out head and shoulders above their private industry counterparts.

28

Laws That Can Help You

Here are some miscellaneous Hoteko's Laws that can help keep you out of harm's way whether on the job, on the road or at home. They have helped me to survive some dangerous overseas situations, avoid complicated union grievances and nasty EEO lawsuits, and they have assisted in advancing my career. Again, they are nothing more than common sense infused with my actual experiences and those of the *ten percenters* I've been fortunate enough to have worked with over the years.

- The tragic events of 9/11 have changed the world forever. We will never feel as safe as we did before that day. As a government manager, however, you maybe required to travel overseas. Beware of the food as much as you fear the terrorist. Both can do you in. One can kill you and the other can make you wish that you were dead.

- When traveling overseas never eat anything when you don't know what it is, where it came from or how it was cooked. If your host seems offended by your refusal to partake of a local delicacy, tell him that it's against your religion. When asked what religion, I always responded that it violates a major dietary law of Hoteko's religion. That answer usually confounded them and it was case closed.

- Overseas learn to drink your scotch neat without ice to avoid ingesting the dastardly microscopic ameba that will repeatedly cause your small and large intestines to evacuate their entire contents immediately, regardless of where you are at the time.

- When traveling on an overseas flight have a mental personal emergency contingency plan in the event of a hijacking. If traveling on government business, always carry your *blue cover tourist* passport. Never surrender your *burgundy cover official* passport to a hijacker. It's bad enough being an American in that situation, but being a government representative means a sure death sentence.

- Book a window seat. If you're hijacked that seat will keep you further away from the bad guys. They tend to pull someone out of the aisle seat first, if they are going to shoot somebody to gain media attention.

- Never make eye contact with them and or bring attention to yourself. Carry pictures of family members even if you don't have a family, get some pictures, if necessary, from other people before you leave. If push comes to shove and they pull you out of your seat, show them the pictures as you plead for mercy, it just might work.

- When overseas always be aware of your surroundings. Know where the nearest U.S. embassy or consulate is located. If walking down a street, always look for an escape route in the event you may be followed. Be aware of and avoid-dead end streets or streets that seem deserted. Trust nobody but yourself and your instincts.

- At your hotel overseas, never tell anyone you work for the government. Have a cover story, practice it and know it by heart. Be wary of strangers, even those who may seem to be American. Keep to your cover story regardless of how friendly other people may seem. They may not be who you think they are.

- The worst case scenario is if your aircraft is hijacked by elements of al-Qaida. If that occurs, you mentally need to prepare for your fate. Nobody who is sane wants to die for their country. Todd Beamer did not want to die on 9/11 and neither did anyone else on United Airlines flight 93. They evaluated their situation, however, and they did what Americans have done throughout history. These heroes gave the ultimate sacrifice and died so others could live. His last recorded words were, "Let's roll!"

- Don't be afraid to make decisions. To try and succeed is good, to try and fail is OK, as long as you give it your best; but not to try at all is totally unacceptable.

- You can never control what other people are going to do or say about you, but you can control your action and reaction to any given situation.

- Surround yourself with good, competent people whether they are your friends or not. Ascertain their individual talents and place them where they will do the most good for not only you, but for the agency and them-selves.

- Don't be afraid to reach out to those who have not yet proven themselves. Give them an opportunity to excel. Give them all the support they need to succeed. Realize, however, that although many will make the grade, some will also fail and don't let that discourage you. Keep up the effort.

- Don't micromanage the organization. Give those around you the latitude they need to do their jobs. You're captain of the ship but that doesn't mean you have to be physically at the helm all the time or in the bowels of the engine room shoveling coal into the boilers. Your job is to see that others keep the ship running and on course.

- Trust the people around you until they give you a reason to break the trust. Don't second guess decisions that have been made if the ship is still on course. Remember it's a learning experience for your crew; they have to make mistakes in order to learn how to captain the ship.

- Remember anybody can do a job in 80 hours a week; it takes a real manager to do it in 40 hours a week. Prioritize, task, oversee and go home at 5 p.m. and trust those at the helm.

- When valued members of your team are ready for the next step, as difficult as it may be, don't hold them back for your own sake. You owe it to them, yourself and the agency to let them move up. That's the only way an organization can grow.

- When they leave for that step up, challenge them to seek out good people and give them a chance to excel. Challenge them to nurture those people with their support, their knowledge and their trust so that one day they may move on and make the organization even better. Encourage them to pass it on.

- Understand that not everyone loves you. Know that there are those who actively, either by jealousy or by reason of some insanity, will try to do you in. This is just part of human nature in the imperfect world in which we live.

- Park your ego at the door. Know the meaning and symptoms of that blinding malady called *delusions of grandeur.*

- Keep notes on anything that the *little guy inside* you warns you to write down. It's better to have a contemporaneous written account of a minor incident or a meeting in order to be able to answer a lawsuit, EEO complaint or union grievance years down the road. Your notes will give you a tremendous creditability in any potential litigation.

- Be wary of one-on-one meetings behind closed doors and avoid them if you can. It's not being paranoid; it's being prudent. A *wacko* can later accuse you of misrepresentation or misconduct. That's why it's wise to keep notes including the time the meeting started, when it ended and what was discussed. It gives you enormous credibility if an issue arises at a later date.

- It is almost inevitable that in being a government manager you will be sued by an employee or an outside interest. Don't take it personally; it comes with the territory. It's business and if you treat it that way everything will come out OK in the end run. If you take it personally, you will lose.

- Most importantly, do not be paranoid, but be cautious of those around you. Many a *ten percenter* has been done in by their friends or those close around them. If you look back in history; Judas committed the ultimate betrayal, Brutus killed Julius Caesar and Deep Throat did in Richard Nixon. The old adage of *keeping your friends close, but keeping your enemies closer* is not only sound judgment; it's a prudent survival tactic.

- Have a good, healthy sense of humor. The proper use of humor can alleviate stress and can actually create a good work environment. An off-color or one-sided sense of humor can cause irreparable damage and subject you to a lawsuit.

- Remember that like beauty, humor is in the eye of the beholder. Tread softly when using humor because not everyone will find what you do or say to be funny. The best gauge of what is humorous is role reversal, i.e., make yourself the butt of the joke and if you still think it's funny, it probably passes the test of being good humor and not of being obnoxious or offensive to others.

- If you work in a law enforcement agency such as Customs, never laugh or belittle someone whom you've just arrested. When a bust goes down, there's a natural urge to let off steam through some whopping and laughing. Resist the urge. Remember that the person arrested is someone's son, daughter, brother, sister, aunt, uncle, father or mother. They're someone who made a mistake, and if convicted in court, will pay the price. Treat them with dignity.

- Remember, any day is a good day to arrest a drug smuggler. I would tell this to the Customs inspectors each day. What I was saying is that you can't wait for opportunity, it may never approach you. You have to go out and do your job, and if you do, you'll be successful.

- Know your employees. Know as much as you can about them, their career goals, their education, their interests and their families.

- Don't be aloof or unapproachable, but don't be one of the boys either. To be successful you have to walk a fine line. They need to know that you care about them, but they also need to know that you have the responsibility to run the show.

- Be fair across the board. Although many may not like your decisions, they will accept the decisions if they know that they apply to one and all. People respect consistency.

- Stand by your employees. If there's a trouble situation, give them the benefit of the doubt until the situation is proven otherwise. Don't give them up at the first sign of trouble.

- Don't be afraid to discipline the troops when it's necessary. Too many managers don't do this because they fear union or other grievance procedures. Many managers look the other way because they want to curry the troops' favor by being a nice guy. If someone is proven to have violated the code of conduct, administer the justice in a fair and consistent way. People respect a captain that runs a tight ship.

- Don't be a perk hog. Pass the perks along. Too many managers take the good temporary duty assignments and conferences and leave the bottom of the barrel for the troops. When you pass out the good with the bad, people will respect you for being fair.

- Above all acknowledge good work. Give credit where credit is due. Let the team know when they've done a good job. Let everyone know when one of the crew has done a job above the call of duty.

- Don't let anybody trash your agency. Avoid the negative when dealing with outside interests. You can always find a positive thing to say about your agency, so say it.

- Don't you yourself trash your agency. Although at times you will be expected to carryout idiotic programs promulgated by a HQ *stargazer*, remember it's your job to do so. Do so with conviction and never ridicule the agency in front of the troops. It's bad for their morale and your morale.

- Always be proud to be in public service, it's a noble career.

- Do your homework before briefing the brass. Know your subject backward and forward. Be assertive, be positive, but be humble too. Maintain eye contact, use some self depreciating humor. This means don't make the boss the butt of your opening joke!

- Don't be intimidated by the brass, but know when it's appropriate to use first names, when to address them by title, such as Mr. Commissioner and when to respectfully call them Mr. Smith.

- Never try bullshitting a bullshitter. If the boss is full of it, let him be full of it. You aren't going to change him, so let him prattle on!

- Don't make a public fool out of yourself when confronted with subject matter you don't know. Keep your mouth shut and let people guess how stupid you are; don't pipe up and publicly prove it.

- Get involved in your work community. Take a leadership role in organizing your agency into giving something back to society. Try and make your work community a better place.

- Above all else, always do the right thing. Many times it's easier to do nothing, to do something halfway or to run and hide. Have the courage to stand up and be counted on to do the right thing.

29

Lunch and Richard Nixon

We had a second-line supervisor named Eddie Roberts (not his real name) who had been in Customs quite a number of years. Eddie was a funny person in many respects, first of all, in looks and in mannerisms. He was a typical Chicago born-and-bred guy who spoke using the unique city vernacular of "dem" guys and "dose" gals. You can take the boy out of Chicago, but you can't take Chicago out of the boy, so to speak.

At the time Eddie was first promoted, there was a so-called Polish Mafia in charge of Customs in Chicago. It seemed that you had to be Polish to gain a promotion, and being from Chicago, I fully understood those politics. In 1967, Customs was freed from the federal political patronage system. Prior to that date the Collector of Customs in each city was appointed by the president and confirmed by the senate. The appointee had to be recommended by the ranking senator of the president's party in that state. This patronage system flowed down the ladder even to the supervisor level. Since, you had to have clout to get ahead then, ability rarely counted.

In today's world Eddie would never have made it past inspector, but he lived in yesterday's world and was promoted twice under the old patronage system. Eddie had limited ability but was an affable person who tried his best. He was a *90 percenter* who was buried in an unimportant job. He had a simple task to do that should have been only an ancillary duty and not a 40-hour-a-week job. Yet, he really thought he was doing a bang-up job and earning his keep. He never comprehended that all he was doing was treading water in a pool and not swimming laps. Eddie Roberts was a true Chicago Customs classic.

◆   ◆   ◆

I once overheard Eddie talking to someone about how long he had known a mutual acquaintance. He said, "Norm, I tink dat da last time I saw Majewski was about a year-and-a-half ago. No, I take dat back; it was 18 months ago."

That was Eddie in a nutshell. He could drive you batty not only with his Chicago-speak, but with his Chicago logic! Eddie wasn't the brightest guy on the block, but as I've stated he was affable and meant no harm. I recall another situation when I had been on the job only a few months.

We had some down-time while we waited for the next international flight to arrive for processing from Europe. I was sitting in the back of the Customs Hall with a fellow inspector named Val Derer. We were the only two there; the rest of the staff was in the break room. I can't recall what we were talking about, but it was late in the evening, about 9 P.M. Roberts had entered the hall and walked toward us.

Eddie lit a cigarette—these were the days when you could smoke a cigar in the airport if you wanted to—and sat down. He took a couple of heavy puffs on his smoke and he said, "Sarge, how are ya liken Customs?"

I told him I was enjoying the job and I was eager to learn more. He spoke a few words to Val. He then looked at us with this wizened look on his face, his keen blue eyes glistening and stated, "I like boat of use guys, so I'm gunna give use some advice about your careers."

Well, we both perked up. Here was a second-level supervisor, albeit somewhat of a character, but none the less here was a guy who was going to tell us the secret of getting ahead. We were all eyes and ears, eager with anticipation not unlike those who are on the verge of discovering the Holy Grail. A heavy silence filled the vast Customs Hall as we waited for his sage advice.

It was then Eddie said, "Always remember to grab a hot lunch. With da hours we work, ya don't know when your gunna get home and be able to eat. So, grab a hot lunch. Dats better dan eaten a cold cheese samitch."

Our bubble was burst. Apparently Eddie thought more about satiating his hunger pains than about the job. This is very typical of the *90 percenters* across the board. They rarely miss a meal. Unfortunately, they rarely make a deadline or a timely decision too. They reduce management down to simple basics, like insuring they eat lunch each day.

◆   ◆   ◆

On the other hand, I remember what Richard Nixon had once said about lunch. He told Bob Haldeman, his iron-fisted chief of staff, that he never spent more than five minutes eating lunch and did so at his desk. He had followed this routine whether in public or private life. He wanted Haldeman to get the word out that the president didn't fool around with a two-martini lunch. Nixon was proud of the job he was doing and thought that the public should know he was giving it a 100 percent effort.

I was intrigued by Nixon's revelation. So, I have created a hypothetical scenario between Nixon and a corporate CEO discussing the merits of his five-minute working lunch. I can imagine the CEO asking him, "Mr. President, why do you do that and what do you get out of it?"

I think Nixon would reply something like this, "Well, I find that I can use my lunch hour for better things. I've found out that when I used to stop for lunch it broke my train of concentration. I would lose an entire hour or hour-and-a-half from my workday. These were some of my most productive hours.

"Many of the lunches would include a drink or glass of wine. When I was lawyer in private practice and out with clients, I had to have a drink. If I didn't, they would feel intimidated, not have their cocktail and feel ill at ease discussing business. When I got back to the office, however, I had lost good time and felt a loss of drive. It would take me an hour or more to get back into gear. By skipping those lunches I accomplished some of my most productive work. I brought that philosophy into the White House with me and it's worked very well."

The Fortune 500 executive took Nixon's advice to heart and at another meeting with the president said something like this, "Mr. President, I took your advice and started having a short lunch at my desk. It was unbelievable what I could get accomplished in my workday! Before my lunches were more lavish than most and we always had a martini or two. When I got back to the office, I had lost two hours.

"I was really unfocused for the rest of the day and usually had my secretary book only meetings rather than serious work in the afternoon. When I got home, which was usually late in the evening, my wife always waited to have dinner with me. We'd sit down and have a drink, but I never enjoyed it because of the two-martini lunch.

"It got to the point I didn't enjoy lunch, a cocktail with my wife or dinner either. When you told me about your point of view, it really changed things for me. Now when I get home I am looking forward to that martini, talking the day over with my wife and having a good glass of wine with dinner too.

"One last thing Mr. President now when I do have a business lunch, which is only once or so a month, I really enjoy the experience and look forward to it. But the five minutes eating at the desk is the best advice I've ever received."

This hypothetical situation was based on Nixon's comments to Haldeman during a TV documentary filmed during his White House years. What Nixon hit upon was time management. He took the full opportunity to control his time and knew when his creative juices where at their peak. He didn't want to lose that competitive edge that would have weakened his ability to challenge the problems at hand. Love him or hate him, Richard Nixon by his steely determination did, in fact, leave a legacy of great accomplishment in the White House. This is reflective of his being one of the best *ten percenter* presidents in modern history.

◆   ◆   ◆

Hoteko's Law: *Decide early on in your career whether you're a hot-lunch guy or a five-minute Nixon time management person. This could be the difference between being a ten percenter or an Eddie Robert's 90 percenter manager.*

30

The Differences

Simply put, there are differences between government and private industry. Some are major, some are minor, some are negligible, some are just a pain and some are very humorous. Many of these differences are not only a burden, but can be a barrier to success. The government manager, the true *ten percenter,* has to overcome obstacles and make sacrifices that a manager in private industry cannot imagine or fathom nor is willing to do.

There are an entire slew of financial differences between the two groups in terms of salary, perks and benefits. The private sector is most generous when rewarding the fruits of labor to their managers. The government, on the other hand, is frugal to say the least and that's the way it should be. When you are using the appropriated tax dollars of hard-working Americans, you have to be prudent because there is only so much money in the till.

The question then arises as to why good people stay in government when they could easily double their salary on the outside. The *ten percenters* who stay do so to serve the American people. The *90 percenters* stay to survive because they can't make it on the outside. A public service career does entail sacrifice in terms of dollars, bonuses and benefits, as well as the absence of that glorious golden parachute severance pay package that lets you gently float into a comfortable retirement. In the end run, however, those of us who serve receive our reward in knowing that we left the government and this country a better place than we found it.

◆   ◆   ◆

Government managers are more readily able to transfer their talents to the private industry than vice-versa. This is one of the big differences between government and private industry managers. A case in point is Brigadier General Robert Wood. In 1925, Sears chairman Julius Rosenwald hired him to help Sears out of their slumping sales. Wood was a West Point graduate, had spent ten years in charge of logistics and supplies while building the Panama Canal and was the Quartermaster General of the army during World War I.

Wood, using his government experience of moving people and supplies through uncharted jungles and over battlefields, could see what the private industry managers couldn't see. The private industry types in Sears were blinded by their own success of selling to rural America and only looked to expand that market. General Wood looked beyond that initial limited horizon, saw an untapped market and readily planned for the future.

Rosenwald, a true *ten percenter* himself, recognized Wood's abilities in moving items to support the troops in France and the workers in Panama. Rosenwald envisioned that Wood would concentrate his efforts on more efficient support of Sears' then core business, supplying rural America. Recognizing Wood's talents, he gave him a free hand. Hence, the general also expanded Sears' base into urban cities. This strategic move, by a government *ten percenter,* opened that untapped market, which ultimately saved the merchandising giant from financial collapse.

◆   ◆   ◆

Many in private industry think that their government counterparts have the same types of benefits as they do and would scoff at the fact that government is so restrictive. Gene Mach was one of the best *ten percenters* in Customs. Gene surrounded himself with good capable people who made any operation he ran successful. Does that sound like the CEO of the Ford Motor Company, Xerox, IBM and other Fortune 500 enterprises? Sure, except that in private industry that's the norm. A CEO gets to handpick his team. The same is true of a newly inaugurated president; he handpicks his cabinet.

Both the CEO and the president either sink or swim by their selection of key personnel. The challenge of recognizing talent and ability is pretty much left up to the TOP DOG in private industry. If he chooses to put his friends on board or in key positions merely for the fact they are his cronies and they fail him, he falls with them. And that's the norm, because in private industry the CEO has to have a free hand in running the company.

Very few people at the CEO level will choose country bumpkins to run key parts of the company. They hire the very best because they want to succeed, for success translates out to seven-figure-salaries and generous stock options. The president does the same thing in choosing his cabinet. He doesn't look for his Treasury Secretary from the ranks of a defensive lineman in the NFL because he went to college with him. He generally looks to Wall Street and a proven track record of fiscal responsibility. He doesn't look to the NFL to the guy who weighs 320 pounds who only knows how to block the player in front of him. That's an economic recipe for disaster.

Yet, in government people like Gene Mach rarely get to pick their entire team. They can select a few good people, but by and large they have to take what's already in place. Why? Well, things like unions, lawsuits, civil service (now OPM) regulations and a myriad of other inane laws that bar you from handpicking your team from among the very best are also in place.

Hence, people like Gene Mach had their hands tied unlike any CEO or president ever has had. Yet, what's more amazing is that Mach was very successful in any area or program that he was responsible for. Yes, he did have his friends working for him, good capable people he trusted and relied upon. They were often referred to as a FOG or Friend of Gene.

Not all people that worked with Mach were his friends. He had to work within the constraints of OPM guidelines and that meant having to take the good with the bad when many times the bad outweighed the good. Can you imagine a Fortune 500 CEO being saddled with a chief financial officer that thought fiduciary responsibility was a rock group from Russia? Or that the president would be stuck with someone at the Pentagon who thought he was named the secretary of D-FENCE as in a defensive line coach in the NFL? Or a person who thought his job was stopping the offense on the one-yard line when it was fourth and goal? I think not.

Yet, despite the handicap of not being able to handpick his team, Gene Mach always came out on top and so did Customs. Why? Because Mach recognized and worked around the *90 percenters,* placing them where they would do the least harm. He then motivated those few *ten percenters* to accomplish the mission in spite of the obstacles in their way. That's a salute to Gene Mach, his *ten percenters* and their commitment to God and country.

◆　　　◆　　　◆

Another difference is in travel. In private industry your company buys your airline ticket, reimburses you for your cab or limo fares, hotel room, meals and other incidental costs associated with a business trip. Most companies only ask that if an expense is over $25 that you submit a receipt to verify and document that fact. In government it's very different.

I was part of a training mission to Barbados in 1988. U.S. Customs conducts antiterrorism and narcotic interdiction training programs for many nations throughout the world. These programs are sponsored and paid for by the State Department. The objective is to train the police, Customs, intelligence agents and others in these countries on how best to combat terrorism and drug smuggling in their nations. The goal is to prevent the export of those criminal activities to the United States.

At the time of this program we were under a per diem system of compensation that allowed for a fixed amount of money for room, board and expenses. The amount was calculated by the State Department for each foreign country and city a government employee would visit on official business. That was the amount you were allowed in excess of your airfare and taxi/limo costs associate with your travel. The amount for Barbados at that time was $118 a day.

This amount had to cover your daily hotel room, all your meals and any other costs such as laundry or dry cleaning. Barbados is a Caribbean resort area; however, we were conducting the training seminar in late September which is off season due to hurricanes and heavy tropical storms in that region. Yet, the daily rate for my room was $110 and that left me with $8 for food and expenses.

Well, $8 didn't even buy you breakfast at the hotel. There wasn't any avenue for appeal of the official State Department per diem subsidy. All you could do was dig into your pocket so you could eat two meager meals a day and to clean your shirts unless you wanted to wear them twice. Do you think an IBM or XEROX manager would be forced to do that? I think not. I didn't think it was fair, but I believed in what I was doing, so I used my own money to eat and clean my clothes.

Our IBM or Xerox chap would never believe that the government would be so stingy or so stupid as to have such an idiotic per diem plan. Yet, that's the way it was for a number of years. Probably until some *90 percenter* or *stargazer* at State woke up or they themselves had to travel on official business to a nation covered by this type of idiotic per diem plan. I'm sure that they screamed bloody murder when they had to fork over $40 a day out of their own pocket to survive.

They did change the per diem plan, making it more equitable, but it still didn't compare with private industry. I remember talking with the then Customs Commissioner Carol Hallett about per diem rates. She related a conversation she had had with a Hewlett Packer executive on a flight to San Francisco. It was eye opening for the private industry computer manager.

As best as I can recall Hallett told me, "Sarge, I was sitting next to this executive from HP. We were talking about business trips, the weariness of travel, hotels and meals. She asked me what type of compensation I received from the government when I traveled to San Francisco. I told her I received $75 a day. She thought that was adequate until I told her that I had to pay for my hotel room and all my meals with that stipend. She was astounded. She thought I received $75 for incidentals, which she was allowed above her hotel room and meals. She then asked me where in heaven's name I could get a hotel room in San Francisco under $75 and how was I supposed to eat?"

◆　　◆　　◆

Another difference was frequent flyer miles. Just before I retired the Controller General issued an opinion that finally allowed government employees to keep and utilize any and all frequent flyer miles they accrued when traveling on official business. Up until 2002, you had to give your miles back to the government or let them lapse. At that time the airline industry standard was any unused miles that were three years old were automatically forfeited.

Now there were some government employees who thumbed their noses at this rule and used the miles for free personal travel. If you did that and were caught, you could be fired. So, I never did that. During my career I lost 100,000 miles with United, over 75,000 with Northwest and over 60,000 miles with American Airlines. I ask you do you think that our IBM or Xerox manager lost any miles? I think not.

The Controller General's opinion was a long time in coming. It recognized that to have parity with private industry and to stop the flow of seasoned managers leaving government due to inane rules, they had to allow us to keep the frequent flyer miles for our own use. They further stated that this benefit was earned since the government employee was often at times under stressful conditions when traveling on official business with weather delays, long time periods away from home and terrorists threats.

◆　　◆　　◆

Nobody goes into government to get rich, but nobody should have to go hungry or be cold while traveling on official business. When I first started flying around the globe for Customs you were authorized business class if your flight was in excess of eight hours. That was a great perk until some ameba-brained idiot over at the State Department decided one day that was wrong.

Our ameba-brain friend apparently devised a new rule. It was called the 14-hour rule, meaning one had to be in flight status in excess of 14 hours to be authorized a business-class seat. This applied only if you were going to be working when you arrived at your foreign destination, i.e., taking a taxi from the Karachi Airport to the U.S. Consulate for a meeting with the DEA country attaché. If you were going directly to your hotel, you were out of luck; it was coach all the way. It was coach all the way home even if you were in flight status 23 hours which I was on a numerous occasions.

I was sent to Pakistan three times to conduct narcotic interdiction and antiterrorism training seminars. From the time I got on an airplane at the Karachi Airport until I landed at O'Hare Airport, 23 hours or more had elapsed. That's a long and exhausting way to spend an entire day in a cramped coach seat, thanks to our ameba-brained idiot over at State. Our IBM and Xerox executive wouldn't tolerate a coach seat for that length of travel, and neither should a government manager, but life's not fair.

Unfortunately, not all government employees are treated the same. If the State Department has a 14 hour-rule then it should apply to all across the board. What's good for the goose is good for the gander. But this is not so. Consider members of congress. Do you think they take business class? Are you kidding? I was on a flight from Washington Dulles to Charles De Gaulle Airport with a number of members of congress and they took up most of first class.

They were on their way to Egypt on a fact-finding mission. I happened to be with them in an airport lounge while we all waited for our connecting flights, them to Cairo and I to Doha, Qatar to work with DEA on a training program. They were quaffing free well-chilled French champagne and shoveling mounds of Russian caviar into their mouths courtesy of United Airlines. They were enthusiastically chatting about seeing the pyramids, exploring Tut's tomb and leisurely cruising down the placid Nile. There was absolutely no talk or even mention about a fact-finding tour or economic mission or the objective. They sounded like a bunch of giddy tourists ready to see all the sights, enjoy the culture and feast on the local delicacies. There are exceptions to all government rules.

◆   ◆   ◆

Until it was changed in the late 1980's, you were allowed only $1.50 for each six-hour period in actual international travel status, i.e., flying to or from your destination. Therefore, on my sojourns around the globe, I was reimbursed $4.50 for food and incidentals on my 23-hour travel day. The reasoning was that I would be fed on the various airplanes and shouldn't be allowed to voucher any meals in an airport while waiting for a flight.

Airline meals are barely edible at best and are usually a conglomeration of mush by the time it gets to your seat. Not that the airlines plan it that way, but simple logistics, overcooking and slow food service on a jam-packed 747 turn them into an unpleasant mass of mixed unidentifiable flavors, shapes and forms, which is hardly an epicurean delight.

I can recall flying to Karachi on Pakistani International Airlines. PIA is the national airline of an Islamic Republic and observes their dietary code. No pork, no booze, just a horrible meal served with lukewarm tea. When I would board a PIA flight to the Asian subcontinent, I always ate a good, substantial meal washed down by a number of cold beers as a defensive measure of survival. My cost for that fare? About $25 of which I was reimbursed the grand total of $4.50! Do you think our IBM or Xerox executives would have to fork over $25 out of their own pocket to avoid the possibility of being poisoned by a PIA meal or go hungry? I think not.

◆   ◆   ◆

Another big difference between private industry and government is gifts. First of all let me mention that I am all for people in private industry being able to accept gifts as long as they cannot be construed as a bribe, because that would be illegal. The point of my mentioning gifts is the restrictions placed upon federal employees. They run the gamut from the sublime to the ridiculous.

When I first started in Customs in the 1970's, you couldn't accept anything of value from anyone who did business with the agency. An airline could give you a pen or a calendar, but it had to be of nominal value. Anything else was strictly prohibited and could cost you your job. It was that plain and simple, and I accepted the policy.

The reason for these strict regulations were to preclude any suggestion of preferential treatment for an airline, Customs broker, importer or others doing business with us. It was a good rule, but it was taken to the extreme, and any time you take anything to the extreme, it becomes ridiculous.

One such absurd situation involved seminars. If there was a seminar open to the public regarding a U.S. Customs topic, regulation or procedure, such as export control being given by a private enterprise, you could attend. You could attend as a guest of the private enterprise to participate as a subject matter expert, as long as Customs agreed that your attendance was in the best interest of the agency. Let's say that the seminar fee for the public was $50 for the day and that included lunch.

Well, you could attend as an invited guest but you were precluded from the lunch since you are prohibited from accepting a gift of more than nominal value. Our fine chaps from IBM or Xerox wouldn't hesitate to belly up to the table and eat their fill. Therefore, what are your choices that day? You starve or buy your own lunch. Many years later a ruling was made that in these types of situations you could accept the free lunch since it would be surmised that you could answer questions about export control while eating and that was in the best interest of the agency.

◆   ◆   ◆

I used to get bottles of liquor from airline managers and the foreign consul general offices during the holiday season each year. It was customary in the diplomatic corps to give a bottle of their country's best to thank your shop for granting them the required privileges during the year regarding expedited clearances of arriving dignitaries. With airline managers it was just the way they did business.

Each year I would have to return the bottles to the airline managers with polite thanks, but no thanks. With the diplomatic corps it would have been a faux pax to do so. They wouldn't understand why you were rebuffing them. So, I had to transmit their bottles of booze to our Fines, Penalties and Forfeiture (FPF) Officer who would then authorize their destruction as abandoned property. Before he could do that, however, he had to place a notice in a public place and publication, to see if anyone would claim the property. If no one did after 30 days, they were then destroyed by pouring the contents out and smashing the bottles.

I know that this makes 100 percent sense to any private industry executive. Doesn't it? Take the liquor as to not offend the consul general, transmit it to the FPF officer, publish the abandonment notice at tax payers' expense and then dump the booze down the toilet. It sure sounds like a good, sound business practice to me.

Again, just years before I retired they modified the rules again. At that time they stated that you could accept a gift valued up to $10 on a single occasion and from a source, as long as the aggregate value in the course of one year didn't exceed $50. Now I don't know what idiot stayed awake how many hours formulating this one, but some *90 percenter* or really wild-eyed *wacko* or higher-than-a-kite *stargazer* thought this one up.

Just walk down the road with this scenario. "Mr. airline manager, thank you for the bottle of German wine. But I have to ask you a question. Is it valued under $10?"

The airline manager replies, "Well, are you talking wholesale, retail or duty-free value? You can buy this in Germany for $9.75, but we sell it in our duty free shop for $8.00 and you can buy it in the local liquor store in Chicago for $11.50. Does that answer your question?"

You smile at him and said, "Well, no, but let's use the $9.75 value, can you add that to my annual total not to exceed $50.00 aggregate value for gifts this year?"

Enough said, it does go from the sublime to the ridiculous.

◆   ◆   ◆

Another really big difference between the two groups is conferences. Everybody runs these things and they do them all over the country. Beside the fact that private industry has theirs in warm climate places during the dead of winter so as to allow their employees the benefit of playing golf or swimming, they also run them at top notch resorts. There's certainly nothing wrong with that. You have to reward the people who keep your company profitable!

I'll illustrate one example of the difference between the groups. Customs was in the midst of the near disastrous reengineering the corporation during the first Clinton administration. All the *stargazers*, *wackos* and *90 percenters* were on board this run away train being driven by the overeager *yes men* to please the president. All managers were required to take a 40-hour course of indoctrination to this new system that HQ deigned would change government for the better forever.

I attended a session in Dallas, Texas. Our keynote speaker or chief motivator was Chuck Winwood, our assistant commissioner. I've known Chuck for years. He is a very dynamic speaker who has a wide range of knowledge and sports a very persuasive personality. Winwood was capable of holding sway over any audience on any topic. He was just that good.

The first thing that Monday morning we were all herded into the grand ballroom of the Adolphus Hotel in downtown Dallas. Chuck was center stage and ready to rock and roll. He charged up and down the aisles expounding the new dogma of government to be run like a private corporation. It was entertaining to watch what I have always called the Winwood show.

We both walked out together and as I headed to my breakout group session he asked me, "Well Sarge, what do you think about the reengineering thing? It's exciting, isn't it?"

I've never been one to mince words and spoke up, "Chuck, what I find troubling is that each time we get a new administration and some *wacko* working out of the White House comes up with his own theory or has an epiphany, we jump on the bandwagon and change everything we're doing. We never stay the course on the basics, we don't have consistency and we wonder why the public and the importing community look at us like idiots. Chuck, fix what's broke, but if it ain't broke, don't fix it!"

That didn't faze Winwood as he said to me, "So, you don't think we can be like big business?"

We had stopped walking and I turned around to illustrate my answer, "Chuck, look at this conference room. I mean look at the hall outside of it. The private company that's holding a meeting there has a full spread of coffee, tea, milk, juices, donuts, sweet rolls, fresh fruit and cereals for their attendees. Now look back at the ballroom we just left. What's outside of it? Coffee, tea or even water? Nothing. Chuck, if we're going to ask our people to walk that extra mile as private industry does, then let's treat them like that. Let's give them a free cup of coffee before we start the meeting and maybe a donut too."

Chuck walked away without a word. Just for the record in the second Clinton administration there wasn't even a whisper about reengineering the corporation. The *ten percenters* regained control and brought sanity back to the government. All the time and money spent on training and reengineering was lost. We went back to our core business of collecting and protecting the revenue and trying to keep drugs off the street, a business we should have never strayed away from. We are a service and not a for-profit enterprise.

◆   ◆   ◆

If the *stargazers* would have had their way incorporating the reengineering theory in Customs, we would also have had titled changes. A chief inspector would have been called a champion and a supervisor would have been called a coach. I could just see myself going into an airline managers meeting and introducing myself, "Good morning, I'm Champion Hoteko from U.S. Customs."

◆   ◆   ◆

One last thought about conferences and coffee. At most of our conferences we always had coffee for the participants. Anyone who has ever run a conference knows the price of coffee is much greater than the price of gasoline. I was paying $50 a gallon for the brew which was the going rate at any hotel. The only problem was I couldn't voucher it that way and get my money back. What we did in government was to beg the hotel manager to let us have the conference room for free since we were guaranteeing X number of hotel rooms for so many nights. We then asked him to have coffee service, but bill it under the guise of the conference room so we could get our money back. Do you think IBM and Xerox have to do this? I think not.

◆   ◆   ◆

These are just some of the idiotic differences between government and private industry. Many are comedic and I've intended it that way to illustrate just what obstacles a good *ten percenter* has to overcome to be successful. Many managers in government just shrug their shoulders and use these obstacles as an excuse as to why they can't do their jobs. These are the *90 percenters* who look for anything or any reason to explain why they can't get the job done. In spite of these situations, the *ten percenters* plow ahead, either around or right through these obstacles to accomplish the mission.

The *ten percenters* never cried over the fact their private industry counterparts were paid more or had better benefits. They just kept doing the job because they chose public service and knew they weren't going to get rich. They didn't focus their energies on things they couldn't change, but instead they focused on getting the job done. To a *ten percenter*, the personal satisfaction is in the challenge of coming in under budget and ahead of schedule on the task they've been assigned.

I believe the government *ten percenters* make better managers than their private industry counterparts. Look back at General Wood at Sears. If he was able to supply the army in the Great War and build the Panama Canal, supplying and expanding Sears' consumer base was a piece of cake. He was used to working around obstacles, both material and human. He knew to succeed you had to adapt, adapt and adapt. Thankfully there are thousands of General Woods in public service, because without them government would come to a screeching halt.

◆   ◆   ◆

Hoteko's Law: *Know the idiosyncrasies of government and don't try to rational-ize that which cannot be rationalized. Know and accept that government is different from private industry. Remember what the Soviet apartment block chairman in Boris Pasternak's famous novel stated to Dr. Zhivago when he returned to Moscow after serving on the front lines during World War I, he said, "I have some advice for you—adapt, comrade, adapt." And if you adapt, you will succeed.*

Epilogue

Now you have it in a nutshell, Hoteko's Laws. I'll leave it up to you to judge the worthiness, the foolishness or the plain commonsense value of my Laws. All I know is that they worked for me most of the time throughout my career. They kept me in the ball game, they protected me and most importantly they helped me to keep my sanity. I think that most successful people have their own law or code of conduct that has helped them through thick and thin over the years. This was mine.

Some of the situations and people I've described may have seemed humorous and some were indeed funny. The sad part is that many of the people who stumbled and failed could have been helped by adhering to my Laws. In fact, some did learn from my ways as I learned from the ways of those blessed *ten percenters* who really ran the government during my career.

As it has been often stated, imitation is the sincerest form of flattery. I've imitated many of the *ten percenters* and have had others imitate me. Perhaps the MBA *eggheads* would call this type of learning process, *monkey-see-monkey-do* on the job training. They are right to a certain extent since they teach researched theories and proven principles of management. I am not a scientist. I take a backseat to these denizens of academia since my Laws are based only on commonsense observation and on trial-and-error worksite application.

◆   ◆   ◆

Peter Drucker who researched and wrote a classic treatise entitled, *Management: Tasks, Responsibilities and Practices*, first published in 1973, is perhaps the most knowledgeable person in America when it comes to dissecting what works and what doesn't work in private industry management. This amazing, selfless man has devoted his life to educating people like you and me on how to succeed in running a complex organization. On June 21, 2002, President George W. Bush honored Dr. Drucker with the Presidential Metal of Freedom at the White House, an honor well earned for a job well done.

His 1973 publication was an eye opener for me. I was taking a course on management from the Chicago Police Department Extension Academy and that was our text book, our bible on the subject. It definitely influenced my thought process and helped me to see and learn from the proven ability of others who have succeeded. I'll never be in the same class as Dr. Drucker, but I'll forever be grateful to him for writing that book!

The gist of my point is that Dr. Drucker firmly believed that at many critical points in the life of a corporation a key person would come in and save the company. A person of vision, courage and savvy with common sense would step up to the plate and hit a grand slam. People like General Wood at Sears or NYPD's Ray Kelly who saved U.S. Customs from the dastardly effects of Clinton's reinvention of government. His book is where I first got the idea to formulate my *ten percenters* theory. So, to Dr. Drucker; a *Doff-O-The-Hat*!

◆   ◆   ◆

There are those in government with great talent and nothing can help them because they are on a road to self-destruction. All you can do is stand back and watch. Oh yes, you can attempt to help them and to point out they're headed for destruction, but it doesn't work.

All they will say to you is, *yeh, yeh, yeh,* and they will continue with their reckless behavior. Someone once stated that power corrupts. I don't buy that. I believe that a person is already corrupted and his elevation into a position of authority finally allows him to exercise his abuse of authority. All you can do is get out of the way so you're not implicated or scorched by his consuming flames when he self-immolates. The only person who can help them is that one person himself and he cannot do that because he cannot contain or alter his self-fulfilling prophesies of destruction.

◆   ◆   ◆

Government is different from private industry. To know that difference provides you with the margin for success. Many of Dr. Drucker's theories work in government; many do not. His is a detailed scientific study and mine is just a blue collar on-the-job learning by the seat of your pants study. There is a big difference between science and conjecture and I'll admit to that premise. All I know is that mine also works and it gets better as time goes on.

Why? Simply because each succeeding *ten percenter* who has learned from my Laws can incorporate his experiences and that can only make it better. It becomes a living entity. I've been retired nearly three years but still maintain contact with many *ten percenters* in government. I can see how some have refined my Laws, focusing their expertise in a way which makes government better, more efficient and effective. I've also seen many of them formulate their own law and I'm impressed at their innovative ability to see what I couldn't see and to do what I didn't do.

Throughout my career I have enjoyed the challenge of running government, of being able to make a positive impact. In public service all you have is your integrity, your dedication to duty and your ability to do the best job you can for the American people. I've always believed that it's a privilege to serve, a sacred trust given to you to protect and defend the constitution of the United States of America. Hoteko's Laws helped me to keep that trust and to serve with honor.

978-0-595-37674-2
0-595-37674-6